TO
ABOLISH
CHILDREN

Books by Karl Shapiro

Poetry
Poems (1935)
The Place of Love (1942)
Person, Place and Thing (1942)
V-Letter (1944)
Essay on Rime (1945)
Trial of a Poet (1947)
Poems 1940-1953 (1953)
Poems of a Jew (1958)
The Bourgeois Poet (1964)

Prose
English Prosody and Modern Poetry (1947)
Beyond Criticism (1953)
In Defense of Ignorance (1960)
A Prosody Handbook (with Robert Beum) (1965)

Edited Works
American Poetry (1960)

TO ABOLISH CHILDREN / AND OTHER ESSAYS / KARL SHAPIRO

CHICAGO / 1968
QUADRANGLE BOOKS

To Teri, who wrote:

*If the bees begin to swarm,
push this button to inform
the management.*

CONTENTS

ACKNOWLEDGMENTS

The author wishes to thank the Library of Congress, which originally published "The Death of Randall Jarrell" as part of a pamphlet; the editors of the *Wilson Library Bulletin* for "The Decolonization of American Literature," *College English* for "Is Poetry an American Art?", the *Earlham Journal* for "A Defense of Bad Poetry," *Liberation* for "To Revive Anarchism," and the *Carleton Miscellany* for "A Malebolge* of Fourteen Hundred Books"; and the following for permission to quote from copyrighted materials: Mrs. Mary Jarrell for quotations from "Moving" and "The State" by Randall Jarrell, from *Selected Poems* and *Woman at the Washington Zoo* (Atheneum), copyright by Mrs. Randall Jarrell; The Macmillan Company for quotations from "Next Day" and "Woman" by Randall Jarrell; and The Viking Press for quotations from "When I Read Shakespeare" and "Peach" by D. H. Lawrence.

TO ABOLISH CHILDREN

To
Abolish
Children

Betrayal is an act of vengeance, obviously. But in an age of betrayal, when men of authority traduce their office and violate the trust placed in their hands, betrayal becomes the official morality. "Official morality" shortly becomes "public immorality"; whereupon the fabric of a society rots before one's eyes. In the years since the end of the Second World War, announced by the drop of the first Ultimate Weapon, the world has been stunned, horrified, and ultimately cajoled and won over to the official morality of America and its corollary of public immorality and anarchy. Hardly a leader, whether president, general, public relations man, professor, publisher, or poet, can be held to be honorable in his intentions. Everywhere lies the hidden premise and the calculated betrayal, the secret and chauvinistic lie.

To what end? Who is the betrayer, and why? Who are the betrayed? In a pyramidal society, a hierarchy, one would know the answers. But in a jungle there are no answers, only cries of victory or death. In the modern American jungle there are no answers.

Must America give birth to fascism? Or can it survive its pristine Constitution? Both issues seem doubtful. Can the economic motive live with the mass monster it has

created? Can the poor white who has sacrificed his brain
to television, or the poor Negro who loots a TV set from
the store, ever again cross the line from somnambulism to
wakeful joy? Can only the modern artist discover beauty
in the twentieth century?

The entire world has become aware of the pervasiveness
of American violence. The Americans were the last to discover it. This is as it should be. A betrayed husband is the
last to know his situation. America is shocked at itself;
someone has handed it a mirror. Instead of the young and
handsome heir of all the ages, with his bathing-beauty con-
sort, winners of Olympic Games, we see the soft and rotten
killer (almost Hemingway style) with his call-girl WASP
girlfriend, wearing a tiny crucifix between her scientifically
measured bosoms. Wars are staged and televised on the
battlefield; all sports are openly and avowedly big business;
all books sell according to the amount of money deposited
for advertising; countries are bought and sold in the stock
market like cattle. Not that any of this is particularly new.
What is new is that it is all now *public* knowledge. And
what is awesome is that nobody cares. Everyone wants
a share of the rot, the *faisandage*. Ours is a gamy culture from top to bottom. Books about the gaminess are
best-sellers.

The goal of any writer or professor nowadays is to defend his—there is an old-fashioned word—honor. Can a
writer write what he wants and in his manner? Can a
teacher teach what he was hired to teach, in his own
manner? Or must he give way to some form of blackmail
from above or below, some Big Brother, who reinterprets
his role for him. But we have heard enough of this structural mechanism from the time of Aldous Huxley, Orwell,
McLuhan, and so forth.

At the bottom of the spectrum of betrayal are the
"Movements," the pseudo-revolutionary insurrections without goals. The purest of these aim at simple theft and
sabotage, such as occur during and after hurricanes. The
more complicated are identified with civil rights and sex,
freedom of drugs and pills of various forms, the right to

unlimited travel vouchers and hospitalization. These are the heirs to the kingdom of Wall Street—the latest generation of betrayers and destroyers. This is the generation that uses the word Love as a synonym for Hate, that practices infantilism on a scale which has never been seen.

In between are the always duped Bourgeoisie, playing both ends against the middle. The bourgeois pays his children off to stay away, horrified at his mistake of educating these free-wheeling organisms equipped with electric guitars.

Possibly because the economic structure has reached the saturation point, the old order of social development is defunct. The pattern roughly used to be: immigrant (or settler), bourgeois, professional man, and artist (or patron). The child enacts the pattern in reverse: the young man or woman aspires to be artist *first*, deploring professionalism and education itself, condemning the standards of safety of the bourgeois (while exploiting the material wealth of the bourgeois exchequer), and eventually achieving the role of pseudo-immigrant or "native." The Beats and Hippies are products of the American aesthetic which has always preached disaffiliation and single combat with the forces of nature and of society. All American dissident movements tend to fall apart as soon as they are organized. Each artist and pseudo-artist is his own Huckleberry Finn, a moral expatriate. All of our best artists have been recluses of one kind or another, Melville, Faulkner, Hemingway, Cummings. The American artist who does not shun the Center is suspect. The dissident, however, misunderstands the commitment of the artist and thinks of this commitment only in terms of rebellion. The failure of the masses of dissidents to evolve a politic is inherent in the national aesthetic of individualism. And because the dissidents offer no organized threat to the existing order, the existing order continues to consolidate its gains and to ignore the threat of blackmail. The dissidents simply supply additional dry rot to the cultural fabric. The burning and looting of slums signify the abysmal failure of imagination of the would-be revolutionaries,

who in fact have no goals. Their only goals are pillage and
revenge. The intellectual infantilism of the American
radical makes him a figure of fun or of affection (or dis-
affection, as the case may be). The most one can say of
an Allen Ginsberg or a Timothy Leary or a LeRoi Jones is
that they are sincere. Children are always sincere.

Dissidence spread to the professoriat with the instal-
lation of artists and writers on the campuses of the nation. (I am one of the writer-professors who encouraged
the moral-intellectual drop-out philosophy for about a
decade.) It was easy and sometimes necessary to equate
the mass university with other forms of the bureaucratic
organism, but the vagueness of the issues involved and the
failure to clarify them simply added up to an abstract
dissent. That a university can be a democracy is patently
absurd. The prattle about Free Speech at Berkeley which
thrilled the sophomores of all ages served simply to de-
base whatever issues were at hand. Professors such as myself had already fought this issue in the courts, and won.
The campus rioters were betraying these gains and taking
a little private revenge on the side.

Vietnam itself is a falsified issue in the dissident "revolutions." The war is one of the most evil adventures in
our history and its evil effects on the American character
are incalculable, but the dissent is largely hypocritical. The
"Underground" did not raise its voice against the Russian
suppression of Hungary; it pursues a hands-off policy vis-
à-vis Castro, even to the endorsement of antique Marxist
slogans; it does not agitate for the overthrow of the last
big brother of the Axis, Francisco Franco. On the contrary,
the dissidents are to be found disporting themselves as
frequently in Spain as in other exotic places, pursuing
their careers and brushing up on the guitar. If it is laudable
to avoid a draft, it is despicable to moralize about it.

The importation of mysticism and pseudo-mysticism
into the West was an early stratagem of withdrawal from
the known modes of communication. Mysticism is simultaneously an insult and a threat to communal behavior.
Mystical evidence is by definition hearsay and inhibits

communication. The conveniences of Zen and the Sutras to the dissidents (who were rarely if ever "believers") were that they opened the door to a counter-culture, one in which consciousness was superseded by unconsciousness, and provisioned their minds with a counter-literature. The literature of the Orient has never been and cannot be naturalized in the West, but the stratagem of the haiku, for instance, is supposed to put the quietus on Western poetry.

But neither poetry nor any of the other arts are essential to the existence and furtherance of the "Movement," as its members refer to it with typical mystification. The Beat poets were the only dissidents who maintained even diplomatic relations with poetry, but their poetry was openly propaganda for the Movement. The planks of the primitive dissident platform were simple and narcissistic: pot, homosexuality, and doom-prophecy, a tame and almost Baptist program. The poetry lacked ambition to rise above these themes.

Because poetry was meaningless as a vehicle or an aesthetic to the Movement, the early Beat poetry took to the drum and trumpet (nineteenth-century symbols of slave revolt). The mixture of jazz and verse laid the groundwork for the dissident aesthetic: volume of noise, mass hypnotism, pure size, all canceled out the possibility of dialogue or even thought. Nor did hatred of the electronic world preclude the utmost exploitation of the amplifier. Herewith began the invasion of parks.

The deliberate and mischievous inversion of modes (anything "adult" was proscribed) opened a Pandora's box for the child mentality which would have driven Lewis Carroll to suicide. The wave of male and female hysterics with guitars and brotherhood lyrics turned into a mass industry, on the one hand, and, on the other, a generation of *révoltés* without goals. The dissident music is verbal—both the music and the language descend to levels of callousness and insensitivity heretofore unknown—but the contents are those of the infant banging its fists on the highchair. It is an amazing phenomenon that this art, pitched directly to the level of the five- or six-year-old, should also be the level of the college student. (Dissidence appears to taper off thereafter.) Dissident sartorial fashion also abolishes distinctions between the sexes; the not very subtle transvestism of the dissident costume situates the Movement in the years prior to puberty. The burlesque Edwardianism of the Beatles expresses a nostalgia for the age of aristocracy and unlimited wealth.

Throughout human history the fine arts have provided the nexus between intuitional insight and civilized hindsight. That is what the arts have been for. But at times when intuition usurps the more wakeful states of mind, the arts plunge into the playpen and the cry of "immediacy" fills the air. Immediacy (as in D. H. Lawrence's "immediate present" or the Zen Now!) cripples hindsight and deliberation and prevents criteria from coming into existence. The failure of the Beat community to create poetry or any of the other arts is the most significant fact about the Movement. The hidden aesthetic premise of the Movement is that art is evil and must be hamstrung. Only states of unconsciousness are valid: drug-states, violence in bed and on the street, secret languages, political nihilism. These are the lingua franca of the Movement.

The drug agitprop of the Movement is widely misinterpreted. The Movement does not want drugs to be legalized for their own use; it wants to convert others to drugs. The drug propaganda is entirely evangelistic: take acid and you will be saved is the same message as Jesus Saves. The counter-violence of the police and the drug authorities is not so much opposed by the drug propagandists as it is courted. Legalization of the drugs would remove the thrill; without the official opposition and the melodrama of rebellion, LSD would be about as attractive as ice cream. But the uses of hallucinogenic materials also provide the necessary escape from creativity, from the action of writing a poem or painting a picture. If you have been to the artificial paradise, why write about it? There all the poems and paintings and music are readymade. There everyone is a Michelangelo, a Mozart, and a

Shakespeare. The Movement maintains its puritanical aversion to alcohol ("Scotch is for fathers"), for alcohol confers only a temporary nonactivity upon the psyche. Hallucinogens show you the Promised Land.

As the students of medieval and Oriental mysticism know, only about one in a hundred thousand mystics has ever recorded his or her "trip" in even mildly impressive prose or poetry. The jottings of drug-takers are even less engaging. The taker of drugs may be trying to force the gates of the imagination, as perhaps was the case with Coleridge, but the mass movement for freedom of unconsciousness is clearly an aesthetic draft-dodge. The aesthetic arrogance of the drug user in any case lacks the substantiation of visible works. Pot-head, show me your book!

The nihilistic mind is a runaway horse. The Movement blots out literature without ever having cracked a book. Or rather, it burns all literature to the ground. The Movement cultivates cultural brainwashing; even advanced university students pretend to be ignorant of what they know. The fear of cultural infection and the demand for "immediacy" immunize their minds to any responses except to the latest fad or artifact. Their speech and writing degenerate into code (at the moment it is the underworld argot of the slum Negro, a genuine proletarian dialect for him which is, however, awkward and inapplicable to well-wishers and fellow-travelers). The Movement's adulation of the Negro slum-dweller as hero-victim leads it with characteristic naiveté to adopt his sublanguage as a generalized medium of communication. The very mystery of this language gives it credence: the terminology and metaphors of jazz, sex, drugs, double-speak, and revenge supply the necessary circuits of sympathy to the adolescent of the upper worlds. You dig?

The jazz put-on is a major form of cultural blackmail by the Movement. Anyone not "with" the jazz is a marked man. The hagiography of jazz is as immense as the Vatican Library. It is all phony, a conglomeration of the Music Corporation of America and the masses of delayed and permanent adolescents. Jazz is only a minor facet of modern folk music. What is beatified about jazz is that it is Negro. The Negro, as the most obvious victim of society since the latest massacre of the Jews, is thought to be universalizing about the human condition in jazz. Nothing could be further from reality. Negro jazz is— Negro jazz: charming, entertaining, hot, cool, abstract, evangelistic, white, black, blue, but never revolutionary. Negro jazz is masochistic, and that is precisely its failure and its appeal to the adolescent. What it lacks in content it makes up for in sentimentality, sexuality, and volume.

The blotting-out of language in jazz lyrics, the accommodation by skillful musical improvisers to cranked-out dollar-making stanzas, many of them half a century old, attests to the deliberate destruction of language as a medium. The nostalgia of the horn takes over; there is a vague reminiscence of language, unbelievably debased to begin with, whether it came from Tin Pan Alley or from Hollywood. The insistence on jazz, as taken over by the Movement, is the insistence on hysteria as a Way of Life. As such it appeals to the American joy in violence.

The Movement nominates Bob Dylan as great poet. The whining puerilities of this phenomenon are not to be taken lightly in the stock market or in the hearts of millions of children bursting with vitamins and cash. Is he the Leader?

The open release of violence is always a surprise to intellectuals. Rebellion without goals is the most fascinating spectacle of all. The Media intone with relentless stupidity: Why? Why? Congresses mourn. Whole cities are put to the torch while children dance and scream as at a jazz festival or an ice capade. Yet violence is inculcated by the elders and is exactly predictable. Violence is the answer to the question, Why?

It is quite natural and expectable in psycho-politics that Negro looters should espouse white genocide and Nazi anti-semitism. It is quite natural that WASP children in posh suburbs should play Nazi, instead of Cowboy and Indian. In a child society the only authentic emotion is hate. In Hippy language Hate is spelled Love; any four-letter word will suffice.

America is the child society *par excellence*, and possibly the only one ever politically arrived at. It is the society of all rights and no obligations, the society of deliberate wreckage and waste, the only society that ever raised gangsterism to the status of myth, and murder to the status of tragedy or politics. The American adulation of the child mentality leads to an industrialized hedonism, on the one hand, and a chauvinistic psychology of greed, on the other. In advertising, anyone over the age of twenty-one or twenty-five is portrayed as an idiot who has got behind in the science and commerce of rejuvenation. This "adult" is appealed to by an almost invisible Big Brother (Mad-Ave or the Executive in the White House) because the "adult" has made the mistake of legal and contractual obligation. Therefore he is an idiot. The costuming of the so-called radical population is a form of jeering: the beard is not only a red flag with certain flickering political messages; it is also the ultimate taunt at the man in the suit. Arson, looting, and murder are also gentle reminders to the fathers that the tumbrils are rolling. (In many of my creative writing classes the students sit in judgment on their parents and make specific judgments about which of the elders will be allowed to live. Confronted with the fact that the elders and the state are paying their way through education, the students snort and sneer at the stupidity of authorities.)

Humanities departments, notoriously the most deprived segment of the American university system, have been powerless to halt the invasion of the child psychosis in higher education. The effeminate backstairs aggressiveness of the Humanities gives way to the Creative Writing Gestalt. "Creative Writing" is to the Humanities as strychnine is to the horse. Any symptom of guilt discerned by the undergraduate on the part of its elders is parlayed into immediate sabotage—a sabotage which stops short of the curtailment of personal benefits, however. The gangsterism of the American youth mind makes it as

easy a prey to the Marine recruiter as it does to the
Creative Writing instructor. The goals are not education
but theft, generally theft of scholarships and undeserved
preferment. As American literature heroizes the outlaw, so
the outlaw student gains advantage over his more serious
companions; the style of contempt, the "cool," deter-
mines to a large extent the amount of loot acquired and the
length of absolution from the institutions which threaten
his freedom of operation.

The cultivation of Youth with a capital Y has kept the
growth of the American mind off balance since perhaps
the early nineteenth century. The trashy frontier mythology, hand-to-hand combat, Horatio Alger, Alger Hiss,
spy-psychology, advertising, Hell's Angels, Beats, Hippies,
Beatles, dropouts, assassins, amnesiac mass murderers,
pseudo-mystics lately from Kyoto or Benares, CIA, Black
Muslims and Black Nazis, these are all part and parcel
of the American dream of Youth. The dream was dreamed
by the fathers, now on the proscribed list.

As Negro anti-semitism is Christian (the only political
training the Negro was ever given was the flaming cross),
so anti-adultism is American flag-waving in reverse. For
this state of affairs there would seem to be no remedy.
And indeed there is not. Should one suggest a program
to slow down or stop the strangulation of American life by
children, it might read:

1. Cut off all sources of economic supply to Youth
except what they earn by physical or observable mental
labor.

2. Deny all higher education except on absolute proof
of ability. No student should be admitted to a college or
university unless he or she has earned a scholarship or has
otherwise demonstrated unusual ability. Public universities
should be more stringent in this respect than private, rich
universities (the private school is unsupervisable).

3. Deny free travel privileges to children. For instance,
raise the age minimum of drivers' licenses to thirty or

forty. Deny foreign travel except to those who have been granted the privilege from their school.

4. Set aside a large land area for all dissidents to reside in, with ingress but no egress. As children think the world is their personal property, give them their acre of personal property. Keep them there.

5. Discourage the cowardice and intimidation of parents and "authorities" by re-educating them to the nature of the Yahoo. Encourage construction of housing, especially suburban housing, to delimit or exclude the child, and to suit the needs and requirements of adults.

6. Disenfranchise those who reject military service, male and female. Why does conscription legislation apply only to male Youth?

7. Abolish the child. Deliberate the intelligent society in which the infant is loved and cared for and controlled until he is ready to be shipped to a place of education, should he be worthy. Consider two types of human beings: the infant and the adult. Destroy all concepts of the adolescent.

Whereupon his "literature" will wither away, his "music," his drugs, his revolutions and murders, his terrorism of everything he lacks the understanding and knowledge to comprehend.

The power-shift lies in this direction. Man is an aesthetic animal. His greatest works are slashed to ribbons by "youth" and will continue to be until Grown Man relinquishes his image of the advertised profile of Youth. As long as Grown Man apes Youth, he will remain the victim of his seed.

The American adult must battle "youth" to the death. "Youth" is a figment of the American imagination which is destroying America itself.

The essays that follow should be read as a documentary. All of them lie in another dimension from the preceding note. For instance, a few years ago I delivered a lecture

at a Negro university in Atlanta in which I stated that
"retribution is not Negro." Not long after, the Negro youth
blew the lid off all over the U.S.A. Here was illiteracy
in action, television come to life, Nazism being born in
full view. The tendency of American politicians and
journalists to look for the "cause" is inherent in the
myopia of the American mythologists and opportunists
who imagine that the status quo is verbalized in the
eighteenth-century Constitution. Yet no generation of
Americans since the signing of that document has regarded it as the rock of ages. Only politicians and law-
makers perpetuate this document in bad faith, encouraging
the unconscionable materialism of the people and inflating
the images of gangster, murderer, and thief. Little wonder
that some of the greatest presidents have fallen to the
youthful assassin, trained in histrionics and expert in
shooting in the back.

These essays are about modern poetry, more or less.
But poetry is always about more, not less.

The Decolonization of American Literature

American literature has been in the throes of decolonization since America first put pen to paper.

This literature began as a country-cousin literature of England. We were beholden to England for "culture" and broke with that culture through politics. For the great literature of this country until lately is political. In fact, it is the great political documents of America which have broken the back of cultural slavery all over the world. The writings of Jefferson, the Constitution, the Emancipation Proclamation are the basic artifacts of American literature. Decolonization is born in these documents. We are just beginning to feel the consequences. We are still at the dawn of those fabulous political words.

Three hundred years passed before the first words of cultural independence were set down, three centuries of holding on to the Old World, the European mother. We might have been a French country or a Spanish country or English like Canada, but we turned out to be none of those. One of the main reasons was that we had slaves, we had Negroes. The presence of slaves forced the ideal of liberty to its conclusion.

When America decolonized itself from Europe, from England, it opened the door to decolonization everywhere. We pressed a button and opened Pandora's box. It is this country that gave France the example of revolution. And even today we are the admiration and the horror of the Old World. We have not broken with those documents.

We were England's, Robert Frost said; we were colonials. When we stopped being colonials, all hell broke loose.

To be colonial means to live in a faraway place and to long for home. American literature was this way until little more than a century ago—until a few writers began to say, like Emerson, Europe is not home; until Thoreau pulled back even from the village of Concord; until Whitman rewrote the Constitution in poetry and sang the one great poem about the death of Abraham Lincoln.

To be colonial means not to cut the umbilical cord with Home and also to create the Native. America created two Natives, the Indian and the Negro. The Indian was banished to the unconscious mind of America (what is left of the Indian is a record of cultural shock which is phenomenal in modern history). But the Negro could not be banished. He was an industrial army, fuel to be burned and to be replenished of itself. He was the American "native." Richard Wright called his first novel *Native Son;* he understood "native."

But we were still colonial when we began to write. We would even send a Negro slave girl to England as a poet in the eighteenth century! I want to quote verbatim the biographical note from an old anthology of Negro poetry, edited by Langston Hughes and Arna Bontemps in 1949. This is colonialism in a nutshell.

Phillis Wheatley (Senegal, West Africa, 1753–84) was captured and sold into slavery in early childhood and brought to Boston in 1761. She became the property of John Wheatley of Boston whose wife and daughter soon noted the alert sensitivity of the

*young African girl and encouraged Phillis's efforts to acquire
learning. Within a few years she was completely at home in the
language and literature of her captors. She began writing poetry,
and in 1770, at the age of seventeen, published, "A Poem, by
Phillis, A Negro Girl in Boston, on the Death of the Reverend
George Whitefield." When her health began to fail, Phillis
was advised by doctors to take a sea voyage. This was arranged
by the kindly mistress, who also gave the girl her freedom
before she sailed for England. In London, Phillis was a success.
It was there that her only collected volume of verse was first
issued under the title* Poems on Various Subjects, Religious
and Moral, 1773. *Then one by one the patrons of this talented
ex-slave girl died and she returned to Boston. Her marriage was
unhappy, and she died as a servant in a cheap lodging house
at the age of thirty-one.*

The ironies of this footnote are staggering and would
require a Dostoevsky to handle them. Phillis Wheatley's
poetry is as bad as all eighteenth-century colonial poetry,
though better than that, say, of the Hartford Wits, which
isn't saying much. Yet this experiment in colonial "culture" contains a message. The message is negative all down
the line: slave girl, Boston at the dawn of revolution,
guilt about rebellion from the Old World, neo-classical
poetry, "the kindly mistress," and so on.

In every case except ours, a new culture is based on
Home Country, Settler, and Native. But in America nobody knows where the Home Country is, for the Settlers
come from Home Countries all over the world; and the
Natives are no more. We have no Natives and no common
Home Country. We have no peasantry. We have only
expatriates and ex-slaves. This is a country of Runaways
and Captives.

When the literature of America got under way it fascinated the world: runaways and captives, cops and
robbers, cowboys and Indians, palefaces and blackskins,
Jews and Goyim, Syndicate and Chamber of Commerce.
Nobody wanted to be a native—the natives were dead and
done for; everybody wanted to be a "settler." Those who
would not "settle" went back to some Old Country of
the mind: Eliot, Santayana, Pound, Hemingway, Henry

James. Others mourned their "rootlessness"; we have a
whole literature of that.

The cultural history of our country is one of decolonization, every element trying to sever itself from its origins.
We are something like the white Australians, who are not
eager to trace their ancestry back more than three or four
generations because their original ancestors will have been
sent over in the "hulks," the convict ships that were sent
from England to the farthest place England could think of.
Every FFV in Australia was a convict. We are in the same
boat; we have only a paper aristocracy, and our aristocrats
were revolutionaries who fought for their lives. In this
sense the Daughters of the American Revolution are subversive. Only they have forgotten what their ancestors
were subversive about.

Our literature took a long time to decolonize from
English literature, and the process hasn't ended yet. In
the beginning we were "Anglo-Saxon," about 90 per cent,
for the blacks were not counted in the population and
the immigrants hadn't arrived. Excuse a few sentences of
facts, which I think mean so much. A generation after
independence the Germans and Irish began to arrive in
force. Before the Civil War, hordes of Irish, Dutch, Danes,
Swedes, Norwegians, Swiss, and Jews swarmed in. Toward
the end of the century came larger waves of Italians,
Russians, Poles, Bohemians, and Hungarians. A smaller
number of Asiatics seeped in, for this country is still anti-
Asiatic (we invented our first concentration camps for
American citizens of Japanese ancestry during the Second
World War). In all this the English element was inun-
dated and, so to speak, contaminated. The language of the
King was lost in the shuffle.

A language in itself is nothing. A literature in itself is
nothing. A literature is the expression of a nation's soul,
and a great literature leaves nothing out—that is its
greatness. But to leave nothing out means to go against
the grain; it means to dissent. Our modern literature is a
literature of dissent, monotonous and endless dissidence.
This dissidence gives modern literature its authenticity.

Yet this literature of dissent is only in its infancy. Dissent is contagious, and every day we find new areas of eruption everywhere in the world. But dissent is also a drop in the bucket of literature, a drop of pigment in the skin or in the blood.

American literature is unique; it is the only literature I have ever heard of in which all elements have tried, more or less simultaneously, to decolonize themselves. It is the only literature which practices cultural amnesia as a doctrine. The few famous American writers who refused to surrender the past, who insisted on memory (Henry James or Eliot), surrendered their nationality to the idea of European cultural supremacy. They could maintain a continuity with Europe only by becoming Europeans again.

English literature is a dead literature in America, a memory. The English language is practically a memory. Only a few English professors in America pretend that English and its great literature are continuous with ours.

A decolonized literature in an African country or in a free Arab country or in Israel is different from ours. Those nations have a culture to go back to. They go back to where they began when history interrupted their life. In Israel the Hebrew language was reinvented overnight after a sleep of two thousand years. It seemed the most natural thing in the world, for it was that language and its great book which held those people together who became the new Israelites. In India people fight in the streets to retain their ancient tongues, the source of their culture. In Africa, French and English will not long remain the medium of literature, not in the European forms at least. But in America we have only vestiges of culture *to which we do not wish to return.* The first thing the American immigrant tried to do was to prevent his children from inheriting the old language, the old culture. (In my case, for instance, Yiddish was used as a private language of jokes and confidences which we, third-generation Americans, were not supposed to know. I have found the same to be true with students of mine who are of

Czech descent or German or Swedish or Dutch or Greek.)

In a sense, all cultural languages are banished from America. A country settled by runaways and slaves did not carry much high culture with it. And the tides of immigration engulfed what high culture there was. The half-educated American has long been a byword abroad; in fact, it is impossible for the American to be educated in the European sense. We cannot be nor do we have to. As I ask my fellow teachers: In what way am I to present, say, English poetry to the grandson of a Latvian farmer from a ranch in western Nebraska? As the poetry of his culture? In what way am I to present Chaucer or T. S. Eliot to my Negro students? Is that their heritage? Is the great complex of European culture their heritage? And do they have any such heritage at all? Even to me, an English professor and a writer of the English tongue, all things English are foreign.

I gather from Sartre's writings about Africa that European culture is no longer capable of influencing world culture. Europe is now the colony. It is European culture which is thirsty for replenishment from outside. American culture shows a similar thirst for replenishment but can slake this thirst from within.

The great theme of American literature is rootlessness. And this fact also makes us unique. Many writers have even said that there is no relationship between the American and the land. It is as if the spirit of place were hostile to us. We become the greatest technicians and mechanics because we fight the spirit of place; we are bent upon conquering place by force. We have never made peace with the land but have taken it by storm. D. H. Lawrence felt this about us; Henry Miller and Faulkner have it in their books; the urban poets, who have forgotten what a tree looks like, substantiate it in their dusty poems.

The price our writers have had to pay for rootlessness, for cutting ties with all the different pasts behind us, is the neuroticism we know so well in our literature. And yet we have no choice; insofar as the American writer is true to his situation, he is a neurotic, ridden with the anxieties

of separateness from the past. Freedom is one of the benef-
icent symptoms of this anxiety. We are suddenly confronted with an alphabet of freedoms ranging from civil
rights to freedom of the banned book and the spoken
obscenity. Our literature is engaging in a Socratic dialogue
with all previous values; we do this with increasing reckless-
ness and frequently with cynicism, for what is there to
lose? The fact is, there is no place to go back to; we have
nowhere to go but forward. We cannot help ourselves;
that is our condition.

So long as America held on to the mother literature it
was colonial. This was the case until the twentieth century
and even into it. The criterion of the poem was the
English poem; of the novel, the English novel. The ex-
ceptions are few and can be counted on one hand. It was
only with the recognition of rootlessness that a strong and
massive American literature came into being. This theme
coincided with all the forms of radicalism that swept
through the intelligentsia in the early years of the century.
Anarchism, various forms of Marxism, and more recently
existentialism are all expressions of the rootless, those
peoples set adrift by history who have nevertheless become
articulate. The Jewish writer was among the first to speak
from this void.

The Jew is the mythic wanderer, but the American Jew
is the one who has forgotten where he wandered from.
The American Jew has no longing for Israel and possibly
only an intellectual sympathy with it. He has little or no
cultural memory of the religion or of the tradition. All he
has is the invisible yellow badge, which still shows up in
certain lights. This badge, this psychology of self-consciousness, makes the Jew want to be absolutely visible.
He insists on his identification. He is the opposite of Ellison's "invisible man." If the Jew does not stick out like
a sore thumb he is very restless. Hence all these books by
and about Jews. Why does the Irishman James Joyce
choose a poor, uninteresting Jew to be his main character
in *Ulysses*? Because Leopold Bloom not only has a faulty
memory of his fabulous past as a Hebrew but is lost.

Bloom is a symbol of the modern bourgeois drifter. He doesn't belong in Ireland or anywhere else. He is cultural ectoplasm.

In America we are all cultural ectoplasm; and the Jew can stick out his sore thumb, look in a mirror, and say like Job: Whence cometh thou?

I don't want to give one more book review of the now famous and brilliant novel *Herzog*, but I can't resist a sentence or two. Herzog, the neurotic professor and intellectual, is having a breakdown, ostensibly because of a busted marriage, but the marriage is secondary. He is having a breakdown because he is Herzog, American-Jewish intellectual. Like Leopold Bloom he is discovering that he is adrift. He has no place to go back to—neither his home, which he has been locked out of by his bitchy wife, nor his world of ideas, which has fallen all over the floor of his study. And all he can do is write letters to the living and the dead, trying to make a contact somewhere along all those broken wires. It is almost a formula of the American novel.

What is the fascination for the Jewish-American writer today? It is the fascination of the American for one of his own type, the man who at last debates with himself the question, What does it mean to be a Jew, an American, a Negro, an American Jew, an American Negro, an Afro-American, an American of Jewish descent, and so on?

What it means, of course, is that the question has been raised. The question was not raised in the nineteenth century, except perhaps by Walt Whitman. And the question refers art back to the political artifacts: Are those things real? Do they mean what I think and hope they mean? The Constitution of the United States has been backed into a corner by writers. No constitution can answer all the questions we are asking it. Every time the Constitution answers a question it asks a new one.

But American-Jewish writing is already obsolete. The Jew qua Jew is no longer a major premise in the creative equation. The Jewish writer can in effect sit back and chew his cud and watch the Negro. The Jew has achieved decolonization in America; though not by himself, it was going to happen somehow. I lived through it and even had a hand in it. Maybe I should explain that.

Very early in life I decided upon being a poet. (I won't go into the motivations of "being a poet," which are very complex and also irrelevant here.) I knew only one language, English, and so fell in love with English poetry. Falling in love with English poetry, which is still my old flame, meant living an imaginary English life. Living an imaginary English life meant living a phony life of the mind, for I was not English in any sense of the word. And living a phony life of the mind meant eventually becoming an English professor. One day, when I had learned how to write poetry, I had to make a decision about my name. Nobody in the *Oxford Book of English Verse* was named Shapiro. In fact, nobody was named Shapiro except tailors and junk dealers. What was I to do? Change my name? This was my first crisis as a poet.

In those days, believe it or not, it was impossible to get a poem published if you did not have an "Anglo-Saxon" name, but I decided to stick to my name; that decision made me "Jewish." And since I had made the decision I wrote poems about Jewishness.

My name itself had no content whatever. Most Jews' names are more recent than the last names of Negroes. That is, most Jews got names when Napoleon broke the ghetto system in Europe and the Jews either were given the names of a German or Polish town or made up one. *Shapiro* comes from a German town named Spira, I am told. I couldn't care less. So it was not the name that held me, as you might hold on to *Vanderbilt* or R. J. *Reynolds*; it was the foreignness of the word. I hung onto that; I wanted to know why my name was a kind of curse.

Years later I published a book called *Poems of a Jew*. That was when I was finally decolonized. When I printed that book I was already American. I was as rootless as a Texas millionaire with Negro and Indian blood in his veins.

When our literature got under way, it began like a

census to list our cultural deaths. There was the grand
gesture of Whitman like a captain on the bridge waving
goodbye to the Past. There was Captain Ahab hunting
down the great white "blood consciousness" and sinking
the ship of white civilization along with it. There was
Huck Finn, who lit out for the wilderness, running for
his life, like his author, from respectability. There followed that long recital of the failure of the American hero
—the epitaphs of Spoon River and Winesburg, Ohio; the
brutal caricatures of the American bourgeois: the salesman,
the evangelist, the politician; the corruption of pioneer and
settler by the rootless materialism of the New World.
Hemingway assaults the virility of the American male;
Faulkner's vast gallery of Southerners portrays the decline
and fall of a world under a curse—he calls it rightly the
curse of slavery. Of the heroes of the American novel, only
the artist is left unscathed. He is Ishmael in the cultural
desert.

It is the motif of rootlessness that gives our literature
its greatness to the outside world. Whatever the value of
literary prizes, consider the names of Americans who have
been awarded the Nobel Prize for literature: Eugene
O'Neill, Pearl Buck, Hemingway, Faulkner, Steinbeck,
and Eliot. These writers deal mainly with modern man
in the void. If they are part of what is called the Western
Tradition, they lie at the very edge of it. Each phase of
American literature marks a further step away from that
Tradition. As each "colonial" group in America finds
its literary voice, we are moved deeper into the void.
Huckleberry Finn, Ahab, Joe Christmas, Herzog—it hardly
matters who the hero is; he leads us on the search for his
authenticity. It is the unauthentic American artist who
reaches back to the Tradition.

The Martinique writer and psychiatrist Frantz Fanon
says in his book *The Wretched of the Earth* that when
the African native "begins to pull on his moorings, and
to cause anxiety to the settler, he is handed over to well-
meaning souls who in cultural congresses point out to him
the specificity and wealth of Western values." And he

adds: "But every time Western values are mentioned they produce in the native a sort of stiffening or muscular lockjaw."

The Culture Conference or Congress is a twentieth-century institution which has never been looked at squarely. I myself make it a point to avoid those conferences, but I have attended enough of them here and abroad to know that they represent a more or less official machine dedicated to the status quo. They seek to hold the line for traditional values. For this reason the Culture Conference is supported by government, by foundations, and by writers and artists who have a stake in the tradition. The Culture Conference is opposed to decolonization, at least the decolonization of culture. The hidden premise on which it operates is the superiority of European culture. It must therefore work hard to reconvert the "native" and bring him back to a sense of cultural inferiority. I once attended one of these conferences in Tokyo, where it was agreed beforehand that politics could not be discussed. Here were a multitude of writers from all over the world, among them some of the most famous and some of the most political, who voluntarily emasculated all discussion at the outset. Instead they talked about the art of translation.

A few years ago you could ask in all seriousness: Is a Negro literature possible in America? The question implied a negative. I am among those who felt that the Negro had nothing to gain by becoming literary, that he had nothing to say according to the tradition of letters as we know this tradition. He could only create a pseudo-literature, the novel and poem according to Uncle Tom. We had seen this happen with Paul Laurence Dunbar and the early slave poets. Between a transliterated Negro dialect (itself a phony dialect) and *Oxford Book* English there seemed no choice. If there were to be an authentic Negro medium, where would it come from? Obviously it could not come from the standard classics of American literature, poetry, or prose. Perhaps something could rise from the church spiritual, a form of poetry which worked

upon secret levels of meaning, or more likely from the
blues. But almost nothing of the sort appeared to be
happening. A literature is not created in a vacuum; it is
created out of love for its medium. Could and should
the Negro love the Anglo-American language? Or was it
possible that he had his own version of it, as the Jewish
writer had his?

But a literature is more than a version of language; a
novel or poem is more than a work of art. Literature is
an accurate transcription of the quality of thought and
feeling of the writer and his people. What audience would
such a literature have, if any? Was there a Negro audience
to read *Native Son* or *Invisible Man* or Tolson's *Libretto*?
You suspected that there wasn't, that such works would
be for a small white or "mixed" audience. The publication
of *Native Son* was a great shock to the white reader, not
only because of what it said but because a Negro had
written it. Negroes didn't produce works of that caliber,
nor did they read them. Literature, so the mythos went,
was white man's business.

Even the books by Richard Wright were in the white
tradition; his audience was the traditional audience, as
were the values implicit in the work. Ellison's *Invisible
Man*, which I wrote about elsewhere as the Great American Novel, is a masterpiece, but again in the white tradition. Ellison might even be called a white Negro. Neither
what he says nor how he says it is without precedent in the
general literary consciousness. Like Wright he corroborates
the white liberal's worst fears; like Wright he illuminates
the guilt of the settler vis-à-vis the native. In fact, it
seems to me there is more *negritude*, if I may use the
word, in Faulkner than in either Wright or Ellison.
Faulkner is better able to present the sensibility of the
Negro, albeit the Mississippi Negro, because Faulkner's
characters are not always at the point of dramatic crisis.

What Wright and Ellison proved was that the Negro
can write a novel as good as a white novel, as good as
anything in the Tradition. But this obviously was not
enough. Especially as the Tradition was beginning to come

apart at the seams. For a Negro literature to come into being, it had to start from the bottom, not from the top. All great poetry comes from the bottom: Homer, Dante, Chaucer, Whitman—all went to the language of the street for their great poems. A Negro poetess could prove that she could win the Pulitzer Prize, but nobody has been able to prove that the Pulitzer Prize is worth winning.

At some time in its career a people makes a decision to embrace the art of writing. It has no obligation to at any time. The Jews produced virtually no literature after the Old Testament except commentaries. The Jews were in a state of cultural withdrawal all during the diaspora. Scholars will disagree but cannot convince me that the Jews produced any literature or art or music worth mentioning until the great revolutions of the eighteenth and nineteenth centuries freed the Jew from cultural bondage. It is in our century that the Jew has suddenly begun to sing and paint and write, for this is the century of cultural liberation all over the world. Ours is one of the greatest periods of art in history, and it is great insofar as we have broken with the Tradition. To break with the Tradition does not mean to annihilate it; it means to place new values upon it. It means to pick up the pieces and maybe throw them down again. Malraux means this when he says about the greatness of modern art: The fragment is king.

Negro literature in America had to begin with the fragment, not with the whole form. Having proved out of pride that it could handle the whole form like Wright or Ellison or Gwendolyn Brooks or Langston Hughes, it must then throw down the forms—from the top of the Empire State Building. I think that is what Baldwin is doing. Critics say what a shame that Baldwin should give up the novel for the polemic and the pamphlet. I don't think that is any of our business. What if the novel has proved unsatisfactory to him? What if the poem has proved the same? Aren't all the great examples of art and literature of our time anti-art?

The greatness as well as the horror of the twentieth

century is that it is a last judgment. It is a time when every value is called into question everywhere and on every level of the human experience. It is the genius of our age to question.

The racial revolutions of our age are more effects than causes. They are the result of universal indignation over the failures of our culture. One country famed for its music and its philosophers tried to destroy a whole nation in its midst by murder. Another country famed for poetry discovered that it held a large part of the world in virtual slavery. Another country famed for its sense of liberty and its adoration of the arts suddenly collapsed from internal weakness and corruption. These were all European countries of great antiquity. In the East rose a superpolice state with a paranoid belief in its historical destiny. In America we assembled and exploded the ultimate weapon.

For many years I have been trying to loosen the hold of the academic or "colonial" mind over poetry. It encourages a poetry as well as an entire literature of reference, the kind that refers back in every case to prior commitments, historical, religious, or philosophical. In a sense it is a useless battle; attacking the Establishment only tends to strengthen it. It would be better to ignore the existence of the literature of reference and to create whatever we think valid than to go on tilting at windmills. This is what the Beat writers did; they were successful because they refused to take part in the academic dialogue. If someone asked one of the usual deathly questions, such as "What is the role of the artist in the modern world?" they would be likely to answer something like "Fried shoes." Refusal to "play the game" kept them safe. Refusal to play the game won freedom for India and is winning freedom for the American South. Refusal to play the game will turn the dehumanized "multiversity" back into a place of learning.

The importance of the Negro writer in the world today is far out of proportion to the number of books we have to go by. But the significance of Negro writing today is paramount because everywhere, not simply in America, the Negro is in the position to ask the questions. The "hyphenated" Jewish writer is no more. Time has solved that problem. The Jewish writer either is assimilated into the modern bourgeois world with all its neuroses or is a settler in the biblical land, carrying on skirmishes against the Philistines or the Egyptians as in the days of old. A few American Jews try to keep alive the mystique of the diaspora, but with little success. Most modern Jews themselves reject the myth of the dispersion for our time. They go to Israel and have a look and then hurry back to Detroit or Omaha. Today the American Negro faces the same dilemma; Richard Wright, Baldwin, Tolson know that Mother Africa is not for them. And the Africans know it too.

Everywhere decolonization is taking place we find the disappointment of the visitor who feels rejected from his dream. But this is part of the awakening, part of the process of freedom itself. If the African looks down on the American Negro, he has earned that right. If the Afro-American feels out of place in Nigeria or even Liberia, he knows at last the limits of his dream.

We can witness at the moment three phases of decolonization in our culture: *nostalgia, assimilation,* and *negritude. Nostalgia* is homesickness not for the good old days but for the bad old days. *Assimilation* means a cultural entente at the expense of any mystique. *Negritude* means assertion of the realities, historical and "mystical" as well.

The early literature of America, all of it, is nostalgic for the worst. It is as true of Anne Bradstreet as of Phillis Wheatley. And in fact the masses of people at any time fear the heavy responsibilities of freedom and pine for the bad old days when all choices were made for them. Not to have to choose is a freedom, the freedom of the slave. The Negro poets who cultivated a "slave" dialect were in fact in accord with their condition; they consented to the cultural authority of the white "prosody," as the white colonials acceded to the cultural authority of the Old World.

But assimilation too is nostalgic. It was often said of

German Jews before Hitler that they were more German
than the Germans. Which didn't stop Hitler from rooting
them out. The nostalgia of the American-Jewish writer who
is assimilated into American literature is curious. I was
talking with a famous American writer who had made
Jewishness the theme in his books. Speaking of the new
Jews, the Israelis, he said: "But they aren't Jews any more!"
I agreed. Those new Jews had lost their consciousness of
the diaspora; they had fought their way back into the
mythical homeland and were lost to the old Jewry. But
cultural assimilation of Jews into American life was rela-
tively easy and has all but been accomplished. A Jew
does not have the problem of the Hindu, the Oriental,
or the Negro; the Jew looks more or less "American" anywhere he goes; even his name is not held against him as
it once was. But cultural assimilation also means national
oblivion for the nation assimilated. You can only pretend
to act like a Jew; the writer or artist can do this easily
because that is his business. The American Jew of average
sensibility, on the other hand, experiences the common
cultural amnesia of Americans of any extraction. While
the American-Jewish figure in fiction has a cultural nervous
breakdown over American twentieth-century values, he
longs for the bad old days when his father was a bootlegger
or a peddler because he was suffering the crucifixion of
the culturally underprivileged; the father would do anything to keep his family Jews, to turn them into doctors
and lawyers or rich merchants. With economic freedom
they could then be Jews. Only it didn't work that way,
for Jewishness meant suffering, and an unsuffering Jew
was an anomaly. An unsuffering Jew is a goy. Hence the
nostalgia of the assimilated.

The Negro is luckier; he can never disappear from his
condition in the Caucasian world any more than a Hindu
or a Japanese. There he is, unassimilable and un-nostalgic,
the biggest fact of life in the modern world.

Our century is very great because with us all the
chickens have come home to roost, because great men of
goodwill—statesmen, presidents, leaders of men, artists,

and young people—have demanded the exaction of promises made to nations by visionaries and the spokesmen of freedom. This is happening under our eyes; we are all a party to it. Nostalgia is obsolete. Assimilation may well be. Neither is of vital importance. I prefer the idea of negritude. At least it is the first great idea or concept that can deal with the biggest fact of modern life without trying to water it down.

I will give three examples: Aimé Césaire, Léopold Senghor, and M. B. Tolson. Césaire is a Caribbean, Senghor is a Senegalese, and Tolson was born in Missouri. The first two use French for poetry; Tolson uses English or American. (My designation of Tolson's language is that he writes in Negro.)

Or rather, all three of these great poets write in Negro. That is what negritude means in literature. It does not mean accommodation to the standards of the settler or to his nostalgia for the mother or father country. It does not mean making peace through disappearance into the scene; nor, as Senghor has shown in his political writings, does it mean war. It means insistence on the pride of selfhood without hatred. No oppressed people in history has had less sense of revenge than the Negro. Retribution is not Negro.

Negritude is simply decolonization under the positive aspect. Senghor has no grudge against the Tradition (as I do) or against modern technology. On the contrary, he welcomes everything that will make possible greater harmony among men. This is the wisdom of the French in the decolonized man, the daring of the French to push an idea into action as far as it will go. There are, I believe, no African poets of the English language of his stature. The English are still the heirs of apartheid.

Césaire's discovery of negritude—he is pinned as the inventor of the name—is that of the disaffected assimilationist, the Parisian from the colonies who became a Marxist and by nomination a surrealist, even though surrealism is a luxury of the white civilization, a toy of people who can afford unconsciousness. It is also a des-

perate attempt to rejoin civilized brilliance with a *raison
d'être*. Surrealism is an adrenaline shot in the heart under
superb cultural conditions. It revives a culture which does
not really want to live. Césaire, as I understand it, did not
rise to the bait when André Breton elected him to the
surrealist school. I am not criticizing surrealism, which is
of fundamental value in all modern arts; I am pointing
out the naiveté of the French in enlisting colonials in
aesthetic causes which were far from the realities of the
African or the American Negro.

Negritude in the famous poem *"Cahier d'un Retour au
Pays Natale"* ("Memorandum on My Martinique" is one
translation)—negritude is the realization of pity for the
modern world with its great inventions and its great
alibis. It shouts hurrah not for the "steel blue speed" of
the modern but for those who have never invented
anything:

> *Hurrah for those who never invented anything*
> *Hurrah for those who never explored anything*
> *Hurrah for those who never conquered anything*

I know of only one American poet who in genius and
experience even approaches the concept—M. B. Tolson.
And Tolson knows that the concept is different with us.
In American culture, according to the ground rules, there
can be no separatism even by race and color. What then?
Is there a long road of assimilation and miscegenation
ahead? Can there be an American negritude?

Tolson is an American who was also the Poet Laureate
of Liberia. He lived in Oklahoma in an all-Negro town
where he was twice mayor. In various capacities as editor,
I have published more poetry by him than anyone in
America. He has a superb reputation among a few poets
and critics but is unknown to students and to the general
reading public. This is not because he is difficult to read
(which he is), for difficulty of text is the stock-in-trade
of the poetry-teaching profession. *Tolson is not read
because he was a Negro.* A blind spot in the white literary
eye will not recognize a great Negro poet.

To complicate matters, Tolson's *Libretto for the Republic of Liberia,* commissioned by the first African republic, has in its American publication an introduction by Allen Tate. Mr. Tate, in my view, is a Confederate of the old school who has no use for Negroes but who will salute an exception to the race. He sees Tolson as an exception because "for the first time . . . a Negro poet has assimilated completely the poetic language of his time and, by implication, the language of the Anglo-American tradition." Mr. Tate invites Mr. Tolson to join his country club. Tate is one of the canniest critics in the business, the American T. S. Eliot, as it were. But the crux of the matter is that Tate says: ". . . the distinguishing Negro quality is not in the language but in the subject matter . . . ," for subject matter can only deal with your suffering and contaminate the beauty of poetry.

I have tried to correct this statement in my own introduction to Tolson's recently published *Harlem Gallery.* Tate considers that the use of Negro subject matter in poetry, which he calls "the tragic aggressiveness of the modern poet," limits the Negro poet to a "provincial mediocrity." I will not trouble you with my opinion of the modern classicism which Mr. Tate represents (I have written more than one book about it) except to point out that this powerful critic does not consider the theme of Negro suffering good enough for the art of poetry, just as though the theme of America was not a good enough theme for the poet Hart Crane. But in trying to assert that Tolson has been assimilated by the Anglo-American tradition, he puts Tolson in quarantine and destroys the value of the poem—possibly this critic's conscious intention. Thus it took a Southern intellectual and poet to introduce Tolson's *Libretto.* That was the only possible literary context for a great Negro poet ten or fifteen years ago: he must in that context be captured and returned to colonization, to that Tradition which had enslaved his ancestors and would continue to do so if it could manage it.

The refusal to see that Tolson's significance lies in his language, Negro, and that only that language can express the poetic sensibility of the Negro at the door of freedom, is a final desperate maneuver to contain the Negro within the traditional culture. And for that it is too late. The Tradition is already antebellum.

The falsification I speak of is that of trying to assimilate Tolson into the Tradition when he was doing the opposite. The fact that Tolson's *Libretto* is unknown by white traditionalists gives the lie to the critic's assertion that Tolson has risen above Negro experience to become an "artist." The facts are that Tolson is a dedicated revolutionist who revolutionizes modern poetry in a language of American negritude. The forms of the *Libretto* and of *Harlem Gallery*, far from being "traditional," are the Negro satire upon the poetic tradition of the Eliots and Tates. The tradition cannot stand being satirized and lampooned and so tries to kick an authentic poet upstairs into the oblivion of acceptance. But the Negro artist won't stay in the attic any more than he stayed in the cellar.

Tolson says it better in his new poem:

> *The Great White World*
> *and the Black Bourgeoisie*
> *have shoved the Negro artist into*
> *the white and not-white dichotomy,*
> *the Afroamerican dilemma in the Arts—*
> *the dialectic of*
> *to be or not to be*
> *a Negro.*

Is Poetry an American Art?

As poet, editor, essayist, anthologist, and professor, I have been involved in American poetry all my life. And as poet, editor, essayist, anthologist, and professor, I have finally had to confront the question, Is poetry an American art? The question implies a negative. If we assume the question has any authenticity—that is, is more than the braying of an amateur critic—what are its implications for the American poet, editor, essayist, anthologist, and professor?

American poetry nowadays has the reputation for having accumulated a large and impressive body of works. In the English language we are said to be the present leader in the art. Numerically as well as qualitatively, we make the best showing. Nevertheless, I believe that American poetry is a European transplantation which has never really taken root with us and never will. Ours is a hothouse poetry, kept alive by artificial respiration and fluorescent light. Otherwise, it is a poetry of brickbats.

We've all heard this *ad nauseam*. Our poetry is either academic or vandalistic. And yet I think it is so.

I remember a remark by the British poet George Barker which used to offend us. Barker said: American poetry is a very easy subject to discuss for the simple reason that

it does not exist. Today, the remark makes better sense
to me. I recall T. S. Eliot's aside which used to rub me
the wrong way. Speaking of Walt Whitman, Eliot said
that he was a great *prose* writer. I did not really understand Eliot's condemnation until I found something like
it in Whitman's own notes. Whitman wrote that the
barriers between prose and poetry must be broken down
once and for all. He said:

*In my opinion the time has arrived to essentially break down
the barriers of form between prose and poetry. I say the latter
is henceforth to win and maintain its character regardless of
rhyme, and the measurement rules of iambic, spondee, dactyl,
etc., and that even if rhyme and those measurements continue
to furnish the medium for inferior writing and themes (especially for persiflage and the comic, as there seems henceforward,
to the perfect taste, something inevitably comic in rhyme,
merely in itself, and anyhow), the truest and greatest poetry
(while subtly and necessarily always rhythmic, and distinguish-
able easily enough), can never again, in the English language
be expressed in arbitrary and rhyming meter, any more than
the greatest eloquence, or the truest power and passion. While
admitting that the venerable and heavenly forms of chiming
versification have in their time play'd great and fitting parts—
that the pensive complaint, the ballads, wars, amours, legends
of Europe, etc., have, many of them, been inevitably render'd
in rhyming verse—that there may have been very illustrious
poets whose shapes the mantle of such verse has beautifully
and appropriately envelopt—and though the mantle has fallen,
with perhaps added beauty, on some of our own age—it is,
notwithstanding, certain to me, that the day of such conventional rhyme is ended. In America, at any rate, and as a
medium of highest aesthetic practical or spiritual expression,
present or future, it palpably fails, and must fail, to serve. The
Muse of the Prairies, of California, Canada, Texas, and of the
peaks of Colorado, dismissing the literary, as well as social
etiquette of over-sea feudalism and caste, joyfully enlarging,
adapting itself to comprehend the size of the whole people,
with the free play, emotions, pride, passions, experiences, that
belong to them, body and soul—to the general globe, and all
its relations in astronomy, as the savants portray them to us—*

*to the modern, the busy Nineteenth century (as grandly poetic
as any, only different) with steamships, railroads, factories,
electric telegraphs, cylinder presses—to the thought of the
solidarity of nations, the brotherhood and sisterhood of the
entire earth—to the dignity and heroism of the practical labor
of farms, factories, foundries, workshops, mines, or on ship-
board, or on lakes and rivers—resumes that other medium of
expression, more flexible, more eligible—soars to the freer, vast,
diviner heaven of prose. . . .*

That last sentence—Faulknerian or something—reduced
to a beginning and end and avoiding the middle reads in
effect: The Muse (of America) soars to the freer, vast,
diviner heaven of prose. . . . In my limited knowledge
Whitman is the first poet ever to speak of the *heaven of
prose,* and I would like to nail that expression on the
desk of every American poet.

Whitman is the one great poet we have produced, and
by that loose term I mean simply a great world poet. He
is also our one innovator. Yet, it was Whitman who demanded the obliteration of the art as it had been known.

We can, I believe, understand the character and importance of American poetry, so-called, when we perceive
that the art is not native to us and that it can be produced only under laboratory conditions. And many corollary facts can be adduced from the same premise, for
example, the fact that most of our poets are products and
functionaries of the university. The fact that this poetry
is almost completely literary, that is, that it depends on
predigested cultural contents for its health. The fact that
self-destruction is more of an occupational hazard among
our poets than among any other writers. (This is not true
of our novelists, for example.) The fact that there is not
and never has been an audience for poetry in the United
States. The fact that we have substituted scientific and
critical analysis of poetry for the use of it, whatever that
might be. The fact that poetry has failed to reach the
drama qua poetry. And the fact that our most influential
poets, such as Pound, Eliot, and Williams, all moved

poetry as far in the direction of prose as they were able but
without succeeding in bringing about a permanent *rap-
prochement* or fusion of the two.

I notice with some wonder that a similar process may
be taking place in England. I have in mind the strange
poem *The Anathemata* which David Jones published
about a decade ago.

This poem by Jones could hardly have been written
without the example of the *Cantos,* to which it is greatly
indebted in form. The poem itself, however, is a Christian
poem, rich in the mythologies and liturgies of Britain. It
is not inconsequential that Eliot and Auden have both
given *The Anathemata* their highest praise. Jones has
very possibly made the kind of breakthrough for English
poetry which the other twentieth-century British poets
failed to do. The true influence of Pound and Eliot may
be felt in England in this way: the mythic form is broken,
prosaic prosody may well be the salvation of English
poetry, which has fallen on hard times, though this form
I think insufficient for the needs of American poets.
Mythography with us is artificial and all but meaningless;
in England it retains its validity. The peculiar situation of
American culture imposes upon us our cultural amnesia,
our most salient and formidable characteristic. Even what
we have left of the classical and religious forms, symbols,
and ikons is blurred and vestigial, in conflict with the
forms and ikons of our actual life. I can now understand
and be more tolerant of W. H. Auden's return to the
English Church. The American Void must have terrified
him, as in fact it terrified Eliot. And Pound's wild-eyed
quest for order led him to a more secular mythos of the
Virtuous Banker and the Precise Definition. Much of
Auden's best poetry, incidentally, is prose, but I doubt if
European poetry can ever be as freewheeling as the American in this respect. It cannot be, in fact. American poetry
must be *sui generis* if it is to progress. I would like to
reintroduce the term *progress* into the literary consciousness, for our poetry has been standing still for generations.

Whitman had the greatest insight after all. This might

account for his monumental unpopularity in America. For Whitman is unpopular not only with Americans at large—*nonexistent* would be a better word—but with poets. Whitman is dangerous to American poets, like a pesticide. Even a poet with the great gifts of Hart Crane could only view Whitman as the good gray poet or great pink mother. For despite his admiration of Whitman, Crane could never free himself from the most formal European poetics, a pseudo-Elizabethan rhetoric and the "iambic" line. Crane is one of our finest twentieth-century poets—and of the most self-destructive variety. And what are we to make of the paradox, for example, of Pound's dependence on Whitman's prosody while rejecting the sense of Whitman's poetry? And Hart Crane's identification with the sense of Whitman while rejecting the revolutionary forms?

In a footnote kind of way, I think also of Eliot's rejection of Milton during his free-verse years and his ultimate acceptance of Milton as Eliot drifted back into the traditional European forms. I beg the theological and psychological questions, not knowing how to deal with them. I'm inclined to judge a poet by his prosody, not his "philosophy." Unless I'm deluding myself, in prosody all the cards are laid on the table. Milton was as revolutionary as Eliot; rather, we might say, Milton is to English poetry what Whitman is to American prose. Both were "translating." Milton was "translating" the idea of the epic. Whitman was "translating" the mystique of American politics. Milton was improvising on pagan rhythms. Whitman was improvising on the Constitution and on the *Brooklyn Eagle.* Both in fact were drifting out of versification at different and appropriate rates of speed. To use a happy vulgarism, we can say both were in orbit. I admire *Paradise Lost* in the same way that I admire *Leaves of Grass,* and I recognize that both books are failures, that is, they are monuments, not living forces. They are the Stone Guests of Anglo-American poetry. They freeze us in our tracks.

American poetry, however, is polarized between Poe

and Whitman, not Milton (until Eliot raised that ghost).
The Poe-Whitman syndrome is the clue to the failure
of our poetry. Or perhaps we should say that because of
Poe and Whitman we have great prose.

Poe is the death of our poetry; Whitman, the midwife
of our prose. Let me fall back on D. H. Lawrence, who
can do this better than I can.

Lawrence is excellent on this theme, and his own
vacillations are very much to the point. Lawrence was
quite American in his disdain for poetry. Poe horrified
him because Poe was pathologically incestuous, tearing
down the delicate barrier between brother and sister,
male and female, past and present. But Whitman dis-
gusted Lawrence also when Whitman spoke of *merging*.
Whitman wanted all mankind to form a kind of daisy
chain of love. Lawrence stamped his foot at that kind of
cowardice. He ended by nominating Poe a ghoul and
Whitman a Great Soul (whatever that is). But Lawrence
had the scent: the purely destructive Poe, with his scientific detachment—the last thin disguise of ego; and Whitman, whirling us into the spiral nebulae—daddy pushing
the cosmic swing, endless rocking. And Lawrence had the
common sense to elicit Whitman, who would go beyond
oneself instead of insisting on oneself.

But Poe had no self. Poe preferred to become potting
soil. Night soil, to borrow a beautiful Irish expression.

It is precisely this circumambience or space program of
Whitman's which accounts for his unpopularity among
our contemporaries. If we leave out the poem about the
learned Astronomer, Whitman is all learned astronomy,
geography, and television. I'm not the first critic to suspect
that the collected poetry of T. S. Eliot and Ezra Pound
is a redaction of *Leaves of Grass*, an attempt to hush up
the joyous sense of vision in order to keep mankind's
nose to the grindstone.

When Poe had successfully and scientifically disin-
tegrated the psyche, he died and went to Paris. And there,
as we know, he was made the patron saint of Symbolism.
This bizarre form of literature is the foundation of modern

poetry, with its belief in nuances, effects, spooks, and cultural memory. We find this Gallicized Poe working a great influence on the moderns, even though the *American* Poe is repudiated by Eliot and the other moderns. The *American* Poe in the United States is, of course, the man of postmortem effects which Lawrence had in mind. And curiously, it is this popular Poe—despised by the Literati —which bears the greatest resemblance to the literature of the absurd. "The Bells" or "Ulalume" or the whodunits are literature of such low caliber that they approximate the anti-literary. Intentionally or not, Poe is still one of the great destructive forces of literature. This explains T. S. Eliot's fear and contempt of Poe, for Eliot would like to salvage and revive literature. Eliot would like to retain the ratiocinative Poe without the romantic slag. And the disembodied, Gallicized Poe is pure in this respect. Poe is the author of the doctrine of the uncontaminated poem, which I refer to as the laboratory poem.

Whitman could not possibly affect Europe. Whitman is more or less on the wavelength of India, the cosmic wavelength, but in Europe it just sounds like a lot of United States static. Swinburne found Whitman attractive for a time but dropped him. Only a dissident European like Lawrence could stomach Walt. And similarly, very few Americans can stomach him either. Our own wavelength as far as poetry is concerned is still European: reason, form, continuity, fear of spontaneity and originality. This is why we can produce only a variant of English poetry and why we have no American poetry except for a few followers of Whitman who are mainly pseudo-Orientals. The pseudo-Orientalism of Whitman and our New England Transcendentalists is repeated by our contemporary Beat poets as Zen or Yoga.

The rational line of modern poetry, when it flirts with the East—the line of Eliot and Pound—is quietistic and orderly and is directed toward a controlled politics and a state church. We get Confucius in Pound, a variant of the eighteenth-century Jefferson, or we get a mysticism of surrender and passivity, as in Eliot.

The irrational line of modern poetry, when it flirts
with the East, is anarchic in politics; it is apolitical and
religiously egocentric. Such is the American variant of Zen,
which sees this psychology rightly or wrongly as a technique
of self-expression. Not as a way of making peace with
nature or history, but as a way of thumbing one's nose at
life and time. American Zen is about on the level of the
American fascination with judo and the haiku; both are
techniques of combat. With my minuscule knowledge of
the Japanese, I yet think we have not understood them
very well.

Nevertheless, the ambition to separate our art from
Europe is a healthy ambition, and the drive to the East
was inevitable. It was equally inevitable in the time of
Whitman and in our time. We must appreciate this intellectual flight in Eliot's Vedism, Pound's Confucianism,
and the Beat writer's Zen. What such writers share is an
intolerance for American hedonism and violence, what is
called The American Way of Life.

Modern American poets, for the rest, have held to an
uneasy compromise with French poetics, in Cummings or
Wallace Stevens, or to a mindless adherence to the standards of English literature. And this Anglo-American poetry,
as I have suggested, is quite naturally the province of our
"English Departments."

American poetry—what there is of it—has a powerful
centrifugal force. It throws itself out of its country. I know
of no other poetry which has done this. Think of the
pride of the British poet for Britain, of the almost religious adoration of the French poet for France, even a
Rimbaud or the poets of the Resistance. Then look at
American poetry with its bitterness, disillusionment, its
striking-back, its treason; it is even in Whitman. What
does it mean? Why is there so little good American poetry
which is not self-consciously anti-American?

A few years ago I put together an anthology of American
poetry for college students. The chronology ran from Anne
Bradstreet to Allen Ginsberg. A secretary at the publishing

house objected so violently to the latter item that she had a nervous breakdown and had to be led away. The Ginsberg poem was "Howl," and the publishers themselves were concerned about sales, especially in parochial schools. They included the poem nevertheless. In compiling this anthology I did my one and only piece of original research. I went back and read all the books of American poetry that had been called that. Little if any of it was. My scoreboard ended up something like this: seventeenth century, Anne Bradstreet and Edward Taylor (no Wigglesworth). Eighteenth century, nothing. Or rather, Philip Freneau, mostly because he had the good sense to ignore the Hartford Wits. He is probably our first American poet, but unfortunately he isn't much of a poet. Nineteenth century, Bryant, Emerson, Longfellow, Whittier, Poe, Holmes, Jones Very, Thoreau, Whitman, Melville (a perfectly awful poet), Bayard Taylor, Henry Timrod, Emily Dickinson, Lanier, and Father Tabb. The rest of the gallery, the bulk of it really, is given over to twentieth-century poets.

It is an extremely unimpressive record for a nation born and conceived to remake the world in its image. Taking a dismal view of the anthology, we might say with accuracy that we have given birth to only one poet before the present century, Walt Whitman. There are a few false starts, such as Poe and Emily Dickinson. The rest is padding.

As far as I can tell, Whitman was the first American writer to be conscious of the fact that the language of England no longer applied to us, though we speak it. It was a language dissolving. A curious linguistic process obtains with us: it is a destructive process and it is fascinating. It works this way. We admit, in greater or lesser numbers, immigrants from all over. We immediately destroy their language, simultaneously destroying our own. What we get rid of are the cultural vestiges and overtones. We cultivate what used to be called broken English. Now, no one seriously suggests that we have a new and separate language or even a derivative language, but everyone agrees tacitly that we have scarcely a language at all but only a medium of communication.

After the Civil War everyone was indoctrinated into the Northern mentality. This meant (aside from the love of the factory and the office, the industrialization of the farm, and the hatred of nature) the accelerated demolition of cultural vestiges. An Old Country language became a matter of shame; the very trace of an accent was distasteful. It has taken a mighty effort on the part of the present government to institute foreign-language programs, for unconsciously we resist them. We do not wish to come that close to the recent and ugly past. Next to the French, with whom we have so much in common, we are linguistically the most intolerant people in the world—and proud of it.

It cannot be said that Americans have a mother tongue. We have removed the singing organ of the nightingale. On the other hand, all the arts in this country *except poetry* are flourishing, as everyone is aware. Painting, sculpture, theater, music, the novel and short story, and much other prose—we are creating very lustily in every direction except that of the poem. Our poetry is still English, still written in the hieratic language which is to us about as meaningful as Etruscan. We speak a variant of English certainly. Yet we associate the language inevitably with its greatest form of expression, English poetry. Now what can English poetry mean to a third-generation Czechoslovakian used-car dealer in Nebraska whose children are my students? For my part, I am on the side of the student.

What is the rationale of visiting this poetry upon millions of central and southern Europeans, Scandinavians, Jews, Negroes, Japanese, or Navajo Indians? Classical Greek would make more sense—or Latin certainly. Yet most English professors in America can't read two words of Greek and only six of Latin. This has never ceased to amaze me. The great bulk of English literature was created by men saturated in the classical languages, men whose sensibilities were shaped by the endless discipline

in those languages. How many English professors know
Italian, and how can one be knowledgeable in English
literature without knowing it? I am speaking as an outsider, an impostor really, for I have too much respect for
the scholar's profession to think that I am any more than
a guest in any university. But as a writer I know that
English poetry was not conceived in a vacuum, that it is
a part and only a part of European literature, and that
American literature is perhaps the first original point of
departure from that great culture.

There is little evidence that Americans have ever
clutched poetry to their hearts. Jefferson was more interested in Italian and German music than in Shakespeare.
Benjamin Franklin packed a copy of *Fanny Hill* in his
luggage when he went abroad as an ambassador. Lincoln,
a great writer, was no literateur. Our great prose writers
of the nineteenth century wrote execrable poetry, for example, Melville and Thoreau; Mark Twain was the opposite of poet (or, from my viewpoint, a great poet who
wouldn't stoop to verses). All of our great writers ("poets"
in quotes, if you like) are prose writers. William Carlos
Williams made English poetry his chief target of abuse.
Cummings tried to veer toward a divorce from English
forms by cultivating the graphic atomic forms of Apollinaire. Stevens beat prosody to a new flatness. The only
good poet in the *English* tradition we have produced in
our time is Robert Frost. I myself have never been able
to see anything in the slightest American about Frost.
Oxford and Cambridge knew this. He was our last Colonial, the shining light of that group of British poets
who called themselves the Georgians. It can scarcely be
said that he lived in America. His habitat was that mythological New England which, since it does not exist, might
as well be Old England. We know very well that Frost is
not read in the United States; he is studied. I won't go
into the question of Frost as our Establishmentarian poet
or Virgil. Or why William Carlos Williams, our most
American poet since Whitman, who was once supposed to
serve as poetry consultant to the Library of Congress, was

unseated before he could exercise that function. The government feels safer with a poet of the Tradition, European tradition, that is.

Frost, it goes without saying, is a master. But it is no accident that he had to go to England for recognition and that to the end, except for the great honor given him by President Kennedy, his audience was English.

I think also of the almost catatonic depression of E. A. Robinson, a poet displaced in America, or the bitter self-hatred of Robinson Jeffers, a Whitman without joy. Jeffers had hoped to spend his life in Ireland and escape this country forever. The fact that Jeffers wrote in Whitman's forms—traducing them, really—only reinforces the irony or paradox of the expression "American poet."

It would be tedious to rehearse the present situation in our poetry, this poetry so endlessly and cruelly satirized by our novelists, and rightly so. The poet in the academy, the Writers Conference or Writers Colony, the Fulbright poet, the poet-critic—these are what posterity shall know us by. I will not discuss this phase of the business but simply touch upon the types of poetry we get from this environment.

First of all, we have many, many poets, all highly trained and expert in the skill of writing poetry. I am not trying to be witty when I say that the average graduate student who works a little at it can write a poem as well as Yeats. My opinion of Yeats has suffered considerably from this discovery. Was Yeats a graduate student?

The huge majority of these poets of ours are nestled in or around a college or university. The American university has taken on the responsibility for the care and feeding of poets. For a long time I admired this hospitality but after engaging in it for a number of years decided that it was a snare and delusion. A poet on an American campus, if he is not a bona fide professor, is no more than an exotic insect, a zoology specimen, a Live One. He exists entirely in the third person. He fled from the town where he had no identity. In the university he has so much identity that he might as well be under a microscope. Freshmen pull his wings off and deans wear him like a scarab. But I am off the subject.

Where are the poems themselves published? In university quarterlies, naturally; in secular monthlies, governed or influenced by university culture; and in magazines such as the *New Yorker*, which entertains a slightly gamy approach to literature. Or else in certain select little magazines far from any public view.

For me it is impossible to distinguish between one of these marvelous mechanical poems and another. They always seem to me to be written by the same person or Thing. I can't name five poets writing in the English or American language today who have enough individuality or style to be distinguished from one another. That some get ahead of others in reputation is purely a matter of chance. Or so I believe.

But there is also a poetry of revolt in the United States. This poetry of revolt is far better, more engaging than the university poetry, but unfortunately it seems to have died an early death. (I'm not sure why it petered out.) In any case there has been little development of this poetry that I know of.

In a larger sense, of course, all our poetry has been a poetry of revolt or at least of complaint. This is the most significant fact of all. Such a poetry rejects the very basis of its existence. It rejects what I call the poetic situation, that which is characteristic or what Williams called the *local*. Our poetry is criticism, very nearly in a technical sense, as our criticism is very nearly philosophy. We have a poetry of violence and a poetry of wit. The violence may be inner or outer in direction. And I notice about my two favorite United States poets, Whitman and Williams, that they report upon the violent but do not themselves become violent. Perhaps it was because Whitman and Williams knew the street and not simply the writer's colony, the European salon, or the academy that they developed a sense of proportion about American life. Whereas the *poète maudit* is committed to cursing a society he does not know, the academic poet is committed to cursing the street. Or rather, he does not curse; he witticizes and versifies. Yet the poetry is good, well made, and made to last. It's for the "quality." And the violence is real and records true horror and frequently ends in blood. But I cannot be content with either poetry. Our poetry reflects only corners of the city; the poet flees from university to university like a pilgrim in the Dark Ages hurrying from one distant cathedral to the next. Our poor modern poet, full of self-pity and champagne, his pockets stuffed with stanzas and passports. Or else he flows from the Left Bank of the Seine to the Left Bank of the Ganges miraculously, being a mendicant. I have no quarrel with any of that except to ask him once in a while: Where are you from? Why don't you sit down and take a load off your feet?

American poetry in our time has been a brilliant form of introspective photography. But the famous photograph album of the modern anthology is only to leaf through in some unborn dentist's office, a momentary and mindless distraction before the consolation of the novocaine. In different ways our opposite poets, the Academes and the Bohemes, are both anesthetized. Isn't this because they are trying to write poetry, on the one hand, and *be poets*, on the other? To *be* a poet in America—what is this like? To write poems in America—isn't that turning back the clock?

Some young poet recently wrote an article in which he was saying about me and others: Leave us alone. Shut up about Whitman and Williams and prose and let us write our poems in peace. Maybe he is right. An overnight collapse of the stanza might be as dangerous as the abolition of the army. Poets still need close-order drill and the barracks mentality. It's too bad that they do. Novelists don't, nor does any other kind of artist I know of. But poets are still the hostages of convention.

What would an American poetry be like should we have one? Certainly it would not be recognizable as such. It would be nonsensical, hilarious, and obscene like us. Absurd like us. It would be marked, as we are, by cultural

forgetfulness and lack of principle. It would be void of
values and ideals, sensual, joyous, bitter, curious, gossipy,
knowledgeable to the last minute detail, ungrammatical,
endlessly celebrating the facts, objects, neuroses, murders,
love affairs, and vulgarities of America. Certainly it would
develop favorite forms, but these would be soluble in
prose. It would be comical and slack and full of junk;
impure, generous, bookish, and cheap. It would be mystical, savage, drab, and as hateful as Joyce Kilmer's "Trees."
As sloppy as Whitman and—well, it would be like the
great American novel which every American poet ends
up writing as a tribute to "the diviner heaven" of prose.

For poetry is—let us admit it—a minor art of America,
like pottery. Our poetry becomes more and more ceramic
as the decades roll by. And outside the pot shop the boys
with their hammers and rocks peer in at the window.
The novelists of this country pay their respects to poetry
out of courtesy and professional *esprit*, but they know, as
we know, that the jig is up. Poetry has long since become
a pastime, a way of puttering around. Henry Miller wrote
me once that he had been puzzled all his life by his suspicions about so much famous poetry and that usually
in his reading he sought great poetry in prose. He admired
certain German, French, and Oriental poets and Whitman in this country. But on the whole, he drew back
from the sacred object called the poem. I had helped him
understand this, he said, for which I felt pleased. And for
myself, I also seek poetry in prose and in foreign poets.
Notice the tremendous pull toward translation in our
time. Our poets, the best of them, have turned translation not into an art but into a new poetic medium. What
does this point to except a failure of our own medium?
Doesn't it mean that our poetry can no longer digest the
contents of our life? For this kind of translation is not
scholarly or even culture-tradition translation; it is a lifeline
or a feeding tube from afar, a temporary supply of life
to revive our sickly poetry. We will translate Cavafy one
day, Catullus the next, Evtushenko, Lorca, or Gottfried
Benn. We do this as if to reassure ourselves that poetry

is possible in the old manner. But at bottom we don't believe it. We don't believe the spatter of questions at the close of "The Waste Land" or the beautiful gleaming lines of Homer and Ovid and Cavalcanti in *The Cantos*. *Dove sta memoria*. But we have no memory. Memory is a luxury Americans cannot afford.

Everything in our literature tends toward the dissolution of what people usually call poetry. We happen to have great literature—the political works, the strange and wonderful novels and tales, the polemics, sermons, speeches, asides, criticism, even journalism and reports —and a few unexpected flashes of poetry. But poetry itself we do not have, except that poetry which flowers under the light of prose. How typical it is of our poetry, even a century back, that it is tortured into existence. Emily Dickinson's heartbreaking style or Emerson's the same, repeated in our time in the exquisite timidities of Marianne Moore and the stylized elegance of our university wits. I suffered through Cummings' struggle against the great monuments of the Tradition and his momentary honeymoon in France, Jeffers' gigantic bitterness, Sandburg's hiding in the shawl of Lincoln, and Roethke's roving back and forth between Yeats, the *New Yorker*, and *Leaves of Grass*. Trying to write poetry in the old manner is murder for us. All of which sounds like the lengthy obituary which Rexroth did when Dylan Thomas died.

We have tried so hard—and failed—to produce a poetry of sensibility. Let us give it up. We have experimented with every extreme to no avail. The art of poetry is foreign to us. To some this is a bitter pill to swallow, but we'd better take our medicine. I think I understand finally the flight of our great exiles, the lonely achievement of Whitman, and the triumph of other arts of language in this country except ours. "The heaven of prose"—that is a corny expression to conjure with and to nail on the walls of Yaddo or the MacDowell Colony. But it makes sense. For if some Tibetan or Amazonian were to ask me to name the great poems of this country I would name a couple of poets and add something as preposterous as the works of Thomas Jefferson and Thoreau, *The Rosy Crucifixion, Huckleberry Finn, Henderson the Rain King,* etc., etc. The poetry might well be placed in the archives of Washington, not even in a library. Nobody reads it except students, who have no choice, and the teachers who think it necessary to talk about. Nobody loves it. Nobody wants it. It's mostly a great stack of Confederate money which you can hold sorrowfully in your hand and wonder: Did people ever really think you could spend it?

As a summing up, I would like to share the responsibility for what I have said. I am in earnest when I argue that American poetry is yet to be born and that what we have optimistically called our poetry is only a garden of chemical flowers. I share the responsibility with Whitman, who laid it on the line when he denied the possibility of a formal poetics in America. I elicit the support of Eliot, who shrewdly named Whitman a great prose writer. Pound, who demonstrated how the Old World forms might be broken. Williams, who struggled so long to locate in language the rhythm of American life at its worst.

I have been trying in my small way for years to help devalue the false currency of our poetry. We need a poetic stock market crash. Yet, we have had it; we had it really at the Boston Tea Party; we have it in every generation which rebels against the Old World cultures. The saying goes: Every nation gets the poetry it deserves. Is this what we deserve? Why don't we turn the question around to ask: Do we deserve a poetry at all? Our history shows very little inclination toward the art. The one brief upsurge of poetry we have had was during the 1920's: Sandburg, Fletcher, Lindsay, easy poets who wanted American listeners. The Americans listened more or less politely and then went about their business. Fletcher killed himself. Lindsay killed himself. Sandburg became a famous historian. It was almost as if the muse of America had muttered: Give them enough rope. . . . Exile or monasticism became the only method of survival for the poet:

abroad or behind the campus wall, anywhere, elsewhere, even Skid Row. The Southern poets exiled themselves to the North.

For years I've battled publishers to print more poets, sometimes succeeding in getting some new man's work in print. Now I don't know but that the publishers weren't right. For generally the publisher is only shamed into printing poetry. The Old World is drilled in the super-stition that poetry is the highest form of art. If so, it is certainly not the highest in this country. Nearly every one of our famous novelists began as a poet and gave it up. I am sometimes inclined to think that literature itself gave up the poem when the novel was invented. Poetry has been fighting for its life for centuries, but in America it never stood a chance. Does this make us a nation of barbarians or what? We consume books but we will simply not consume poetry. Spoon-feed it as we teachers will, it refuses to go down the body politic. Pediatrically, I would advise this: We'd better change the formula.

Perhaps we should teach our children that once upon a time there was a thing called poetry, that it was very beautiful, and that people tried to bring it to our shores in boats but it died. And a few people couldn't live without it, so they went back to the Old World to see it. And others built elaborate greenhouses, called English Departments, where they kept it breathing. And they watered it with the most expensive electricity, but it didn't like it here and died anyhow. And some fractious students lost their tempers and began to smash the greenhouse windows. And then everybody started reading prose.

A Defense
of
Bad Poetry

I am going to start with a quotation from a poet who
has been trying to learn how to write Bad Poetry. This
is from a magazine called *The Noble Savage* (the poet's
name is Louis Simpson):

*A few years ago I was able to begin and finish a poem. I found
that the poem was directed by certain external forces toward a
certain end. But one day I found that the ideas were better
expressed in prose. No, it was more than that. I found that
I no longer wished to please. . . . I found myself wanting to
write bad poems—poems that did not depend on stock responses. I wanted to write poems that would not please. For
the last three years I have been learning to write this new kind
of poem. The most important change is in the content (whether
one writes "in form" or "out of form" is not an essential question). Instead of statements which reassure the reader by their
familiarity, or shock him by their strangeness—instead of opinions, there are only images and reverberations. I can never
finish these poems. I wrestle with them and leave off when I
am exhausted. Frequently all that remains is a handful of
phrases.*

This statement I find very appealing. It makes more sense
to me as a writer than anything I have read about poetry

in a long time, because I have been going through the
same process myself for years.

When a poet says he wants to write bad poems, after
he has succeeded in writing "good" ones, he is kicking
over the traces. When he says that change must come in
content, he is asking for a revolt against his own values
not only in literature but in everything else. He has come
to doubt the values not only in literature but in everything else. He has come to doubt the value of accepted
literary "contents" and of his own psychic contents. He is
in full revolt; he is trying to break out.

I too find myself wanting to write Bad Poetry, poetry
that will not please, poetry that will subvert the standards.
The built-in convenience of the term *bad* doesn't matter
and in fact is a help. We who belong to this revolt feel
an obligation to refute reputation itself, our own, whatever it is; to turn our backs on our successes in order to
survive as artists. To the Serious World this looks like
suicide as well as vandalism. And it may be. The kindergarten term *bad* carries a powerful charge of meaning on
all levels of the Serious World. In religion it may mean
the damned; in morality, the illicit; and in aesthetics,
the hopelessly inferior. Ordinarily when we say a poem is
bad we mean at least that many things: it is wicked, it is
contrary to right behavior, and it is substandard. But we
who defend the Bad question all that. We question the
religious dichotomy of good and evil, the legal and ethical
dichotomy of right and wrong, and the aesthetic scale of
valuation also. We are in the Void. But we do not mean
that there are no longer standards of judgment, only that
standards are arbitrary. This is why we oppose Tradition
and consider ourselves the enemy of institutions.

Blasting away at institutions is old stuff for artists of
all kinds. A generation ago we had the revolts of Bohemia,
Greenwich Village, Bloomsbury, expatriation to the Left
Bank, and so on. A generation before that there was the
Decadent upsurge in France and elsewhere. And a generation before that we had such famous smashers of institutions as Baudelaire on one side of the ocean and Walt

Whitman and Thoreau on this side. It's not too much of an exaggeration to say that every literary generation is a generation of revolt. The revolt is invariably against standards and rules and regulations which seem just about on the verge of being fixed. Consequently, many historians of literature regard this revolt of the generations as something natural and inevitable. They expect the young to kick over the traces, and they know that in good time the new revolt will slow down and take on the set features of an institution, while it is being blasted at by the next generation. Beat poetry, it appears, is partly institutionalized already and preparing to defend itself against a new uprising.

This anyhow is the common historical view of poetry and art, and I hold it to be completely false. I have never been convinced that the battle of the generations explains anything of importance or even deals with the facts. Yet we are so historically conditioned that we tend to see even poetry as a series of historical struggles, with gains, losses, and casualties. To escape from this time-psychology once and for all seems to me one of the paramount tasks facing the artist. Rebelliousness may be one of the characteristics of poetry, but it is not its aim. Our unfortunate tendency to think of the arts in negative terms does in fact create negation in art; we have come to expect it. Art as protest always attracts the most attention, just as a plane crash is more attractive to a journalist than the unveiling of a masterpiece.

As long as we abide by the concepts of good and bad, major and minor, great and not great—these rules of thumb used in desperation by teachers as a framework for literary education—we perpetuate the literature of protest. Such terms as *bad, evil, great* are very powerful images that create realities. Winston Churchill once pointed to a place in Europe and said: There is an iron curtain across Europe. What a fine image, said the history-minded on both sides of the remark, and they all proceeded to build one to specification.

We have evolved a value system for the arts which is

untenable. The revolt of the generations is proof of that. It is typical of this kind of thinking also that every revolt is eventually forgiven. If we skip a generation, going back to the Victorian, say, we begin to assert not only that they weren't so bad but even that they were extremely good. Even old movies, which were known to be junk when they were first screened, are called classics two film generations later.

Suppose we could free ourselves from conventional valuation in poetry or any art and assign a zero to the term *bad* as to the term *good*. Suppose, in other words, we stopped looking at poetry aesthetically, religiously, morally. Then, instead of these endless abstract generalizations or bigoted opinions about a poem or a painting, we would have nothing but the poem or the painting itself. We might be able to look at it with the honesty of a man from Mars or with the sincerity of a child. Artists, by the way, are constantly dependent on the perceptions of children.

My point is that most of the art and literature of the world, if seen outside religious, moral, and aesthetic convention, habit, and prejudice, would disintegrate into dust. For a tremendous quantity of what we call art and literature is little more than the projections of outworn values of one kind or another.

The twentieth century has been the first to question wholesale the validity of those values. We are the first people who place the art of savages (so called) on a par with learned and sophisticated art. We are the first to take the creations of children seriously. We are the first to recognize the genius of the insane. We are the first to pay homage to the writings of the criminal and to works previously condemned for obscenity or what the law books call sexual aberration. Ours are the first artists to visit the junkyard and there discover beauty. (This is quite a different thing from digging up the busted statuary of Greece.) We are the first to search the scientist's laboratory for new and unheard-of kinds of music and design. On these levels we have already left conventional Good and Bad behind.

The true modern artist and poet knows that values will be assigned to his work, but he himself is not concerned with that. A poem may be value-creating, but that is an accident, an unfortunate accident, like the money value attached to a painting. The artist knows that he cannot prevent this making and counterfeiting of value, but he does his best to ignore it.

In his personal life the modern artist's greatest job is to escape the Evaluators, these pawnbrokers and Shylocks of good and bad, major and minor, great and ungreat.

Curiously enough, the marketplace of aesthetic value is the school, any school from grammar to university. The Evaluators are most prevalent in the graduate colleges of literature and history. I've written about this sociological phenomenon elsewhere and have earned myself the name of the Trojan Horse in the English department. For it has struck me in many years of teaching that my colleagues who are English or history professors are the real Aesthetic Tories of the University. Their fear and even hatred of science and technology, for instance, are attitudes I cannot share.

In practice, modern arts have freed themselves from religious dogma, moral fiats, and aesthetic prejudice. But Theory follows hard behind, always on the poet's heels. The artist has a hard time escaping his Evaluators. Much of the time he uses up all his energy doing just that. A young writer I know who went to a writer's colony (or an asylum for the creative) told me that all the people who went there spent their first two weeks—you'd never guess what they spent their first two weeks doing—*sleeping*. Alone. Then one day they awoke and assaulted the typewriter.

The one thing never granted the writer in this society is the one thing he needs, and the only thing: time to do his work. The moment he writes one successful poem or paints one successful picture or writes one successful composition, he is finished. The Evaluators and curators have got his number. Every kind of snare is loosed to capture the goose that laid the golden egg.

So the writer takes off to the north woods. And if he can afford it he will erect an electrified fence around his hut that would kill an elk at a hundred yards.

Or he will hit the highway literally or otherwise. I am speaking on a low level at the moment, the level of survival. Artists have a very low survival level. Money has nothing to do with it. To surive as an artist or craftsman or inventor, a person of imagination, whether scientist or artist, you need only the respect of privacy. Respect for the possibility of successes or failure. Nothing else. Rewards are fine but meaningless, as every honest craftsman knows.

A man who wants to write Bad Poetry, anti-theater, the artist who decides upon anti-art, the composer like Charles Ives (to name an early example) who prefers cacophony to melody—not only are these people making technical experiments but they are barricading themselves and their work against the tried and accepted values of the past.

The way I'm trying to use the word *Bad* is as a synonym for *Good*; so that a Bad poem, if it is Bad enough, will drive out "good" poetry. For example (I think Auden said this one time), the "poesy" poems in the *New Yorker* (poems written in country newspapers by hillbillies, etc.) are frequently better than the high-paid poems in the same magazine written by famous poets. There is a sense in which Joyce Kilmer's "Trees" is better than "The Waste Land" because it is so truly bad, it is true to its badness, while "The Waste Land" is a poem in bad faith, really an essay and not a work of poetry. Well, what a man like Simpson is saying is that "good poetry" has become so predictable that you might as well give it up and let the anthologist write it. Literature has become so literary that the literary work is almost bound to be born dead; and all the midwifery of criticism and pedagogy can't bring it back to life.

Now, that is exactly the pickle the poet is in today. He cannot write *his* poem without somebody's immediately assigning it either to a class or to a category. The poem must somehow escape the deep freeze of classification if it is to function. The poet tends to react in two ways in this situation in which he knows his poem is going to be trapped: either he goes into a Protest Tantrum (even protesting against his own standards, since they have failed him into "success") or he ditches the Standards completely. In protest he becomes an anti-poet, a revolutionary, an avant-gardist; and in abdicating from standards altogether he becomes Bad.

So, anti-poetry is not enough and is in fact grist for the mills of the Evaluators. Gerard Manley Hopkins makes the *Oxford Book of English Verse,* and so forth. The aim is to stay out of the anthology, any anthology, not because they don't want you but because you are *Bad.* Hence the compulsions of the Bad poet to be "obscene" or nonsensical or Dadaist.

Anti-poetry is not really different from any poetry of Protest, and Protest poetry is nothing new. You might say Wilfred Owen was an anti-poet: when he put that little twist into rhyme he was not just making war noises as a protest against war, he was also making war on rhyme. It was like saying: If you pretend to make harmonious sounds nowadays, you are lying. Cummings was an anti-poet, protesting against the forms of sentiment, whether in himself or in versification. So were they all, the good poets of our century, anti-poets and protesters. Even Eliot protested in his earliest and best work. But everyone knows that when Protest becomes an end in itself it loses meaning. The trouble with Protest is that it's only Loyal Opposition. Simpson's remark that the change must come in the content is right. Protest poetry is mostly a change in the externals. But what if Cummings, to take an example, instead of lampooning the forms so obsessively with such baroque elegance had broken out of the forms altogether, which psychologically he could not quite do. Protest poetry is a protest against form only. Auden's old line about new styles of architecture pops into my head. Maybe that was the trouble with Marxism: it was only a protest against a style of architecture. They got their new architecture, with the same kind of management running the building. But what if the Marxists had had a real revolution, a revolution in content? Anyhow, anti-poetry is always betraying us with its deathbed conversions and ending up as the Loyal Opposition. To my way of thinking, Protest poetry and anti-poetry are the same thing, a battle against forms or habits without any real uprooting of the contents. In the long run anti-poetry only confirms the Tradition, only gives new form to Form itself.

I seem to be setting up a thesis that there are three kinds of poetry: Formalistic poetry, the poetry of limited Yes; Protest poetry, the poetry of No in various registers of thunder; and Bad poetry. But by *Bad* I mean *Good*. That is not very rational, but I will try to clear it up. Presumably, Formalistic poetry has form as an end in itself. Protest poetry vandalistically tries to break up or sabotage the forms, and sometimes the protest also becomes an end in itself. (Literary history is fascinated by this cobra-mongoose struggle and can't take its eyes off it.) And then there is Bad poetry, which Mr. Simpson and I want to write and which I will try to describe. We might just as well call it the poetry of the absurd, to get off the ambiguity of *Bad*. First, let me say something about modern Formalistic poetry, which is, as critics have been saying for a long time, a period piece. Our period.

Some people blame it on the Iowa writer's workshop. Somebody coined the expression "corn-belt metaphysical," but you could just as accurately call it Bennington Metaphysical or the Yale Conceit. Modern Formalistic is a national school of poetry.

Modern Formalistic is in fact Literature, with all the pretensions of that establishment and the life expectancy which surrounds anything that can afford the best doctors and lawyers. It is the poetry of the American age. Metaphysical it isn't; yet this poetry is so loaded with literary assumptions that it bears a shallow relationship to the school of poetry that goes under that name. A true metaphysical poetry would, on the contrary, be absurd: the cultural contents would have long since dissolved; the values implicit in mythological quotations, for instance, would no longer be present. The absurd artist ideally can say Leda and the Swan without even knowing that there were or were not such characters. Any poem by the same name would seem to him an artifact of the Serious World, hence inconsequential.

The best example of absurd or Bad poetry in America today is the poetry of William Carlos Williams. But in order to talk about this kind of poetry I will have to talk about other arts (as Williams always did). And in order to propagandize for this kind of art I will have to employ the service of Albert Camus, especially as he deals with the absurd in his early book *The Myth of Sisyphus*. I am not taking a philosophical position. I have no knowledge of philosophy, and I am even given to understand that Camus departed from his original thesis in *The Myth of Sisyphus*. That is not my concern. It is what he says about the absurd that I understand—in blinding flashes—and that illuminates my own feelings and prejudices about poetry.

Very briefly, Sisyphus is the absurd hero. "His scorn for the gods, his hatred for death, and passion for life won him that unspeakable penalty in which the whole being is exerted toward accomplishing nothing," Camus says. For various acts of disobedience to the gods, Sisyphus is condemned to push an enormous boulder up a mountain, only to see it roll back again when he reaches the top. Camus follows him down the hill: that is the moment of glory before Sisyphus must begin to push the rock skyward again. But it is at that moment of awareness when the victim feels his powerlessness and his fate that he is most grief-stricken and most joyous. As Camus puts it, "One does not discover the absurd without being tempted to write a manual of happiness. . . . One must imagine Sisyphus happy."

Camus wrote this book during what he called the European Disaster, and on one level it was a powerful diatribe against tyranny. Philosophically it was a treatise on sui-

cide: it answers in the affirmative the question, Is life
worth living? I find this work even more valid today than
in 1942 when it was written. Today we are all facing the
Void, all in revolt against the gods, passionately clinging
to life while we are aware that life is meaningless. Or
rather, whatever meaning it has is given by us. And in
poetry this means that the gods of value are dead. All
values are equal. Consequently, we can talk about Bad
poetry and strive for it, either on the level of protest or on
the existential level of questioning value out of existence.
Nietzsche, of course, is an absurd hero. So is Céline, who
helped invent the anti-hero. So is Henry Miller.

Not the *best* living, but the *most* living is one way of
putting the absurd. Value judgments are discarded in
favor of factual judgments. Metaphor has to go; the symbol has to go; myth itself has to go, except, as Camus says,
myth "with no other depth than that of human suffering,
and like it, inexhaustible. Not the divine fable that amuses
and blinds, but the terrestrial face, gesture, and drama in
which are summed up a difficult wisdom and an ephemeral
passion." Modern poetics is basically a theology, for the use
of mythology descended from religion, whether it comes
from Homer or the Bible or *The Golden Bough*, and will
revert to a religion. A secular myth like Usura can become
a quasi-religious symbol in no time. An absurd poetics, on
the other hand, would prefer quantity to quality, a difficult wisdom and the ephemeral passion, rather than the
one undying, immortal passion for God or for a member
of the opposite sex. Camus singles out Don Giovanni as
an example of the absurd hero.

He says about Don Giovanni (he is speaking of the
one who is the twentieth-century favorite, Mozart's and
Da Ponte's Don) that as seducers go he is an ordinary one.
Or rather, the difference between him and the ordinary
seducer is that Don Giovanni is conscious, and that is
why he is absurd. That is what makes him different from,
say, a goat. Don Giovanni has no use for gods, he worships
life, and he laughs at the Stone Guest, the symbol of
Death who leaves the graveyard to come to dinner and to

drag Don Giovanni through the opera house floor into the flames of hell. This ending, of course, is for the clergy and the usherettes. Above all, Don Giovanni does not believe in the profound meaning of things; he has no scale of values, unless it be that a fat girl is more comfortable in the winter than a skinny one. *The absurd poet, like the Don, has no sense of unity.* He doesn't try to put his life back together again every ten minutes. The "form" of his life will take care of itself.

In the libretto it isn't Don Giovanni who keeps the little black book with all the phone numbers in it; it is the pious and rascally valet Leporello who hypocritically impresses the ladies with this document. Don Giovanni multiplies what he cannot unify; to him nature is bountiful with women. He probably doesn't even know the little black book exists.

The clue to the marvelous and beloved absurdity of Don Giovanni is quantity as against the ideal—Maud Gonne, for instance, who was Yeats's ideal. The ideal love belongs to the Serious World, which is to say the phony world, the world in bad faith. Imagine how much famous literature would go by the board if we were to apply the criteria of absurdity instead of that of value, permanence, universality, and immortality. Practically all of it.

One of the great absurd artists of our time, a quantitivist if there ever was one, is Picasso. I know that his popularity is held against him and that in some quarters he is regarded as an interior decorator for motels—Ezra Pound dismisses him as a financial genius—but I find him absurd in the best sense. I see no reason to evaluate him, this man who has been in flight from values all his life. Picasso is very Chaplinesque, a great clown; he has lived a vast succession of presents, which is more than we can say of most artists. I like to believe that his dealers are Leporellos who keep his little black account books. And it is a foregone conclusion that he will have a state funeral —the one thing that will make him turn over in his grave —that Malraux will pronounce the benediction (and say that he was not really a communist or a millionaire) and

that de Gaulle will salute this Spanish peasant in the name
of France when they press the button and he descends
to his worm farm.

Picasso is typical of the plight of the poet today: hopping around like a flea to escape being caught and ticketed.
Just like Chaplin hopping to Switzerland with his nest
egg, another millionaire communist. But with Picasso it
is the aesthetic Evaluators, not the Bureau of Internal
Revenue, that are on his trail. And there's no way to out-
wit them except by reinventing the present over and
over in a million different disguises. The absurd genius
is a practical joker, the man who laughs. Chaplin is funnier than his movies and probably knows it. And the
difference between Céline and Henry Miller is laughter.
The laughter of Don Giovanni is not that of the villain
twirling his mustaches, an interpretation made available
for fathers; it is pure golden laughter, absolute quantita-
tive delight. Like Picasso plates. Or William Carlos Williams' scribbly poems.

The example of Louis-Ferdinand Céline is still with us
as the novelist of the absurd anti-hero; *Journey to the
End of Night* is still one of the bitterest, most absurd
books of the age. It is the Bad Novel (like the Bad Poem
I mentioned) *par excellence*. Céline was one of the first
French novelists to use the language of the street as a
narrative vehicle. That was absurd enough. The tale
proper is a parody of the romantic voyage with the hero
stripped of every vestige of heroism. Bardamu spends his
whole life escaping: from the Western Front in the First
World War, from an insane asylum, from a jungle outpost
in Africa, from a galley which takes him to America as a
galley slave, and from the production line of the Ford
Motor Company. Every institution of modern life, beginning with war and colonialism and coming down to
smaller personal institutions like love and murder, is de-
nounced brutally. The point is that you are left with
nothing of the values; you are left only with this anti-
hero, this Sisyphus without joy. The book is a merciless
comedy of ourselves with not a single second of relief

that I can remember. Céline has to go back and destroy the conventions of Beauty, as Rimbaud must, as all anti-poets have to. "One night I seated Beauty on my knees. And I found her bitter. And I cursed her."

There was a phase in modern poetry, still going on by fits and starts, called the anti-poetic, but this was naive: looking for the least "poetic" object and making it the center of attention. This is a step in the right direction, but it is a baby step. The Céline way, the Rimbaud way was a bigger step: wiping the whole scale of values off the slate. Even that is also poetry vis-à-vis something. An even bigger step is taken, I think, in the theater of the absurd or in abstract expressionism, Op, Pop, Minim, etc.

In recent years American-type painting, as one art critic calls it, has become the dominant painting in the world. It is the first time American art has taken the lead over European painting, or so I've read. I would call abstract or non-objective art absurd; you can almost turn back the clock a few years and hear people like de Kooning or Rothko or Pollock saying, "I want to paint bad paintings, paintings that do not please." I suppose that the idealization of the object was the point of opposition: the death of allegory (though it survives in surrealism), of representation of things or figures for the sake of representing, but especially the abandonment of symbols and symbolic objects —all these were moves away from the secure world. You need no longer fall on your knees before a picture, whether the Madonna or her opposite, the Mona Lisa.

I relate the nonsensical, the hilarious, and the obscene as three qualities of the absurd. Nonobjective painting is, the Serious World tells us, certainly nonsensical. It puts the trained artist in the same category as the child artist and the primitive, if not the chimpanzee. It explores the moment of the present instead of trying to manipulate the present toward the future, the ideal. To sit on top of a ladder and drip paint becomes as valid a skill as the finest calligraphy. Speed is a factor of this kind of art. We have seen Japanese artists who do abstract brush paintings of written characters; how fast they attack the paper with

the brush has much to do with the success of the painting.
Chance has much to do with it. Without becoming mystical, we can say that the absurd reintroduced the element
of chance into art: the printer's error, the spot of paint
from nowhere, the worm holes in the wood, the old poster
peeling off the wall; we have discovered the scrap heap
and found it good. It is jabberwocky but even without the
story and the moral.

So with the *objet trouvé*. If you pick up an object in
the woods or on the beach and put it down in a certain
place in your house it is to that extent an absurd work.
I don't mean seashells; those are readymades, like the
urinal Marcel Duchamp tried to enter in an art show.
The real *objet trouvé* has something wrong with it, like
the crack in the Liberty Bell. Only it has no patriotic or
other sentimental associations. It is valueless except as it
contradicts value.

Take compressed automobiles. Some artist thought of
mashing up cars in a hydraulic press, not for the purpose of melting them down for more cars, but for the
sake of mashing and mounting. It is neither a social criticism, poetry of protest, nor mashing for mashing's sake,
Formalism. It is absurd. In looking at a compressed Pon-
tiac we must not think of General Motors and the horrors
of industrialism; on the other hand, we need not forget
that this is a car, though mashed. It is something like the
stage direction given in one of the absurd plays: "The
actor kisses or does not kiss Miss Jones."

Let me go out on a limb a little further and give you
the outlines of an absurd poem. This is going to be a
Bad poem in the absurd sense, although it is probably
also a lousy poem. There's no question about it. What I
have done here is to take three advertising slogans which
are now dead, that is, obsolete; they are *objets trouvés*.
They are tied together by one line which happens to describe the pen I was holding when I wrote the poem. A
critic would give this quatrain a bad reading if he remembered the ads too well: he would be associating or reacting.
Instead, the reader should merely be conscious that three

of the lines were once ads; he is not too sure what they are trying to sell even though the objects are or are not mentioned. Then the old dead ads are joined by a fourth made-up line. Here is a skeleton of an absurd poem:

> *Hickock Belt Buckle and Beltogram;*
> *Eversharp Pen and Pencil Set;*
> *This smooth gold reminds me of my Bar Mitzvah;*
> *Ask the man who owns one.*

It's a collage, and it would be all right with me for the reader to say it is a recollection of the 1920's. But I am not going to do an *explication de texte* on this quatrain. Besides, every piece of nonsense is a Rorschach Test. But I guess it would be better to call it a Mashed Poem. A great deal has been written about nonsense, and I have nothing to add except that in a work of art the artist is *conscious* of the nonsense. A lunatic, on the other hand, is not. The art of the asylum has a great deal to tell us, but it must always stop short of telling us it is art. Child art, however, *is* conscious. Even though a child does not know the meaning of words, he is using them consciously for the fun of it. I am speaking of poetry. I subscribe to the hey-nonny-nonny school of poetics. This the child knows: All language is hey-nonny-nonny. Every poet spends a lifetime battling against the encroachment of meaning. Someone is always coming up and explaining that he knows the meaning of hey-nonny-nonny. For a simple definition, poetry is language in the meaning of hey-nonny-nonny. By this definition, every good line of poetry is absurd.

The absurdity of the obscene works the same way: you remove the meaning, usually "moral," and you are left with the word out of context. Minus its moral contents you put it back into action. It begins to make a new kind of sense. This is what Henry Miller is all about: he has changed the content of the novel by ignoring the morality of social forms. He remembers what it means to have had those words be obscene, and they retain a kind of vestigial obscenity, but he has moved the words a big

step away from their activity. The dirty words or slogans
or ads have lost their radioactivity: they are still but yet
no longer dirty words; the author's reorientation or disillusionment has changed all that. Lawrence was trying to
do the same thing but rather quaintly, making the dirty
word pretty as a dialect. Not so with Joyce: to Joyce the
dirty word was a dirty word and that was that. Joyce was
still stuck with the contents of the Dublin mentality.

You wonder whether the judges who have lately been
so liberal about the so-called obscene books are not wiser
than the authors themselves; for in saying that a work is
not evil even though it contains elements of the obscene,
they are making a transvaluation. They have left the moral
question behind and have conceded the change in moral
contents. No matter how much malarky the court hides
behind in suggesting that such works of art are healthy
for the body politic, it seems to me that they are really
admitting the devaluation of moral standards, to the point
at which the obscene is on the verge of becoming the
polite. Which is absurd.

Not to linger over this commonplace subject, I don't
want to leave it without making the usual distinction between the obscene, which is absurd, and the pornographic,
which is not. I would say that de Sade is obscene and
absurd, for one thing because he was such a "bad" writer.
Baudelaire seems to me pornographic, as he does to Sartre. He is an onanist. The Earl of Rochester would seem
to be a pornographer on the basis of his deathbed conversion; a true Rabelaisian or Don Giovanni cannot be saved:
they have to come and get him. And yet if you take the
side of the absurd you cannot moralize about pornography
either. Sooner or later even the pornographic must enter
the realm of the absurd. But it will first have to lose its
propagandistic tone.

As for hilarity, that speaks for itself. Hilarity is related
to nonsense and is a second cousin of the obscene. There
is a point at which the most solemn moment decides to
become the most ridiculous. Possibly the reason for ritual
is that ritual prevents this from happening. Anybody

caught laughing during "The Star Spangled Banner" just before the football game is certain to be hustled out of the stands more dead than alive. Yet nothing could be funnier than this particular ritual. I won't offend anybody by listing more solemn occasions, though folklore and literature and old wives' tales are full of assaults on church ritual and funerals. So is drama itself. The classical separation of tragedy and comedy was finally overcome by the Elizabethans, who were considered by certain critics as savages for that reason. Hamlet, after all, is as absurd as you can get; he makes no sense whatever, and that is precisely his charm. Though possibly he is more of a protest character than an absurd. But the last scene of the play is definitely hilarious and might have been written by Red Skelton.

Poetry should be zany. Not only should it frolic, as Camus says, but it should cavort, stumble, trip, fall flat on its face, get up, slither, fly, soar, dazzle, gloom, and lash out. But it has a fatal tendency to sulk and be melancholy or to be pompous and asinine. The dreariness and pomposity of *Paradise Lost* is compensated for only by Milton's zaniness of language. Whitman is saved after all by his sense of the comic, his sense of the absurdity of America. His failings are too well known to mention, but there is no question that he one day said to himself, "I want to write Bad poetry," and so forth. And he did, and we are all thankful for that.

Poetry has a lot to learn; it is a backward art. It learns from modern painting, from music, jazz and electronic music, from the anti-novel of the anti-heroic, from the picaresque and the primitive, from the theater of the absurd. It learns from the popular and the corrupt arts. The popular arts, say, television, have a brutalizing quality which frustrates people to the point of absurdity, even though the net effect is to make people who watch it homicidal. The sadism of popular art can be *materia poetica* also. Instead of writing poems which say loftily, "I hate television," the poet can write about the lines on the screen or what the TV mechanic calls "snow."

I saw a good Bad poem recently by a Beat poet which
absurdly described the beauty of a B-59 bomber. It was
a big step away from the poetry of Strontium 90, which
is poetry of the Serious World.

The absurd poet does not attempt to unify; he is content with multiplicity. The very number of poets in this
country today should be a comfort to everybody. Instead
of an elite we have a populace of the creative. We will
leave the relative quality of the poets to those who make
it their business to candle poems. I read in a recent interview with Ezra Pound that he didn't have time to read
new poetry but that he had appointed a representative
to pick out a few new things to show him now and then.
A kind of IBM machine of an adviser. In the long critical
career of T. S. Eliot there aren't more than two or three
contemporary poets who are ever mentioned. Both of
these major lights would contend that there is entirely
too much poetry in the twentieth century and that there
just isn't that much room at the top of the obelisk. They
get around the problem by disqualifying all the competi-
tors on various grounds or by pretending to ignore their
existence, like Pound, who probably stopped reading poetry with fresh ink somewhere around 1910. But now the
quantity increases and with it—or, as I would say, *because*
of it—the quality. It's as simple as arithmetic: the more
the merrier. For the minute you say the word *quality* you
are setting up standards, and that is what you must not
do. That's jumping the gun. Standards will be perceived
all too soon; it's the works that matter. And each generation will pick its own works for the past because it has its
own reasons, absurd reasons, and not because Dr. Johnson
has flourished a cane.

There is one final thing I want to mention in connec-
tion with absurd poetry, this poetry which I can only
adumbrate and not define. In fact, it must remain inde-
finable, not because of any ecclesiastical mystery but because of the nature of change. Art is constantly and er-
ratically moving toward a state in which it will cease to
exist; that is, man may someday be so happy that he will

not even need music, so conscious that only children will write great poetry. But for the time being poetry is flowing in the direction of prose, instead of away from it as it has done for so long. We have seen this all through the twentieth century (and earlier) and have been afraid of it. We should not be afraid of it. We are gradually losing the line of demarcation between prose and poetry, and we are almost at the point of asking perhaps for the last time: What is prose? What is poetry? And are almost at the point of answering: There isn't any. The contents of poetry have already become "contaminated" with the nonsensical, the hilarious, the obscene. This is as it should be. It happens that prose for centuries has moved closer and closer to the conditions of human life and poetry farther and farther away. Now it appears that poetry is also flowing in the direction of human experience and away from the ideal. Or so we hope.

The Image
of the Poet
in America

One of the saddest things that has happened in this country recently is the debasement of the word *image*, a word long dear to artists and of the deepest significance to them. The word has now been kidnapped by Madison Avenue, broken in half, and shared with the government. Poets can no longer use the word without hesitation; the crude alloys of greed and propaganda have been added. The word is already counterfeit.

But I am going to use the word in its present debased state of meaning, as it is used by advertisers when they say "public image." And I am going to use it to talk about the poet. In this sense of the word it would mean: What does the poet look like to People? What "image" do Americans have of the poet today?

To answer this question we must say that we have been given two images of the poet. (A) The good old man standing on a windswept platform and asserting his patriotism. This is the Frost-Sandburg image. And (B) the short, sweaty, bearded, and unwashed pro-Castro-anti-American youth. This is the Ginsberg-Corso-Ferlinghetti image. (And the question immediately arises: Why didn't Frost and Sandburg wear beards? Which may be the most crucial critical question of the day.) Image B has now been stylized in the press as the Hippy poet—but there are no examples presented.

I am pretty sure that the iconography and symbolism of the beard have been thoroughly analyzed by our sociologists and cultural anthropologists. But I would like to offer an aside or two of my own on this important subject: namely, that the beard, which always in the past was a symbol of fatherliness, paternity, goodness, and moral rightness, today signifies the opposite. The beard today stands for youth, rebelliousness, license, immorality, and sabotage. The beard today is a red flag waved in the face of the bourgeoisie. Charles Baudelaire is said to have dyed his hair green. Modern beard, red flag, green hair are all the same thing.

"Communications" being what they are in America— the absence of an independent press is our largest present difficulty in getting information distributed—we are all victims of an image-making machine called the newspaper and an image-making institution called the office of publicity. The public does not have the power in the twentieth century to create its own images; rather, the images are piped into the home by various well-known devices and corroborated in the neatly folded pile of newsprint which lies at every doorstep at dawn and at dusk. Just as in a police state history is rewritten at whim by those in charge of Truth services, so in the free world, as we are constantly reminded it is, any image can be redrawn, touched up, glorified, or exalted, depending on the mood of Publicity. For the American public to be able to tolerate two images of the poet, and opposite ones at that, points to a degree of sophistication which is new for us. And to these two images, the bearded rebel and the elder patriot, we are now adding a third: that of the academic poet, the poet housebroken by a college or university. The mood of Publicity is such that the public can now make these two or three valuations about the poet in America: there is the Grand Old Man, who has served his country well; there is the Beat poet, who is an enemy of our way of life; and there is the academic poet, who,

if he behaves himself over a sufficient span of time, may
himself become a Grand Old Man.

Notice that none of these valuations has anything to
do with poetry. They have to do with the *image*. It is
enough for the Medium to show a face underneath which
are printed a few well-chosen adjectives to convey the
message, the entire content of which is: This is a poet.
Usually the picture is enough to carry the valuation; and
the words are added for those who are not as highly
image-trained as others. Needless to say, these images of
the poet are not true, and when they are, the truth is
incidental to some larger consideration, such as politics
or religion, depending on what Publicity has in store for
us at the moment.

The public has already forgotten—if in fact it ever
knew—why a couple of poets were seen rubbing shoulders
with Presidents, chief justices, and generals. The public
is said to have said: What a fine thing! Recognition of
culture at last! When of course it wasn't a fine thing
at all. It was a very dangerous thing for artists, however
well meant such a gesture might have been. The image
of the poet was immediately gilded and enshrined. Suddenly we had something the equivalent of the King's
Canary, as the British Poet Laureate is usually called. And
of course it was not in the least an innocent gesture, an
expression of love and admiration for a couple of our
finest poets. It was much more. It was the beginning of
a political cultural policy, the exploitation of the artist
for prestige and propaganda. We are just at the beginning of this movement, and it is hard to see how far it
will go, whether we will have a Minister of Culture
sitting in the Cabinet, whether we will set up a National
Academy with ribbons of honor, pensions, and White
House odes. Traditionally, White House culture has been
a private affair and one that never ceased to amuse us.
For myself I prefer the good old days when White House
culture was limited to such pagan rites as the Easter egg
roll and the lighting of the Christmas tree. But nowadays
even New Critics are invited to dine, not to mention

foreign ministers of Culture to whom we have to show off our own elites.

The public is not given the "specifics" of the inner culture gatherings and meetings. It is not interested, and besides, Publicity is satisfied if only the general outlines are presented. But for those who are concerned (say, artists who have not been invited), a certain protocol is indicated. For instance, a poet with a questionable political past or one allied with the new rebels would not be likely to attend. A certain amount of screening, we must assume, operates in these functions. I think we can take this for granted.

I was talking recently with a State Department man who had once sent me on a lecture tour of India, about the use of artists in the propaganda war. I suggested that if we sent enough poets to Russia we could possibly produce a revolution under the noses of the police and the commissars. My statement was probably quite true but so hypothetical and academic that it was meaningless. The reason is that most of our poets would never get the sanction of our government to be sent abroad in any semi-official capacity. Only a minute fraction could ever be considered, not because of their politics—very few poets nowadays have any—but because most poets are opposed to the "image" of America itself. The anti-American-way-of-life theme is probably the most prevalent theme of our contemporary poetry. It's not good for export. Imagine using E. E. Cummings for this office; he must have been asked before he died. (Cummings, I heard, refused an invitation to the White House, as did William Faulkner, though Cummings was the more anti-establishment man of the two.) Officialdom is severely limited in its choice of representatives. I very much doubt whether Walt Whitman could pass muster as a Culture Representative today.

One of the reasons we have to use the Old Poet image in government is that he *is* old and safe or, to use the newspaper's word, mature. The Byrons, Shelleys, and Dylan Thomases we have to leave at home. They would give the wrong image abroad. The American poetic image

is so badly distorted in the public prints and in other
forms of Communication that we would be better off
without any "image" at all. Or so it seems to me. We are
after all a people without a literary past, certainly without
a common literary past, and it is quite easy for publicists
to make up an image of the poet out of whole cloth. The
whole story of literary expatriation, as far back as writers
like Henry James, tells us that the American writer has
often felt the desperation of rootlessness. Frequently he
finds himself driven back to the shores of his forebears,
real or cultural. These are only a few cases of American
citizens surrendering their citizenship to become British
subjects or followers of a foreign leader, but there are
scores of cases of American poets, painters, and novelists
who ran away from America in a panic in order to survive
as artists. The process is still going on, although today,
instead of all of our expatriates congregating in Paris in
one or two Bohemian quarters, they are as likely to turn
up in Algiers, Kyoto, Mexico City, Majorca, Athens, or
Missoula, Montana.

It takes a good deal of courage (either that or a powerful inertia) for the poet to remain in America. I mean,
and remain a poet, not a Sunday versifier. We live in
what is probably the most unpoetic climate the world
has ever seen, in spite of the fact (or because?) that we
have probably more people writing poetry of some kind
than in the rest of the world put together. Judging from
my own experience as an editor of literary magazines, I
would guess that the poetry population is bigger here than
it has ever been, except in Oriental countries where everyone, I have heard, writes some kind of poem. Living in an
anti-poetic climate, in fact, is our chief form of poetic
stimulation. An anthology of twentieth-century United
States poetry will bear this out. Thematically, the poems
are almost all of a piece: life in the land of the air-
conditioned nightmare. That twentieth-century poetry has
been content to exploit this theme almost exclusively
is one of the chief weaknesses of our poetry. I don't mean
that it is all poetry about the gleaming kitchen (some-

times called the White Rhinoceros) or other American artifacts, but it is all related to the horrors of Progress, the puritanism of hard work, the failure of success, the betrayal of the social character, and so on. We are a very social-minded bunch of poets, carrying a burden of historical guilt which is way out of proportion to our sins. And whether we are talking about Robert Frost or Edgar Lee Masters or E. E. Cummings or Kenneth Rexroth or Theodore Roethke, it is the same cry of historical anguish that we hear. It is instilled in the American poet at a very early age that something is anti-poetic in the state of America. Some poets pin it on the social system; some, on the economic system; some, on the failure of spiritual belief; some, on the religion of science; but all use the Way of Life as a target.

A lot of this antagonism is conventional; some of it is a pose; yet even when the poet tries to break away from the clichés of negation he finds he can't. His conscience won't let him. Without resorting to political knowledge or ideology the poet finds himself outside the pale of the Establishment. This is quite as true for the Academic poet as for the Beat poet. It is not true of the Official or Government poet, but then we don't really have one of those. Tea and cake at the White House don't make a Poet Laureate. The only two bona fide Government poets we have produced in our century are both, in different meanings of the words, enemies of their country. I mean Eliot and Pound. Both believed in the social hierarchy which limits education to the few and makes the poet into a kind of priest who works at the top echelons of government to help fix cultural standards. It is a very curious fact that these two men have provided the American publicists with their most frequent images. The Luce magazines piously pronounced Pound a great poet and helped secure his release from the hospital-prison where he was kept to everyone's embarrassment for so many years. Eliot was universally acclaimed in this country as the chief man of letters of our time, this acclaim being fostered by a handful of scholars and editors and a small, powerful religious

contingent which uses his works as an apology for religion. Very few poets in America subscribe to the Eliot
myth; many more subscribe to the Pound myth, largely
for aesthetic reasons. Pound actually advanced poetic style
on our century. Eliot made a few timid advances in his
youth and then drew in his horns.

But both are Government poets in the strict sense. No
one would have been surprised to see Eliot elevated to
Poet Laureate of England. Pound, had his side won the
Second World War, would most certainly have been
made American Culture and Education Minister. To people who argue that Eliot's Christian and Royalist beliefs
are his own business, my reply is that his lifelong attempts
to undermine freedom of religion and freedom of government and education are most emphatically everybody's
business. I find it distressing that even in the 1960's the
image of Eliot still looms over our literature, Big Brother
to poetry.

The total rejection of America by these two poets is
fundamentally different from the negation of American
material progress by most of our younger poets. It is
different from Walt Whitman's bitter criticism of the
corruption of the nation's character by businessmen and
politicians. Both Eliot and Pound wanted to see some
form of aristocracy instituted in the New World, if only
what they call a cultural aristocracy, while most of the
twentieth-century American poets want to see *more* freedom, not less. Our criticism of the Way of Life, which
is shared by all artists of any kind in our day, is that our
freedoms are quietly being stolen away from us: by in-
creased invasion of individual privacy, by more and more
standardization of ideas, by the presence of the military
in our midst and the terrorization of the people by scientists and diplomats, by various forms of intellectual regi-
mentation at almost every level of society, and by the
destruction of sensibility through image-making machines
and institutions.

The Eliot-Pound kind of thing is obsolete. We should
put it back in the history books where it belongs. What

is more important today is the threat to poetry by the robot element of the population—advertisers, journalists, scientists, militarists, and politicians whose initial objective is to turn all of us into smoothly reacting automatons that will buy what is flashed in front of the eye, believe what jumps out of the headlines, cheer when the missile screams into the atmosphere, die when and where we are ordered, and vote whether there is anything to vote for or not. Anyone who refuses to perform these duties is an odd-ball and an anarchist. It is all too easy for the artist to fall into attitudes of negation, condemning society and its tendencies, and it is the worst thing that can happen to him. But in a time when the Way-of-Lifers virtually dictate the terms of day-to-day existence, the poet has no alternative but to protest and withdraw. And this is exactly what he has done, whether he has withdrawn to the university or to skid row. A generation or two ago the poet fled abroad to find a more congenial atmosphere in which to write. Today he withdraws from the encroachments of the Establishment upon his own personality and aspirations, seeking for companionship among other artists or teachers or people who by virtue of circumstance have no stake in the Way of Life. I refer to outcasts, individualists, "drifters," and even psychopaths and criminals, though the latter are rarely in evidence, except in the imagination of the poet.

I would like to correct the popular image of the poet as it is given us by the instruments of Publicity. In place of the Old Poet standing shoulder to shoulder with the chiefs of state, instead of the Beatnik poet hurling obscenities from the platform, instead of the university wit muttering involved and perfect stanzas, I see a slightly different picture. I see the Anti-Poet, who does not really exist in this country; the literary anarchists, calling themselves the holy barbarians; and the modernists, mostly the poets in or around institutions of learning.

The Anti-Poet does not really exist in America but would like to. The Anti-Poet—Robert Graves pinned the label on Virgil—almost existed below the Mason-Dixon line for a while but never got far. I am talking about a Southern poetry which never quite came into being but almost certainly would have had the South survived as a separate nation. As it is, we have a twentieth-century variant of the vestigial aristocratic tradition. It is primarily a literature of nostalgia and apparently it has lost its *raison d'être*, but it numbers among its school the novelist Faulkner and poets such as Allen Tate and John Crowe Ransom (possibly Robert Penn Warren), and in a slightly different dimension dramatists such as Tennessee Williams. It is therefore a considerable literature of its own, even though it belongs somehow to a century that does not exist. And it will probably continue to hang on as a literary growth of its own without much reference to the world of our time. It is significant that what is or was once called the New Criticism had as its main faction in this country the Southern branch of our literature. Insofar as this criticism is foreign, hierarchical, and hieratic (the brainchild of Hulme, Pound, Eliot, Ransom, Richards, Tate, Empson, Brooks, and Warren) it fits into "Southern" thinking. And insofar as it is Southern it is somewhat British, British cultural attitudes of the eighteenth and nineteenth centuries having survived much longer in the South than elsewhere. The very concept of "gentleman," which in America is always coupled with "Southern," signifies the class structure which still hangs on crazily. When Ransom uses the word *lady* in a poem it carries quite a different and older meaning from its usage in the North. *Lady* is not a title in his poetry, but it has not quite lost the quality of superiority. And both *lady* and *gentleman* have implications of lineage as well as of pigmentation.

I am sorry to deal in superficialities, but I am trying to point to a condition of sensibility which indicates an aristocratic and therefore non-American mode of literature. It was at the University of Virginia that T. S. Eliot a generation ago delivered a series of lectures in which he advised the exclusion of too many liberals and freethinkers from the State. We cannot suppose that the same lectures would have been delivered in New York or Chicago. We recall also Faulkner's failure to take any clear stand on freedom of education for Negroes. Both are instances of the aristocratic mind showing its reluctance to give up authority.

Robert Graves gives us a pretty picture of the Anti-Poet in the person of Virgil himself. Graves speaks of Virgil's "pliability; his subservience; his narrowness; his denial of that stubborn imaginative freedom that the true poets who had preceded him had valued; his perfect lack of originality, courage, humor, or even animal spirits." The Virgilian poet is and always has been the Government poet; but as I have said, we seem thus far to have avoided this phenomenon in our country. And we can leave the subject there, somewhat doubtfully.

Let me mention the Academic poets second. I refer to these poets in universities as Modernists instead of in the usual terms: campus poets, university wits, or whatever.

The poet laureate on the campus is pretty much an American invention (even though John Skelton actually carried such a title from Oxford and Cambridge almost five hundred years ago). In America during the present generation we have made a universal practice of keeping the poet within the institutional walls. According to many authorities, this makes the poet a figure of fun for everybody else, especially writers outside the walls. And of course there is a paradox in the freest of man residing voluntarily in captivity, teaching literature courses, attending committee meetings, and in general behaving like a lapdog. Worse, the campus poet tends to be influenced by his teaching, developing a reflexive sensibility and ending up as a traditionalist among traditionalists.

By and large, this image is correct. The poet in the university is like a fly in honey and is likely to die of hospitality. But if we shift our attention from the poet in the institution to the institution itself, we see a different picture. We see the American college or university assimilating artists of all kinds for the purpose of having them teach what they know of their craft. This is perhaps an idealization of the actual conditions, but it is also the intention of the Academy. The revolution here is not in poetry but in education.

This is a big subject and we can't go into it here. But briefly what has occurred is this. Public education in a democracy has burst the confines of the curriculum and taken over the creative element of the community. In a country too large to have a culture capital, too rich to limit education to the few, too experimental to be content with previously tried methods, in a country, moreover, where a new language is in the making (and is at least as fluid as Middle English was in the time of Chaucer), where publication of almost anything is commonplace, and where all cultures flow into one another—under these circumstances the university has turned into the culture community serving not only its students but also the people outside its walls. This is already the pattern of the American university, with its art galleries, music schools, theaters, public lecture halls, dancing studios, and writing classes. And here too reside the poet, painter, and composer.

From some observation, it seems to me that the university poet is theoretically in a good spot, but not in reality. Usually he is attached to an English department, whether or not he is trained for scholarship. (He seldom is.) As a consequence he seems to turn into a kind of quasi-professor, an exponent of those phases of literature which are recent enough or characteristic enough to be called modern. I call him a Modern-ist, that is, an apologist for that body of poetry and criticism which happens to be dominant in the twentieth century. Some people call this literature Neo-Classical or Classicist or Baroque or Alexandrian or something. But the words all mean the same thing and refer to the literature of intellectual retrenchment. I know of very few poets in the Academy who do not purvey this type of literature and who are not personally infected by it. To espouse Modernism or the Tradition also makes the poet acceptable to the scholars themselves, who perforce deal in the continuity of culture. Today we find the same articles on the same subjects in both the scholarly journals and the university literary quarterlies. There is a slight difference in tone and detail; the subject matter flows together. The poetry—and this is what is disturbing—reflects the scholarship: it is almost always formalistic, objective, learned to some degree, arch, ironic, coy (when it is not stilted or brittle), and in any case bookish. Bookish, literary literature is the end.

I see here a confusion of motives, and I think the remedy must be to give the poet in the school at least as much latitude as is supposedly given to the composer, sculptor, dramatist, and so on.

In any case, the poet would do better to turn his back on literature and simply demonstrate the process of creation as he has experienced it. Intellectualizing about it is not his business, nor is scholarship. To a certain degree criticism is not his affair, if by criticism we mean valuation. Aesthetics is definitely not his dish.

The Academy being in an extremely liberal frame of mind these days, it should be the poet's turn to take the initiative as a man practicing an art, a craftsman, a workman, no more. Every vital artist has students in school or out. Teaching is as natural to the creator as creation itself. But what he teaches should be his art and not the many other things he is expected to do because he is on an institutional payroll.

But let us make no mistake about it: the Academy is an organic part of society, by definition and in fact. As such it is in certain of its basic attitudes as inimical to the artist today as it was in the days of Shelley or in any time when the university was a branch of the church. What we hope for is the continued intelligent liberalization of the Academy with its adoption of the artist as the living evidence of the creative spirit. That sounds a little like keeping him in a zoo, but we'd better settle for at least that.

Every campus should be able to boast at least one poet—
the only living poet in captivity.

Finally, the image of the Beat or "anarchist" poet. These
poets, insofar as they constitute a school or "movement,"
have been called the only interesting rebellion around.
Now, rebellion is a condition of modern literature and
has been for more than a hundred years. There is a cliché
that every revolution contains the germ of its own failure;
and we can anticipate the failure of the "Movement," if
we believe the proverb. I don't. In the historical process,
it seems to me, a revolution always makes a slight advance.
The counterrevolutionary process seems to destroy the
gain; yet something has been ineradicably changed. Only
a permanent police state can prevent historical progress,
to us an old-fashioned term. The USSR successfully destroyed poetry beginning in 1917: Essenin and Mayakov-
sky, the two chief Bolshevik poets, both committed suicide.
Now the Russians, partly because of the Pasternak scandal, have allowed one or two poets to show themselves.
It is too early to say whether Evtushenko is a Government
Poet or a true muse poet, but giving him the benefit of
the doubt, I believe he is perhaps the most dangerous
man in Russia for the Russians. In a state as puritanical
as the USSR, where modern painting and jazz were
banned until recently, the appearance of a single poet
could be the signal for a generalized revolt. Actual revolt,
of course, must be prepared for by a psychological revolution, such as took place in Russia in the days of Tolstoy
and Dostoevsky; and a revolution in thinking must necessarily be articulated by artists and intellectuals. The presence of the artist in a police state is a sign of weakness
in the police.

The image of the Beat poet in America is distorted in
several ways. First, he is not just an American phenomenon. He came into the European scene long before his
San Francisco counterpart. He is in fact part of a world
rebellion of a generation, the generation too young to
engage in the Second World War and the Resistance

movements in Europe. It appeared to writers my age after the Second World War that we were rearing what some people called a Silent Generation, a generation of do-nothings, ostriches, isolationists, and pleasure-loving non-entities. This seems to have been the frame of mind of the first atomic generation (to give them a slightly horrifying label). And it was out of that state of mind that the Beat writer erupted. The caricature of the Beat is well known everywhere: the beard and sandals, signifying asceticism or a kind of primitive brotherhood, like the early Christians, and signifying also disaffiliation from established society. Along with the costume and the bare dwelling place are supposed to go the love of cool, abstract jazz, the dogma of Hip or psychosexual relaxation, with the Negro as the prototype of the natural man; the use of a wide range of hallucinogenic drugs and the practice of certain Oriental disciplines, such as Yoga, Zen, and the physical-mental exercises of the Greek monk Gurdjieff. Their art is confined almost entirely to literature, the most outspoken characteristic of which is the use of obscenity and the violation of time-honored rules of Taste. In addition, according to the public image of the Beat, he or she is usually childless and is probably homosexual. Politically, he would be called something like Marxist-anarchist. (There is by now a whole literature of description of the Beat, mostly unfavorable.)

The description I have given is not far wrong in its details but is, in my judgment, wrong in the interpretation given it by the press and by the Academy. It is interesting to watch the reaction of the Academy to the Beat; on the whole it is infuriated and contemptuous, even though here and there it recognizes a poem or a novel of power. If it is true, as William Carlos Williams once said, that T. S. Eliot gave literature back to the Academy, the Academy now feels itself threatened by the Beat, who number the university among their foremost enemies.

The real difference between the Beat and the old-style Greenwich Villager, Left Bank decadent artist, or Blooms-

bury bohemian is that those groups moved outside society
in order to govern it intellectually from the periphery.
The Beat do not wish to govern anything; they oppose
government or any other establishment meant to maintain law and order. To the degree that they are disengaged
they resemble some of the extreme Existentialists, such as
Genet. Sabotage is a positive form of action with them.

I find a good deal of unity of theory and practice in
their works and ways. But I do not see a literary school.
The breadth of their view precludes a writing program.
In fact, they are not at all programmatic in the usual
sense, say, the way Pound-Eliot-Yeats-Joyce evolved an
aesthetic to serve a traditional ethic. If anything, their
attitude tends toward the destruction of poetry as it has
been known, a kind of withering away of the literary state
once their rebellion is accomplished. Here we run into
the psychology of the anarchist, the contemplative, and
the primitive. Poetry is neither an art nor an end in itself
but a kind of biological function which may be displaced
altogether when man enters a higher phase of consciousness and truth. It is too bad, in a sense, that the Beat has
become public. He must now wrestle with a kind of self-
consciousness which has always afflicted the establishmentarian artist. Self-consciousness is the one form of behavior
he cannot permit; yet, being famous, he must be forced
to imitate himself to his own peril.

The revolt consists of several operations: The rebellion
against consciousness, achieved naturally or artificially,
legally or illegally. The sexual revolution, as it is sometimes
called, that is, the abolition of all morally oriented sex.
Disaffiliation from politics and all other institutions of the
civilized state; America and Russia are both considered
politically evil; a Gandhian-Tolstoyan-Thoreauvian politics
is the ideal. Finally, the literary revolt, which is indi-
vidualistic, anti-classicist, and personal, drawing heavily on
such figures as Rimbaud, Shelley, and Whitman. There
are some oddities in this picture: for instance, we find a
tremendous respect and discipleship for Ezra Pound, evi-

dently on grounds of technique and individualism. It is ironical that Pound's first group of followers spring up among poets whose ideas and principles he would be the first to condemn.

In addition to these forms of revolt, there is an aura of something like mysticism surrounding the Beat. It is not religious but metaphysical mysticism, beginning with the doctrines of Japanese Zen Buddhism, which is less a religion than a psychology and aesthetic, and ending in the realms of consciousness psychology with a deliberate exploitation of drug states and experimentation with automatic writing, Dada, surrealism, dream transcription, and other techniques which have been in operation since the twenties.

Here are a couple of quotations from a "political" talk between two Beat poets. They are talking about the war:

"The Berlin question has nothing to do with the Berlin question."

"Maybe then the solution is to do away with solutions."

"I think a real revolution of interpersonal relations is at hand —individuals must seize control over the means of communications. . . . The techniques applied by poets for altering the world of literature can be easily applied over telephone lines, radio stations, TV control rooms, wire services, newspaper desks, movie sets and projectors, all the way down to the minutest ramifications of the vast electronic spiderweb network that controls all civilized portions of the globe. . . . The war's a by-product of universal mass communication centralized direction of madmen."

[We need] *"universal strike on purely personal basis in your own area of activity without waiting for any central orders or program other than the promptings of your own conscience. . . ."* [The new conscience or consciousness is] *"a mutation of the functioning of the brain, physiologically, to accommodate a wider field of personal consciousness than human beings have been historically aware of."* [Follows a list of new drugs which are quicker and more "civilized" than breathing exercises of Yoga and other vision techniques.]

"The earth is now falling off a cliff and so the whole earth is having a vision of the Cosmos."

This conversation ends with a surrealist suggestion that the two present heads of state engage in a cold war—by taking, say, mescaline, and locking themselves up naked in a TV studio, "yakking at each other in public till they figured out what they are doing. TV maybe could be adapted for human use."

Here we get a return to the one-man revolution of Whitman or that of Thoreau, Gandhi, Tolstoy, or, for that matter, Martin Luther King. What cannot be done by organization can be accomplished by the individual. The power of the individual, long lost in the modern wilderness of communications, is reasserted. The person is the only potency left. The right action of the one can electrify the many, as happened with Gandhi, whose fight for Indian freedom was virtually his personal affair. The individual can effect a poetic revolution, indeed, as he always has in the past, simply by acting the truth. If the truth involves harshness, bad taste, obscenity, and worse, it must still be asserted.

It is startling to think that today there is an even wider gulf between poetry and the public than there has ever been. And it is a bitter irony that this gulf has been widened by what our society calls Communications. The ease with which man now "communicates" has only served to limit what is communicated to the few who control the talk machines. Now and then we see on a television program a strange, uninvited figure, like the Wedding Guest in Coleridge's great poem; he leaps in front of the fabulously expensive and intricate cameras waving his arms, but before he is able to speak he is gently but firmly collared and rushed away—who knows where? And what is he trying to tell us? He is so much like the poet, pathetic, ridiculous, risking his sanity for the gesture of honesty. Of all the thousands of television programs I am ashamed to say I have watched, this image is the only one I can remember. That and two science-fiction movies which scared me to death.

We are pretty certain by now that the image of the

poet as we have it impressed on our consciousness is not going to improve the state of poetry or of anything else. The Government poet will become more and more familiar, whoever he happens to be, but people will read his face and not his poems. The Modernist poet of the Academy will continue to write for his fellow academicians and continue his life of uneasy happiness in the class-room and the publisher's office. Only the anarchist Beat poet seems to have a real, live audience of any size or vitality. We had better get used to this fact if we are to understand what is happening in literature in this country today.

Among other things, we can foresee the end of the poem as we know it, the formalized, autotelic, interior mono-logue, art-for-art's-sake object of beauty which has been the favorite form of narcissism of the poet for many, many years. For it appears to me that the poem is already in fusion with the prose forms, the novel, drama, auto-biography, and so on. Whitman predicted this new art form a century ago; it is now coming into being. It is the poetry itself, regardless of techniques, the poetry of per-ception, such as we had it in Rimbaud and in quite a few French poets of the last century, which has almost never occurred in England but which seems destined to flower in America. I don't want to "project" too much about this new poetry. All I know is that it won't look like poetry or maybe even sound like it, but it will express perceptions in a new language of consciousness far out of reach of our present limited sensibility.

Poetry in America has been going around in circles for almost two generations. There started to be a breakthrough around 1915 when an authentic American poetry got loose. But this poetry was almost immediately kidnapped and carried abroad where it was tamed and taught table man-ners. Once in a while there was a rumble of revolt, as when an Outside poet like Dylan Thomas stirred up a lyric frenzy or when a group of poets tried to push the Square World over the cliff. All the same, poetry is the weakest of the arts in America in a time when all our arts have influenced the world: arts of jazz, films, fiction, painting, and what not. What authentic American poetry there is is unknown or predated, circa 1915. The rest, as a French poet once said about the same thing, is Literature.

In this country too we have to go outside Literature to obtain poetry. And that is what the poet's struggle is all about in America—how to get Outside. Every poet who is a poet today is some kind of Outsider, some kind of runaway escaping from the images set up to look like him. So in a way we are in a good position as poets; we are starting all over. We are on our own, and we are honestly obsessed with the making of our own image in the image of nothing else that has ever existed.

A Party
in Milo

(*A Fragment of a Novel in Progress*)

When he and Inge parked across from the Janiczek house, Edsel said, "Sit for a minute." Inge stiffened and sat still.

"It's only that I've got a crazy feeling," he said, "that in there I'm going into the waxworks of my life in Milo; that I'm going to encounter the fuck-up of what they call the best years of my life. In fact, I feel like I'm going to a sacrifice and I'm the . . ."

Inge relaxed. "Lamb?" she laughed. "Or bull?"

"Prime rib of poet," he quipped, and lit a cigarette. "There goes Bumpy Harrington and her surgeon," he said. "Followed by Hugh Gilchrist—you know, the monk fellow who is handy with a mimeograph and such instruments of total destruction."

The street was filling up with cars of all vintages, and shadows could be seen making their way on both sides toward the stately little bungalow. No sound could be heard from the interior, but then the house was well back from the street,

"Quiet as a whorehouse," said Edsel.

There was a roar and a wild flash of lights as three motorcycles riding abreast neatly made a right turn and jounced over the curb and came to a halt against the porch of the house. With a wild symphony of farts they subsided while their drivers hunched lackadaisically through the front door. "That's the first echelon of the wave of the future," Edsel announced. He felt nervous and wanted a drink. "Let's go in, Inge," he said. "You know, like the time has come."

"You really take this thing seriously," she said.

"This party has farewell written all over it. Just a prophecy," he said.

Inge had dredged up a serape from somewhere in her Colorado past and was wearing it like a shawl. Edsel thought it a perfect disguise for the company ahead. Her hair was drawn back into a knot, but she wore two-inch-long wooden earrings that flicked when she walked. Edsel still had on his almost-white cords and his fifty-dollar gondolier shirt. He had decided not to shave and wore a salt-and-pepper stubble on his face. They passed through a spacious vestibule into the semi-darkness of the first living room. Since the four Janiczek children (by various marriages) were all ensconced in various way-out schools around the United States, all the former bedrooms had become "other" living rooms. In fact, the only bed in the house was in the Brom and Karen bedroom where Edsel had watched the flamenco demonstration. "This generation has abolished the bed," Brom had told him at one of the parties. "Part of the tribalism," he added, and jerked his head; "they've rediscovered the floor." "You can say that again," Edsel had replied.

All the rooms were semi-lit but seemingly in different colors. A bluish light leaked from one doorway, a reddish glow from another, a cold fluorescent white from a third. If you whipped your head around quickly it was like the American flag. "Don't say it," Edsel told Inge, " 'The Masque of the Red Death.' " She laughed dutifully. "Liquor for grownups back here," he pointed. "Children bring their own."

They went down a narrow hall toward the back of the house and could hear soul music driving out of an old-fashioned gramophone horn which, Edsel noticed, had been expertly remodeled to conceal some pretty sophisti-

cated electronic equipment. Brom greeted him and was
introduced to Inge, "my secretary and defender of the
faithful." Brom introduced them to the "adult" liquor
cabinet, a scrolly walnut armory which Brom had rebuilt
on the interior with heavy shelves to hold his gallon-size
booze bottles, mixing liquids, and a trough in which ice
cubes made themselves gaily and plentifully. Edsel asked
Brom what the going beverage was; Brom suggested
bourbon, and they took large tumblers and splashed
bourbon over the blue cubes.

"Let's wander," Edsel said to Inge. She wanted to look
first into the room where the music was pulsating. It was
a huge glassed-in sun porch at the back of the house and
there were no lights at all.

"In this case," said Edsel sourly, "you don't see; you
smell." They stood outside the door and could feel the
floor moving in a four-four rhythm up and down—or so
Edsel imagined. A strange zoolike odor filled the room in
which they were standing—the dining room—but there
was no dining furniture visible.

"What is the smell?" Inge asked.

"It's a medley," Edsel answered. "Cheap Chinese in-
cense to cover up the marijuana, cheap cologne to cover
up the sweat, darkness to cover up the Jamaicans, and
the sour smell of soul music. Had enough?" Inge shud-
dered, not at what he had said but because he had said
it. They moved toward the more lighted rooms.

They entered the "blue" room and Edsel saw practically his whole Creative Writing class seated on the floor
in a kind of semicircle. As he entered with Inge they
applauded. "Oh my God," he groaned. "One of Brom's
goddam gaietés parisiennes." He waved a smily phony
wave and asked to whom or to what he owed this honor.
He was angry and some of his bourbon sloshed into his
shoe.

"Mr. Lazerow, sit down with us," called the white-haired
book-clutching person of no known sexual denomination.
"We want to—commune!" he giggled.

Edsel looked desperately at Inge, who was smiling

distantly as if to say, "Pass your own tests; don't include
me in." He sat on one arm of a fat cracked-leather chair
which had belonged to Karen's grandfather; Inge perched
on the other arm, looking at the students.

Christ, it really is my class, thought Edsel, as he saw
Chris Jaffe raising his hand in mock permission to speak.
He was draped with Indian beads which he had bought
at Durd's Drug, and around and over them he wore a
tallith. Edsel bristled at this self-insult. It was okay to play
the Indian bit, but to sport the prayer shawl of the Jew
in a hippy outfit—Edsel didn't swallow that.

"Speak, Jaffe," said Edsel, trying to remain calm and
humorous. "As one must at a party," he counseled heavily.

"Well, it's this, sir," said Jaffe, with a pencil-line sneer
which Edsel hoped he was imagining. "We of the tribe,
sir, we teach as well as learn. We give as well as take,
because we are the believers in the Immediate Present."
With his right hand he began slipping the prayer shawl
from his neck, very slowly. The worn silk tassels dragged
on the bare polished floor. "But one must give slowly, as
one must learn by inches." The tallith lay across his lap,
and Edsel thought this obscene little clown was going
to make him a present of it, with some little idiotic
speech. Instead of which, Jaffe brought one end of the
shawl to his beard and to his lips, and in an ancient
gesture of reverence kissed it, and then with both hands
ripped it longitudinally down the middle.

Inge leaped to her feet and snatched it from him and
slapped him with all her might across his mouth. "You
stinking little turd!" she screamed at him, and began
whipping him across the face with the silk shawl. Edsel
had turned to stone and sat perched on the arm of the
chair. Inge caught herself with hand raised and dropped
the tallith gingerly, and catching Edsel's eye motioned
him out of the "chamber," as Edsel thought of it after-
ward. He stood against the wall outside the room for a
time. He felt icy and somehow clean, as if he had just
passed inspection for cleaning and oiling his forty-five,

which he had had to carry when he was in the Army. And
suddenly he felt thoroughly drunk, as if all the liquor he
had downed since he had landed back in Milo had risen
up at one fell swoop to belt him in the head. Inge was
leaning against the wall herself, muttering, "I hate rotten-
ness, I hate cruelty, I hate it, I hate it." He looked at her
and she was white.

"How did you know what it was?" he asked curiously,
coming out of his spin.

"I knew it was some religious thing," she said, "with
all that Hebrew writing. And I know you don't give a
damn about all that, and I know you goddam well don't
go around looking for insults from those spoiled little
pricks. Piss on him!"

At that moment the monkish student sidled out of
the door.

"Mr. Lazerow," he said timidly, "Chris is drunk, that's
what happened. Well, Chris is a Jew—that is, he was
born . . ."

"Skip it, Hugh," said Edsel, and walked off with Inge.
"Why don't we try the red room," he announced to her.
"Krishna only knows what we'll find in that malebolge."

"You're gibbering," said Inge, which was true enough.
They moved toward the red glow, the immemorial aura
of temptation. A six-foot scarecrow, skinny as a question
mark, with watery blue eyes and a wisp of blond beard,
collided with Edsel at the door. He leaned over the poet
all a-tremble and whispered, "She's doing it! She's doing
it! Hurry!" and lurched through the hall.

Edsel had stopped at the annnouncement and Inge
asked, "What? Who's doing what?"

"Listen, Inge," he said. "Did you ever go to the car-
nival?"

"Millions," she answered, getting her laugh back.

"And the sideshows?" he asked.

"That's what carnivals are for," she answered.

"Okay," he said, "wait till you see this freak."

They stepped inside the room which was deathly quiet

except for one contralto monotone; the voice came from
the corner away from the door, and about twenty people
sitting and standing faced a woman in a motionless
tableau.

Her name was Catherine House. She was in her late
twenties and had the horsefaced handsomeness of an
English matron. She was elegantly dressed in a burgundy
velvet skirt with a white silk blouse open at the neck. She
wore a large gold-rimmed cameo over her bosom and no
makeup on her face. Her shoes were what Edsel remembered hearing described as "sensible." He had heard
rumors of her acts at parties but could never quite believe
them. After all, she was a faculty wife; her husband
taught scientific classical Greek at the Dental College and
to pre-meds. Why hadn't she been put away, or why
hadn't House been fired for encouraging this termagant?
Nobody knew.

"Because," said the elegant Catherine in her throaty
voice, "I am the only doer and *you* are all chicken-shit.
Male and female the same." She raised her hand and
began to point in a manner reminiscent of a regal gesture.
"You, Margaret. You, Howard. You, Dale. You, Merle.
You, Harlan. You, Clare. You, Marie. You, Scotty. You,
Oscar. You, Gustav. You, Miriam. You, Douane. You,
Cynthia. You, Ape. You, Cletas. You, Dotsy. You, Emil.
You—whatever you call yourself. You, Barb." She had
come to the end of the roster and spotted Edsel. "And
of course you, Mr. Lazerow. Chicken-shit. And I'll include
your friend."

"Go, baby, go," said Oscar, who was evidently enjoying
the scene immensely. Catherine gave him a withering
glance. "You, you—capon-shit!" There was a spatter of
laughter, but the tableau remained in place like a high
school stage set.

Without knowing he was saying anything, Edsel said,
"That chair doesn't become you, Mrs. House." It was one
of those old overstuffed chairs which had once been considered the height of posterior fashion in men's clubs.

"I like it," said Mrs. House pettishly and, straddling one of the threadbare arms, began to ride up on it, as it were.

What happened was that she masturbated for the assembled company, cursing them for watching and for not joining in. Her husband Howard smiled and scanned the faces of the audience. Catherine rode her chair under her velvet skirt, modestly concealing her flesh. Her eyes were closed in a squint as her rhythm settled into a jog. The chair creaked and groaned with its unaccustomed load. The company, her intimate audience, began to encourage her with a communal wavelike sound of "Shhh! Shhh! Shhh!" each time she thrust.

Inge grabbed Edsel by the elbow and whispered, "I'm going to vomit," and rushed through the door. He piloted her to the porch railing and she threw up vigorously and heaved and spat down into the marigolds. He gave her two handkerchiefs—he always carried a spare—and she wiped her mouth with one and her eyes with the other. After a minute of swaying silence she sought out a glider on the porch and sank down. He dropped the handkerchiefs over the rail and sat beside her. Neither had anything to say. It was dark where they were and they watched cars parking and unparking, people in curious dress coming and going, but everything in a kind of silence. An ugly quiet, thought Edsel. He suggested another drink, tentatively; Inge wanted to wait a little.

A police car beacon was whipping around a couple of blocks away, and they watched it approach and slow down and double park in front of the house. An officer with a good deal of gold on his hat mounted the porch with difficulty and rang the bell. Edsel and Inge sat still. The police officer asked to speak to Mr. Janiczek on the porch —"and no cause for alarm," he said, and waited.

Brom emerged with a clinking glass and asked the Chief, as he called him, to come in. "No need, no need," said Slezak. "I just wanted to tip you that that drug preacher, Akiba Mame, is heading for your house with his crowd. We got a call from the state line and you know, Brom, it's our job to give him surveillance. You understand." Brom tried to assure Slezak that everything would be in order, that there were just a bunch of college students dancing in there and that he and Karen were definitely in charge.

"The only thing of it is, Brom," said the Chief, "we have to check his wagon for drugs, because there's a report out on him and his crowd. Will you care if we question him here if we can't locate him on the highway?"

"Well, Chief," said Janiczek, "you are as welcome here as always, and I don't think you'll find anything illegal about those boys. They're just religionists, good kids, take my word for it, and wouldn't hurt a fly. You can even wait if you want; they've got nothing to conceal."

The police chief would rather not wait and said he would come back maybe in an hour. Brom offered him a drink which he refused, but he took Brom's glass and had a swallow. "See you later, Brom."

Word spread through the house at electronic speed that Akiba Mem and friends were definitely en route to Milo and would pay a visit to the Janiczeks. Two of the black-jacket motorcycle set sped through the screen door, leaped on their bikes, and vanished down the lawn and the silent street in a roar. Edsel turned to Inge and said, "The message is abroad. Do you want to stay or go?"

"Stay," she said laconically. They sat quietly for about five minutes before Inge decided she was recovered enough to re-enter the den.

"Are you ready for another exhibit?" he asked. Inge apologized for being so squeamish, and laughed. "I never knew little old Milo had so much nightclubbing to offer. From a prayer-shawl-ripping to a public masturbation in two minutes. Lead on, Boss, but get me a motion sickness sack just in case."

"This one won't be so bad," said Edsel, "except for me." She looked at him doubtfully. And he added, "Can you see in the dark?"

Inge took this to mean they were going to watch, or imagine they were watching, the Jamaicans with the college girls and the faculty wives. They moved toward the throb and wail of the soul music records, but the adjoining room was already jammed with spectators and auditors and it was hard to get close to the darkened sun porch where the action was. Bumpy Harrington was elbowing her way to the front, her husband standing uncomfortably in the middle of a herd of what seemed to him to be aspiring cowboys and Indians. Edsel spoke to Doc Harrington.

"Have you bonded any yet?" he laughed.

Harrington shook hands and suggested that he had told Bumpy this was no place or time to get a foreign student to live in, but that Bumpy, "you know Bumpy," said it was precisely and scientifically the time and place and "just you see, Doctor Harrington." By now Bumpy had wiggled into the other room and was in total darkness.

Actually, there were only seven Jamaicans, plus several native U.S. Negroes and two Africans wearing the embroidered fez. But the dance program was apparently arranged by the West Indians, who always traveled to parties in a body and danced in the same room and with the same ground rules. They picked the records and set the volume and one of their number had the job of operating the light switch. The overhead lights would flash on before and after each dance, at which time the Caribbeans (Edsel called them The Blues) would crowd at the doorway and leer at the available white meat. Now and then during a record the lights would flash on for a brief second, as if to give the girls a preview of the paradise to come. Edsel wondered how Bean Harrington was taking to this Walpurgisnacht, but when he turned to see his face, Bean had disappeared.

"What do you think?" he asked Inge.

"Just dancing," she answered, and leaning toward his ear added, "with a dry fuck here and there." The music was pounding like the Grand Coulee Dam, and suddenly

the lights flashed on in the dance pavillion. In front of
the dancers a white girl or woman was standing on her
hands, her feet held up by a grinning Blue. The woman's
skirt was over her head, making her face invisible. She
was naked under her clothes. The lights flashed off so
quickly that nobody was sure he had seen what he had
seen. Inge had regained her composure and was laughing
again.

"For your edification," Edsel said to her, "that was
Wanda."

"I wouldn't be surprised," she answered, and told Edsel
she had seen enough of that sideshow and why not make
them both a new drink. They worked their way back to
the armory-bar, where Brom was still hosting the adults,
making drinks, and discussing fire rites among the Bantu
tribes with a pretty graduate student named Deirdre.
She was leaning against the sink admiring his handlebar
mustaches and not hearing a word.

"They say you may have a visit from the Dali Lama,"
Edsel said, as Brom handed them their drinks. Karen
suddenly appeared at Edsel's ear like Ariel and whispered,
"We arranged it, Ed, *arranged* it!" and gave a *Wuthering
Heights* laugh. "And he said he was coming especially to
see you, Ed. *You*. So don't get any notions about leaving,
Ed."

Edsel laughed and said, "Well, I don't see why I have
to have my soul beholden to that phony ex-Hebrew LSD
soixante-neuf queersville public relations genius with a
beard of egg noodles and pubic hair . . ." Karen squealed
with delight, Brom chuckled, the graduate student named
Deirdre opened her mouth to reveal—braces!—and Inge
kicked him playfully on the calf. It was at this moment
that Wanda appeared, moving Edsel and Inge just
enough apart to confront Brom and demand Scotch.
"No," she said, "two scotch, one for me, one for Indian."
While he was obliging her she turned to Inge.

"Are you the It?" she said. Inge turned a shade pale.
She said nothing. Whereupon Wanda wheeled on Edsel.
"Nice going, Edsel," she said, slightly drunk or dizzy.

"Nice fucking going, *Edsel*," she ended, in what was intended to be an icy tone, and stalked off with a drink in each hand.

Inge had fair recuperative powers and was slightly flushed from her brief encounter with Wanda. A bit of fire shone from her eyes and Edsel worried what the next brush with Wanda might bring. He toyed with the idea of escaping the party but was too curious about Karen's remark to want to leave so early

"What time do you figure the Christ and his apostles will descend?" he asked Karen.

As usual, Karen coiled near his ear and whispered, "Gimpy Slezak, our faithful fuzz, said they were about fifty miles into the state already. Don't you think that's metaphorical, Ed?" She reared back and laughed at her own joke. "Give or take an hour, they'll be here. And listen to this, Ed. Akiba is bringing the tapes of his mass rally from yesterday and he said he wouldn't play them unless you sat on the floor with him and listened to every last millimeter."

"Dolce, dolce," he answered. "You mean I can't wait and read it in *Flowering Banana?* or *Pottie?* or *All-Day Sucker?* or whatever he calls his magazine?" He began to think seriously of leaving this time and asked Inge her opinion. She flattened an open palm downward against the air and said, "We'll stay. My education is at stake." Edsel shrugged and they walked off toward the white room.

The white room looked like a secondhand electrical appliance shop. There were beat-up fluorescent desk lamps on the floor and on all the tables, some turned upward toward the ceiling, some facing walls, some turned to shine out of the door. They were all buzzing like trapped New Jersey mosquitoes; Edsel wondered how so many hideous fixtures had found their way together and what message they might be trying to convey. It seemed to be an every-man-for-himself department in here. In a corner sat a drunken Air Force sergeant with his shirt open and out, bent over what looked like a Nazi souvenir

bayonet. He was spitting on the blue blade and honing
it on his boot. Edsel walked near and spotted the neat
little swastika on the hilt. The sergeant didn't bother to
look up at the stranger. In the second corner stood a girl
with her face to the wall, as if, thought Edsel, she was
being punished for not being able to spell *transcendental*.
But it wasn't as simple as that: she was stark naked and
was in the process of being painted orange and gold. The
huge bald-shaven halfback known lovingly to Milo as
The Ape was swabbing her buttocks and legs with wide
housepainting brushes, waiting a little after each stroke
for the paint to dry. The Ape turned around when Edsel
and Inge approached and made as if to rise, but, changing
his mind, just grinned and went back to his labors. In the
center of the room a black-belt Judo, real honest-to-God
Japanese, was demonstrating the graceful art of splitting
two one-inch boards with the edge of his hand; his ap-
prentice was a tiny gnome of a student who was actually
twenty-one years old but looked nine or ten, a well-
known glandular case of some variety. Edsel knew the
Japanese, an instructor in geology, and had met him at
the Yamoshiras. Rumor had it that he was a nobleman
of the ancien régime, had been an aide-de-camp of
Hirohito, and was even on board the *Missouri* during the
surrender to the Americans. His English was practically
nonexistent, which Edsel attributed to his nostalgia for
the good old days.

"I'll hold the other end, Shiki," said Edsel. Shiki
turned and greeted him and nodded. Shiki did the expected: let out a scream of "Hai! Hai!" and split the two
boards with a clip of his hand.

"You try?" Shiki asked Edsel.

"Me," said Edsel, "I couldn't break a matzoh." Shiki
naturally didn't catch the reference and Edsel amended,
"Cracker," and pretended to bite and masticate. They
both laughed.

There was a drumming of heels. Edsel turned slightly
and watched Kaz flamenco into the room, arms akimbo.
"Nice party, professor," he said, machine-gunning past

Edsel, then circled Inge three hundred and sixty degrees, stopped in front of her, and bowed.

"Would you like to dance?" he asked.

"Where?" she answered in a fainting voice.

"Where? Where the action is," said Kaz.

"Thanks. No," she said, and took a step closer to Edsel.

"Drink then?" he asked, offering a half-pint bottle from a back pocket.

"I have one already," she said, holding up her glass. He flicked the cap off his little bottle, took a discreet swallow while starting up his heels again, took another, and glided out of the door with the bottle vertical against his mouth.

"What's he want?" asked Inge. She was a little frightened.

"It's not you, Inge," he said. "Just a message to me from the Black Widow." He quoted a few lines from Melvin Tolson:

> *The black widow spider gets rid of her man,*
> *gets rid of her daddy as fast as she can.*
> *If you fool around, I know what I'll do—*
> *like the black widow spider I'll get rid of you.*

Inge let out a small scream. Edsel jerked around. The Air Force sergeant had lurched to his feet and was stumbling toward Shiki, pointing his Nazi bayonet.

"Dirty rotten mother-fucking Gook bastard!" he yelled. Shiki stood still and let the soldier come within distance. In one motion he had the bayonet in one hand and had seated the sergeant on his prat with a trick of the foot. The soldier sat stupidly weaving on the floor and began to sob.

Edsel touched Shiki on the back and gave him a wink; he said to Inge, "I forgot. There's a basement as big as a house in this joint. Lots of guitars no doubt, and candlelight. I hope Janiczek has insurance."

But Inge wanted to try the porch again. "Got to process my data," she laughed. They were going through the door and as if by telepathy Brom arrived and wordlessly took the bayonet which Shiki held out to him handle-ward. The sergeant keeled over with a horrible knock of his head on the wood floor and lay apparently un-conscious. As Edsel glanced back he saw Shiki holding the sergeant up and slapping him lightly across the cheeks.

"Love thine enemy," said Edsel. "Not for me. Shiki should have him swallow the bayonet, swastika and all." They sat down again on the cooling porch. "Pseudo-children," said Edsel, and they subsided into their own thoughts.

Traffic was getting heavier up and down the Janiczek front steps and someone switched on the porch light. He saw Grace and Atwood Tremaine coming up the walk, dressed normally, as if they were attending a neighbor-hood cocktail party. They spotted Edsel and came to say hello. "Be careful in there, Tremaine," said Edsel fol-lowing the introductions. "It's Durd's Drug come to life. Like 'The Nutcracker Suite.' "

"Which only goes to demonstrate," said Tremaine, bending gracefully down, "that nature imitates art even in this day and age. Why, where would these drab little citizens get their imagination if not from books? Left to themselves they'd remain the field mice that they are."

"The mice are dead. Long live the mice," answered Edsel.

Tremaine leaned again and said in a stately manner, "Perhaps what we want is the Pied Piper, Edsel?"

"I think he's due here tonight," said Edsel, and men-tioned the oncoming caravan. Tremaine raised his eye-brows and gave a smile which might have symptomized delight. The pair entered the house with an air of gravity.

"Poor Grace," Edsel said half to himself. "Always the spectator."

"I hope she gets away with it in there," laughed Inge.

"No danger," he answered. "A woman like that could walk through the fiery furnace and come out without a hair mussed. Cool as a firewalker. Only I always wonder why."

They chatted about virgin immunity until Karen came out wreathed in smiles. "The kids are going to line the walk with candles, Ed, holding them."

"You mean like Rush Week, Karen?" Edsel asked incredulously. "Maybe they'll bring Akiba in on a bed of nails and we can all throw away our crutches."

Karen laughed at what she thought of as Edsel's barbed-wire wit and waved herself back into the party. Pretty soon a line of boys and girls, carrying candle stubs of various sizes and shapes, emerged from the screen door and sat down on both sides of the walk. Karen expected a call from Akiba from the outskirts and had told the faithful she would signal them when to light up. It was a sweet windless night and leaves seesawed down around them.

"It's pretty," said Inge. Something about the scene touched her.

"And funny," said Edsel. "Those kids would rather be crucified than step inside a church, and here they are starting a religion from scratch. They call it love but it has all the earmarks of hate to me. A little crop of corn-ball Nazis waiting for instructions from headquarters. Don't think our hosts haven't tipped everybody off about the confrontation between the Cupidons and the Cossacks. Don't think they all aren't dying to be arrested. How else would they have any identity?"

Inge said that Edsel was sounding embittered because of the student who ripped up the prayer shawl. "Yes," he said, "him and the army killer and the Judo king and the flamenco buff and the I'm-better-than-you-are-niggers from Jamaica and Tremaine Atwood—Dr. Livingston, I presume—and the whole rotten hick scene lying in wait for the kike messiah who's going to give them a treat of Hindu wrist bells and maybe even a picture in *Lux* magazine. Look at these denizens of the woodwork who've crawled out tonight to confront what they think is

Authority. Tonight their atrophied little imaginations will
shine in candlelight and in what Harry Peltz, I mean
Mahatma Schlock, calls poetry and love. They've got to
make a politick of love too. Like Miss Milo in there getting her ass painted by that Polack mutant."

He started to laugh. "Jesus," he said, "you're right. I
am taking this seriously. They all look like cockroaches to
me. I'm in love."

Inge turned and looked at him in the porch light. His
face looked far away. He felt her look and her tenseness
and turned to meet her gaze.

"A woman nobody knows around here," he explained,
"and I hope they'll never know

Inge sighed, "with relief," Edsel thought and hoped.
He patted her gratefully on the hand and said he would
go and fix their drinks.

"Pardon the confessionalism," he said. Inge reached
out and caught his hand as he was getting up.

"Boss," she said, "I'm so glad. I mean—that you are
—in love. Hide it because, you damn well know, in this
burg . . ."

"I know," he said, and squeezed her hand gratefully
and went for their drinks. Know what? he said to himself
as he made his way through the now excited crowd to
the bar. All I know is, Inge is right. If anybody rises above
himself in this town he's clobbered. Definition of the
province. Stay in line. Like these stinky little boy-girl-
scouts are forming a corporation to keep everybody in
line and their boss is coming to give them a Christmas
bonus and a few preferential fucks and a few sticks of
weed and the gospel according to Saint Smegma.

Brom was again stationed at the bar and engaged in
an animated conversation with Bumpy. "They are now
superior to equality," Brom was saying. "They don't mind
the houseboy bit, but it has to be on the condition that
you are inferior; not at their mercy, mind you, but mor-
ally-culturally responsible. You *know*," he ended know-
ingly.

"Silly man," said Bumpy. "I have three offers already; it's a buyer's market." She garnered two drinks and turned around to face Edsel.

"Aha," she cooed, "there's the man with the blue guitar," and gave Edsel a grin and a buss. Bumpy was proud of her memory of the names of "significant" modern poems and used them to goose appropriate friends and acquaintances.

"How's the hiring going?" asked Edsel.

"It's all but accomplished," she answered. "And the one I want—you'll never guess his name. Rodney William Penn!" She laughed gleefully and announced that Rodney was a direct descendant of the English admiral.

"Pretty unlikely," corrected Brom. "That was the Penn that chased the blacks up into the hills for a century. He's putting you on."

Bumpy thought that was perfectly delightful, and if she were a Negro she'd give herself a put-on name too. At this moment Karen came floating into the room and announced in a stage whisper that Akiba had called from the highway outside of Milo to alert the party and to make sure that Edsel was still among the company. "It's grand!" she emoted, and swept out onto the lawn to tell the welcoming committee to light their candles in exactly four minutes. Edsel made his way back to Inge with their bourbon to watch the candle-lighting.

"Nervous?" asked Inge.

"I don't know why I should be, but I am," he answered. "I've never had anything to do with him actually, and the last time I saw him was just before the day he woke up famous. He was brought to my house by Hal Beechnut, the Providence poet. I was teaching at Mills that year and Beechnut wanted me to meet this genius named Peltz. Akiba was a later name. Anyhow, nothing happened; Akiba didn't open his trap but just stalked up and down my living room, clean shaven and in horn-rimmed glasses, looking like he wanted to bite somebody, probably me. Amazing thing was this kid had never published a line, and a few days later he was being seen and heard on TV, radio, and every front page in the country."

"I remember something about it," Inge said, "but never got the point."

"The point was," said Edsel laughing, "that Akiba and three cronies, all dressed in pleated Greek military skirts, climbed up inside the head of the Statue of Liberty and found an open barrier and showered the populace below with Akiba's poem 'The Bitch of Bedloe's Island.' The first line was enough to start a riot: 'Imperial virgin whore of Wall Street shore, Whitman and Hart and I Akiba scream no more no more no more to the American gulls of clap and shit,' and such paeans. When they were arrested they claimed their goal was to remove the bronze sonnet on the statue and replace it with Truth. Akiba meanwhile had lined up thirty English professors over the country, including Beechnut, to pay for an ad for his defense. They didn't need the ad: every veterans' outfit in the country took to the air to denounce the sacrilege; Akiba himself published a book of editorials attacking him, or rather pirated the stuff and had to be bailed out by softheaded pinko well-wishers. That poem sold a hundred thousand copies in a matter of weeks and another hundred thou when the California court banned it as obscene. The whole thing was a miracle of planning."

The people on the lawn were standing up and lighting one another's candles. There was a gentle tinkle of Indian bells. Karen had dug strands of little cowbells out of a trunk and passed them around; they were evidently a great hit. Edsel had to admit to himself that it was an attractive scene, reminding him vaguely of childhood Fourth of July's which he had always loved.

At the far end of the street a car turned toward them flashing its headlights bright-dim, bright-dim, bright-dim. In a moment another car turned behind it, swinging the thick white beacon of police authority like a lasso. The candle people rose and lined the sidewalk. The party began

to crowd out of the house onto the porch and lawn. Inge
and Edsel stood against the rail to watch.

The double doors of the poet's yellow Microbus swung
open and the visitors burst out and stood for a moment
at the curb. Brom and Karen both marched down the
walk while cameras and flashbulbs popped. From the
lawn others began popping; Edsel thought he spotted
two local newspaper guys with professional stance and
equipment. The candle holders meanwhile raised their
lights and began to tinkle their bells and sway and chant:
Harry Krishna, Harry Krishna! They didn't know what
the words meant but they did know they were Akiba's
battle cry. Akiba would give them the correct pronunciation later.

The police car had pulled up behind the Microbus and
switched off its beacon.

"Harry Peltz Krishna," said Edsel, staring.

Nobody got out of the police car, and the arriving
dignitaries began up the walk. Coming within range,
Akiba did in fact look impressive. He wore some kind of
faded Russian ballet shirt with billowing sleeves and what
might be embroidery. Long loops of seed-beads hung
around his neck, which was wreathed with whiskers. He
stopped every few feet and spoke to his greeters, sometimes bowing, sometimes clasping a candle-holding boy or
girl, sometimes lifting an arm in a gesture of weary delight. Behind him came two tall lads dressed as American
Indians, or so Edsel surmised; they wore tightly braided
hair which hung down in snaky ropes, and they sported
fringed white-leather jackets. Bringing up the rear were
two college student types in shirts and jackets without
ties and with neatly mussed hair, between them a kind
of stumbling creature which might have been anything
from a trained chimp to a liberated basket case.

Brom and Karen intercepted the delegation as it neared
the porch steps and all shook hands vigorously. Suddenly Akiba raised his voice and called:

"Edsel, my friend! I came to see you. Where are you?"

"Go on," said Inge.

"Don't push me," answered Edsel, and walked to the steps and down.

The guru stood still and waited until Edsel had made his descent. Goddamit, he thought, why do I have to come down to his level? The holders of the candles had circled over the lawn and made an enclave around the Janiczeks, the new guests, and Edsel. Camera bulbs popped again. As Edsel approached, Akiba spread his arms out like the wings of a totem pole. Edsel walked into them deliberately, and they clasped each other like long-lost brothers. A cheer and clapping and ringing of Hindu cowbells came from the audience.

Akiba took a step back and said, "But you look so distinguished, Edsel, like a person of wisdom. The white hair of the suffering. I have come to visit you."

Edsel said, "You have changed yourself, Akiba" (he wasn't ready to say Harry). They proceeded side by side up the steps and into the house, saying nothing.

In the back of the house the Jamaican contingent was still holding forth, and the beat of the folk-rock had switched to a more intelligible Calypso. Somebody was having fun with Brom's collection of antique records. Akiba winced as he entered the hall and faced the patri-otic-looking lighting and the sound of "camp." He excused himself and disappeared toward the dancing academy. Inge appeared at Edsel's side and he beckoned her. "Come with me," he said. He led her to the blue room where Brom and Karen kept their "classical" col-lection and where the master phonograph was housed. He grabbed an album at random and slapped a record down and turned the volume up full force, then pulled her back into the hall to wait for the guru. As Akiba emerged with his arm around a glistening Jamaican who was dragging Wanda in tow, they met with the blast of the "Dies Irae" of the Verdi *Requiem.* The volume was blinding and Akiba, who had just succeeded in turning off the music in the back of the house, seemed to stagger slightly. But Karen had already rushed to the rescue and yanked out the wall plug; she was sweating slightly when she apologized to Akiba. "Some child," she said, "trying for attention." Akiba gave her a mincing smile. He turned to one of his henchmen.

"Govinda," he said, "the tape recorder."

Govinda, of lank braids and fringed Custer's-last-stand jacket, handed Akiba a leather-bound tape recorder which Edsel judged must have cost someone about eight hundred dollars. Karen thought the blue room would be the ideal place for the recital and she led the company through the door. Akiba slipped the handsome machine from its case and plugged it in.

"Sit by me, Edsel," he said, and lowered himself to the floor. "Less light," he commanded Karen, who switched off all but one.

Edsel called to Inge who was leaning against the wall. "Get me a bottle from Brom, please," and gave her a wink with both eyes. She sidled out of the door and returned shortly with an uncapped fifth of blended scotch.

"We don't drink, Edsel," said Akiba, "but with you I drink." He seized the fifth and upended it against his mouth and took a healthy drag, and handed the bottle to Edsel. Edsel took a healthier swallow and set the scotch between his legs.

The room had become crowded with standees, and in the hall faces were peering over one another, staring at the university poet and the guru seated on the floor.

"Not only *with* you but *to* you I drink," said Akiba, and put his arm around Edsel. "Because I love you," said the itinerant mystic. "Tell me, now, what are you writing?" Akiba said this with an air of a creative writing teacher who had just returned from a Fulbright and was speaking in secret to his favorite student.

Edsel in turn had thrown his arm around Akiba and gave him a kiss on the beard. Akiba immediately smoothed it out with his hand. Edsel had the fleeting impression that Akiba had just come from the beauty parlor and thought he could smell the aroma of the hair dryer.

"I've just finished my verse play," said Edsel, "about

Snorri Sturluson the skald. He was such a talented bastard, whether more bastard than talented being the subject."

Akiba looked grave. "You know, Edsel," he said, "I follow you, I have always followed you, worried about you. I worry about your joking, your failure of seriousness, your departure from the—well, why can't I say it to you? —the sacred. Our art is holy ground, as well you know. I came to you about this, to return your art to prayer, invocation, to the *semplicita*." Edsel was touched by the music of the Italian word and hated Akiba for having just returned from the Spoleto festival while he had been grinding out lectures in Hamburg and Frankfurt.

Edsel laughed and took a swig of the scotch and handed Akiba the bottle. "But there's nothing simple about you, Harry Peltz," Edsel said. Akiba smiled and squeezed his hand.

At this moment there was a kind of rumpus on the outer porch and a shuffling of persons in the hallway, along with a few muffled cries of what might have been indignation or fright; and the chief of the Milo police limped into the doorway of the blue room. Brom Janiczek followed and gave Akiba a pay-no-attention wave.

"Mr. Mame?" asked Chief Slezak. Akiba rose to his feet, handling his beard and smiling.

"My name is Mem, Akiba Mem, officer." He smiled and held out his hand.

"Mr. Mam," said Chief Slezak, compromising on the pronunciation. "Sorry to be of bother. May I speak to you privately?"

Akiba leaned over and with one hand behind him lifted the microphone of his tape recorder before his mouth like a lollypop.

"There is nothing private between us, officer," he said in a calming voice. "If you wish to ask me anything, I want you to ask in front of my dear friends."

Gimpy Slezak lurched back on his short leg and peered at Brom who said, "I told you he's okay, Chief. Just ask

him whatever you have to and he'll give you full satisfaction."

The police chief had never been separated from his
subject by a microphone except in his own office with
witnesses, and he asked Akiba why the microphone.

"Sir," said Akiba, "for my rights and for your rights,
and no harm done. Besides, I am a traveler, as you know,
and I like to keep a record of my experiences."

"Okay," said the chief. "I have a search warrant for
your car. Suspicion of carrying drugs. Have to check that
out. Is that all right with you?"

"The car is right there, Chief," said Akiba, "and you
have my blessing to search it for whatever you want."
Akiba took a step toward the officer, who took a step
back.

"Second," said Slezak, "I want to know how long you
expect to be in Milo and where you and your passengers
are residing."

Akiba glanced at Brom who came forward, put his
arm on Slezak's, and said, "Chief, these students are my
guests, Mr. Mem and the four with him—not the whole
party, Chief, for God's sake—and they have my hospitality."

"Thank you, Professor," said Akiba. "A day, two days;
we're not traveling salesmen and we love the country . . ."

Slezak and Brom stepped into the hall and conferred
for a few minutes. Brom returned by himself and winked
at Akiba and motioned him to resume his sitting posture
and to forget the late unpleasantness.

Akiba replaced the microphone in the case and produced a pair of Hindu bells from his pockets. He closed
his eyes and began to sway silently at first, then quietly
let the little bells tinkle. Slowly he began to chant:

"Hari, Hari, Krishna, Krishna."

Suddenly his eyes flew open and he addressed the
assembly.

"The word is not Harry, please. It is Harr-ii. You have
to roll the 'r.' Try putting a 'd' before the 'r' or after

the 'r.' It is difficult to do. But it's definitely not Harry
—like I'm just wild about Harry." He let his hands flow
in the position of a decaying lotus. "Harrdi, Harrdi, Krishna, Krishna," and he let the bells tinkle and his eyes close
and his body sway.

"Oh come, oh come, oh dance, oh dance," he chanted,
"Chanting Harrdi's name with fervor!
What does it matter that you struck me?
What does it matter that you fuck me?
Dance, dear friends, in Harrdi's name!
Sing the name of our beloved!
He'll embrace you in his rapture!
Weep and chant the name of Harrdi,
Harrdi, Harrdi, Krishna, Krishna,
And you will see your very moon-soul;
Harrdi's name is love I give you.
Give me Krishna, bring me Krishna,
Krishna, Krishna, Harrdi, Harrdi!"

Akiba's company had begun their tinkling and chanting also, and soon the entire group was locking arms and
chanting "Harrdi, Harrdi, Krishna, Krishna." Edsel was
being bumped by Akiba's sidewise swaying and shut his
eyes and let the music flow over him.

Akiba had the genius of attention and co-attention; he
knew when to entrance one person and when to engage a
sea of faces. Tonight the house party was of no consequence; he had come to enlist Edsel in some cause or
other, or to neutralize him, "sting me into acceptance,"
Edsel thought. The chanting and bell-ringing stopped
abruptly, and Akiba gave Edsel a knowing Ramakrishna
smile and fished out a huge spool of tape from the pocket
of his tape-recording apparatus.

"What, no samadhi?" asked Edsel.

"I was close. I am always very close," said Mem. "Like
orgasm at will. I know, I know, like wet dream, like
bed-wetting." Edsel knew, from having read Akiba's poems,
his tricks of ellipsis, which was what his style consisted of.
It enabled Akiba to sound "oriental" or "foreign" or "with

it" all at once, without having to construct anything out of his mind. Edsel thought to himself that Akiba's gift was Broken Esperanto.

The tape was in place and Akiba had his hand on the On button. He held his finger poised and lowered his voice and leaned into Edsel's face and said:

"I come here, Edsel, to have you hear me. I know you will hear me. That is why you are here beside me. I am nothing. I am nobody. I am a face, a faceless nonentity. Who is therefore everything. But all over the world I am flocked to. All over the world I am photographed and debated. Why? Why? Now you listen to this piece of plastic tape and tell me why. And tell me who. Or, if you are wise, say nothing or anything. But don't be able to deny that the truth speaks out of me."

He gave Edsel a shy smile and switched on the tape of his last lecture. There was a roar from the amplifier, a mixture of applause and boos. The boos definitely had it. "Listen," said Akiba, "they are booing and hissing me. But not for long," and he started to jingle his wrist bells quietly. Akiba leaned his head back and smiled, closing his eyes to slits. When the roaring of the mass audience had subsided, Akiba's taped speech began.

"Resistance is good, resistance is honorable, resistance is authentic," he began. "I respect you and love you for it, even if my presence displeases, even if my appearance is strange and makes you laugh and cringe, even if you would like to kill me. I have come for you, have come to win you, to win with the help of your beautiful resistance, help of your beauty, your and my youth. If you did not resist you would be dead; I kiss my hands to your resistance. I bring your own love to this community, yes, communion of lovers. I dig your youth, you dig my beard, or you would not come at all and you would not cringe with hiss and booings. Soon you will not see my beard and Govinda's pigtails and fringes of the holy Indian of our blood-drenched United States soil. The mystics call it One. I will One with you—it's a paradise verb—I will One you

and be your One and together we shall see through and
beyond, together we shall resist and together we shall ball
the Absolute."

An outbreak of more boos and a few obscene shouts of
"Beat it out of here, kike!" "Take it off!" "Show us the
fur!" "Call the cops!" Akiba smiled while he listened
to the demonstration subside. He reminded the audience
that this was a religious part of U.S. geography, these
sacred plains where the food animals and gods of the red-
hued owners had been slaughtered and driven into limbo,
where punishment religions, as he called them, had grown
up and made robots of the white men. He reminded them
of freedom of religion which had made this country great
and powerful and spoke of the universal religion of love
and multiplicity which he was about to introduce them to,
the vast and ageless wisdom of the high Himalayas, of the
Christian martyrs, of the Hasidic Jews, of the Mayan worship of the obsidian knife, of sexual sacrifice and of "the
joy of the land of Fuck." "I bring you God," he said, "the
god of cock and cunt, of Yin and Yang, of Sin and Bang,
holy, holy, holy of nakedness."

The blend of evangelism and fraternity language shut the
objectors into silence and Akiba continued in a soft and
cajoling tone. "I bring you the freedom to fuck, I bring
you the freedom to suck, I bring you the freedom to shit
and piss. I bless the holy, holy, holy words and give them
back to you and give back their power to your hands and
mouths and loins and buttocks." The jingling of bells began louder this time, and Akiba went into his Hindu
prayers, chanting wildly, rising to booming crescendos, and
calling for everyone to join in the Harrdi Krishna refrain.
The singing and bell-ringing went on for what must have
been twenty minutes, and when it was over there was a
dead silence while Akiba meditated wordlessly. Now and
then a bell would jingle, as in a Catholic Mass.

"You mean the university let that go on?" Edsel asked
incredulously.

"That shows what cowardice is," said Akiba. "The

power structure is crippled by its own power. Its hands and feet are tied. They preach free speech in the universities but they've preached it once too often. When we get up and demonstrate it, the cops and the trustees just skulk in the corridors, not knowing which way to turn. Yes. They had a warrant for our arrest but were afraid to use it. After what we did at Berkeley you can hardly blame them. All the fuzz did was to search the car and our bodies for grass, as if we aren't better at hiding than the cops are at finding. Now listen to this, Edsel; here you can see the total impotence of the Establishment." He bent forward to hear what was coming.

Apparently it was a dialogue between Akiba and Govinda, his favorite lover. The two had taped what Akiba called their love diary, in and out of bed. The tape recorded and described their grunts and curses and positions, their ablutions and advice to each other and to the world about the care and cleaning of genitalia and sphincters. Akiba ran in a little sermon on venereal disease and quoted his slogan: If you love your lover enough to ball him, don't give him V.D.

This chapter of the sermon was followed by a noisy and incoherent replay of a daisy chain or gang-shag, with much screaming of lines of poetry from Whitman and shouts of "At exactly five o'clock in the afternoon!"

"Louder," said a hoarse voice, which Edsel recognized as Wanda's. Akiba turned up the volume.

The second tape was an elaborate apologia for the use of drugs to expand consciousness, how and where to get them, make them, and use them. Akiba told his audience he was passing out pamphlets at the door, which he himself had had printed, about the laws of drug use, state by state, "and for the love of God, my resisters and angels, be careful. We need every chick, we need every guy, to stay out of the Black Maria. We need you, mes anges, to help spread total and universal consciousness and to assist in the cure of the disease called America. As we love and adore our land, so must we save her, just as we save our

mothers in the flesh. With ancient and godly drugs, with
modern test tubes and hallucinogens, we shall save our
mother Liberty from rape and rapine."

The introduction of the Statue of Liberty led naturally
into the "political" segment of the revival and began with
another invocation to Krishna, some quotes from *Walden*
and the declining Tolstoy, and the recitation of a terrorist
poem by the Negro anarchist Nebuchadnezzar Thomas.
The Nebb Thomas poem began: "If this America is hell,
where are the fires!/Who burned you black, you spade!/
Burn, hot nigger, your fat is in the fire!/Light the fires of
liberty hell!/Shoot off, O Afric cock!/Shoot off your bleed-
ing balls in Charlie's cunt!"—and such invocations.

Akiba carefully explained the dangers of pure hate but
rationalized the poem with a sad shrug of words, "for that
is how we freed the chattels," he said. "We must and will
suffer with them, aid and abet if need be, and show them
our hearts and our sex."

From racial hysteria he moved to a defense of Cuba
and the South American revolts. We are all part of the
same thing, intoned Akiba: the sexual revolution, the drug
revolution, the jazz revolution, all leading to the total and
complete moral and political overthrow of the Establishment. "No more university, no more chancellory, no
White House, no Black House, no Red House, but love of
soul for soul and cock for cock and cunt for cunt and all
for all in the Open Air!"

"Aren't you riding Whitman a little hard?" asked Edsel.

"I ride him and ride him," smiled Akiba with a saccharine grin. "Walt is the gland of our movement."

It was announced that political and race-struggle pamphlets were available in the lobby. Proceeds were to go to
Akiba's foundation, which paid for many things: bail for
drug users and freedom fighters, but mostly to give scholarships to Kyoto and Benares, where the new mysticism
was operating full speed ahead. Akiba gave a few ele-
mentary lessons on starting an underground newspaper
to give the Movement a link with the town and university
he was addressing. He asked those interested to meet him

and his friends in front of the main campus gate where, as he pointed out, the traffic was heaviest.

There followed a lively rock session by the Liver-Pudds, which Akiba himself had taped in England. Tapes within tapes, thought Edsel, drinking from the green bottle and passing it mechanically to Akiba. Mem continued to drink up, contrary to his principles and to show good faith with Edsel.

The final tape was Akiba's poetry reading. He had composed new poems on his tape recorder riding through the nights of the great plains, labeling each village and farm, hamlet and city, some version of Rome or Carthage or Babylon and reeling off the sins and crimes of the inhabitants. It smacked a little of the *Spoon River Anthology*, "but that figures," thought Edsel. The reading was expert, a mixture of recitative and high oratory, plainsong and operatic roaring. Akiba tapered off with the Harrdi-Krishna psalm and ended almost inaudibly with a rhythmic tinkle of the Hindu bells. There was a dead silence on the tape and finally the longest and most bloodcurdling cheer Edsel could remember. Akiba let the cheer roll on and on until the tape ran out, then leaned over and pressed the rewind button, threw his arms around Edsel and hugged him. "Marvelous," said Akiba about his own performance. He seemed genuinely moved.

"No more," said Akiba, refusing the bottle which Edsel had motioned at him. "I want to meet your friends," he added.

"I don't know them, only a few," said Edsel. "Brom will take care of that."

Akiba rose and smoothed his beard and, giving Edsel a cherubic grin, made his way to the door where Brom and Karen stood with arms around each other, enraptured with the performance. As Akiba approached, Karen burst into tears and smothered the mystic with a hug. "Oh Akiba," she snuffled, "you have made this house a holy ground. None of us will ever be the same." Akiba responded silently, detaching himself deftly from the anthropologist's clutch. The music had started up again in the rear of the dwelling and the bang of guitars could be heard from the basement below. The blue room emptied.

"What do you think?" Edsel asked Inge who had sat on the floor beside him.

"I can't," she answered, laughing. "You do have patience, Boss. What's next on the program?"

"What happens from here on in," said Edsel, "is purely below the belt. Or that's my guess. The Indians will add as many notches to their jocks as they can stomach, the Jamaicans will forsake the dance for the fertility rite, Mrs. House will masturbate on the totem pole, Wanda will solve the race problem in the only way she knows how, the Air Force will start smashing objets d'art while Akiba gives a footnote on the evils of the demon rum, the marijuana will be broken out, the motorcycle riders will pass around their rusty hypo needles, the painted lady will shimmy under the fluorescent lights, everybody under twenty will get the dry heaves, and Kaz will do the Mexican hat dance on the kitchen table. And tomorrow this party will be consecrated as the greatest event in Milo since the James Brothers rode through and killed fifteen alley cats from horseback."

They had decided they had just as well leave, and Edsel debated whether to say goodbye to anybody. He was afraid that if he didn't Akiba would come rolling up to his house with his cargo of human suffering. As he and Inge pushed their way to the kitchen they heard the noise of scuffling and cursing and a bottle smashing. Govinda, who carried an American flag as a handkerchief, had made a point of blowing his nose in it to amuse the admiring students.

"Wipe your ass with your draft card," said Govinda, "like I do this." He had dropped his trousers and was bending down with the flag scrunched in his hand. But at that moment Kaz had grabbed Govinda's arm and twisted it behind his back, snatching the flag with his other hand. From somewhere the Air Force sergeant appeared and smashed his fist into Govinda's mouth. Edsel thought he saw teeth flying as the braided would-be Indian folded up on the floor, unconscious.

That was the beginning. Akiba was holding Govinda's head and sobbing and kissing the bloody mouth. The Jamaicans appeared from nowhere and started swinging at everything white. Ape Koslow, in an effort at peace-making, was flinging all combatants against the wall. Karen was screaming and holding her ears. Four teen-agers were rifling the liquor armory. "Turn the music up loud, loud!" Brom was bellowing, as all the lights in the house went dark and the pandemonium mounted. "Quick," said Edsel in Inge's ear, "follow me." They edged toward where they had last seen the kitchen door and slipped out onto the back porch. They raced around to the street and got in Edsel's car as the police beacon made its appearance around the corner at the far end of the street. Edsel started his motor and made a quick U-turn to head in the other direction and turned down the first cross street he came to. Several blocks away he turned slowly back. "Got to see," he said.

He passed within a block of the Janiczek house which was crawling with police lights. Suddenly he said, "My God!" and saw a burst of flame from the high Victorian window on the side. Simultaneously he heard the fire engines; he started his motor again and slid down the darkened street without turning his lights on.

The Death
of
Randall Jarrell

This is not a eulogy, not a memorial, not one of those exercises in the objective perception of value for which the age of criticism is justly infamous. Randall Jarrell was not my friend, nor was he my enemy. But he was the poet whose poetry I admired and looked up to most after William Carlos Williams. This I said many times in many ways in my criticism. I praised his poetry more and more wholeheartedly than any other of his contemporaries. My praise, it may be, did not sit comfortably with him, for he spotted me as an outsider, or one who was constantly battling to get on the outside. Jarrell was very much an insider. There was a terrible conflict in his soul between his instinct for freedom and his desire for cultural asylum. This conflict gave him his style, his literary style, his life-style. It is a style deceptively free. His bookplate might be the question mark. The most common and significant expression he uses at crucial points in his poetry and in his prose is *and yet*. . . . I thought of naming this essay "Randall Jarrell—And Yet," but I decided to be more ambitious. I shall try to situate Randall Jarrell among his fellows rather than doing his portrait. I think there is a message in his death, for me and for this generation.

Let me dispose of a little personal data first, a few

observations which will perhaps illumine my not too extensive relationship with him. When I was editing *Poetry* magazine, and after I had published hundreds—could it have been thousands?—of poets, I noted that the manuscripts of Randall Jarrell, whether poems or prose, were the only perfect manuscripts I ever saw. I mean that they were letter-perfect. There was no question of a typo or any other kind of graphical error. He was my only scrupulous poet, for most poets write the way they dress and their manuscripts look like somebody else's laundry, thank God. And this minor perfection of Jarrell's was reflected in the precision of thought, especially in his prose, which all the same sometimes took on a slightly euphuistic contour. I think euphuistic is the word; *baroque* describes certain of his stylistic processes, a style of inlay in which quotation is so exquisitely handled that everything Jarrell quotes sounds as if he wrote it. He was a great, you might say a dangerous, listener. And yet his style of reportage is comic, for he fears loftiness and bombast like the plague. One looks forward to the publication of his letters. We can be sure that the voice of the poet and of the cultural gossip is there. Charm is overwhelming in all his writing; *wit* is too platitudinous a word for his work, and the sharply outlined involutions of his thought deserve a better word than *wisdom*.

He gave a marvelous summation of contemporary poetry in a lecture four years ago. I asked him if I could publish it in the *Prairie Schooner*, which I then edited. His reply was: "I'd be delighted for you to print the lecture in the *Prairie Schooner*. You've always been my favorite editor because you're not like an editor at all." I put the best construction on this remark that I could, especially as I knew it to be true, more than true, a complimentary reprimand of *my* style of life and letters. Except for an early merciless review of one of my books, he was always understanding about me—and acidulous. We were of the same group, so to speak, and had fought all the same wars, and he had a right to cry *Whoa!* when I came galloping by.

All the poets sat on the edge of their seats while Jarrell, whom everybody had to admit had earned the right to do so, put together the jigsaw puzzle of modern poetry in front of our eyes. When I was finally fitted into place, with a splash of color, I felt a relief that I *fitted* and a regret that that puzzle had been solved. I will repeat what he said of me because it is germane to my evaluation of Jarrell: "Karl Shapiro's poems are fresh and young and rash and live; their hard clear outlines, their flat bold colors create a world like that of a knowing and skillful neo-primitive painting, without any of the confusion or profundity of atmosphere, of aerial perspective, but with notable visual and satiric force." He then goes on to mention my influences, Auden, Rilke, Whitman, and he does not need to say that these are also his influences, more his than mine, because Jarrell assimilated his Auden and Rilke and Whitman, along with his Corbière and Grimm and even Robert Frost. I assimilated nothing but was only influenced by. I rejected Influence out of hand and waged a one-man children's crusade against the Past, the Graeco-Judaeo-Christian thingamajig, so that Jarrell could say of me with amused amazement: "Both in verse and in prose Shapiro loves, partly out of indignation and partly out of sheer mischievousness, to tell the naked truths or half-truths or quarter-truths that will make anybody's hair stand on end; he is always crying: 'But he hasn't any clothes on!' about an emperor who is half the time surprisingly well dressed." There is a slight concession here: Jarrell admits that the emperor is dressed like an emperor only *half* the time, while I contend that he is badly dressed even when he is naked.

I will be done with this "interrelationship" in a moment, but I am leading up to something important, a whole or half- or quarter-truth which I am bound to utter. I will read a poem I wrote about Jarrell; it is a prose-poem, as prosodists say when they run out of verbiage, and is in my last book. I don't remember Jarrell's reaction to the poem, but I aimed to please him when I wrote it.

*Randall, I like your poetry terribly, yet I'm afraid to say so.
Not that my praise keeps you awake—though I'm afraid it does.
I can't help liking them. I even like the whine, the make-
believe whiplash with the actual wire in it. Once when you
reviewed me badly (you must) I wrote you: "I felt as if I had
been run over but not hurt." That made you laugh. I was
happy. It wasn't much of a triumph but it worked. When
people ask about you I am inclined to say: He's an assassin (a
word I never use). I'm inclined to say: Why are you always
yourself? Your love of Rilke—if it's love—your intimacy with
German and God knows what all, your tenderness and terrorization, your prose sentences—like Bernini graves, staggeringly
expensive, Italianate, warm, sentences once-and-for-all. All the
verses you leave half-finished in mid-air—I once knew a woman
who never finished a sentence. Your mind is always at its best,
your craft the finest craft "money can buy," you would say
with a barb. I'm afraid of you. Who wouldn't be? But I rush
to read you, whatever you print. That's news.*

And this is also news. I am quoting from the News
Notes section of *Poetry* magazine of last spring. "There
was a public ceremony at Yale on February 28th to honor
the memory of Randall Jarrell, who was killed last autumn
in an automobile accident. John Berryman, Richard Eberhart, John Hollander, Stanley Kunitz, Robert Lowell,
William Meredith, Adrienne Rich, Robert Penn Warren,
Richard Wilbur, and Peter Taylor came together at Yale
to participate in the tribute, for which the chairman was
Norman Holmes Pearson. Mary Jarrell, widow of the poet,
read 'the last recently written poem that truly pleased him,'
'The Player Piano,' as yet unpublished. The Yale *Daily
News* reports that she 'received an impassioned standing
ovation as she walked to the lectern.' Elizabeth Bishop,
Cleanth Brooks, Robert Fitzgerald, Marianne Moore, John
Crowe Ransom, and Allen Tate, who could not attend,
sent testimonials which Professor Pearson read. . . ."

When I read this little notice in *Poetry* I was dismayed
at my conspicuous absence from the list. Had Jarrell left
it in his will to keep me off the Yale campus? Impossible.
I had a blood-boiling moment of suspicion or paranoia
that the Bollingen Committee or Professor Pearson or

Robert Lowell had blackballed me from the club. My anti-cultural-committee activities span many years, and I have tried to sabotage organized culture whenever possible—not always successfully, of course. When the National Institute of Arts and Letters elected me as a member, I declined. But when their officers called me and said nobody had had that much cheek since Sinclair Lewis declined, and who the hell did I think I was, I chickened out and let them enroll me. When I went to watch the President sign the Arts and Humanities bill, some writer said: What are you doing here? Spying, was all I could say. And now Randall had been organized in death by some cultural subcommittee and all I could think was: Now he knows what it feels like to turn over in his grave.

Between the instinct for freedom and the desire for cultural asylum others can make a choice, and always do. Culture Committees love funerals. There is, even in one's fellow poets, a touch of the vulture; when the poet lies on the roof of the Tower of Silence you can hear the shuddering of ragged wings.

I remember once that Robert Lowell and Randall Jarrell were playing a game. The game was Who's First and it was Lowell's game. The idea is to grade the poets until the downgrading wipes most of the competition off the board. Two or three remaining contenders then engage in a death struggle. Jarrell played this game with a will, but his winning instinct was no match for Lowell.

In Jarrell's bibliography published in 1958 there is a good introduction which contains this sentence: "Most critics predicted the emerging greatness of a Robert Lowell or a Karl Shapiro, but few guessed that Jarrell would outstrip them, especially in so short a time." This judgment is sound as far as I am concerned and certainly as far as Lowell is concerned. I'm not playing Who's First, I hope, because I don't think the game is worth my time or anyone else's. Comparisons of Lowell and Jarrell are irrelevant anyhow. Lowell is primarily a figurehead which he himself personally carved out of solid rock. The effort was immense, Churchillian in blood, sweat, and tears.

But one feels that Lowell writes poetry to *get even*, while Jarrell became a poet because he couldn't help it.

Some years ago I volunteered to write an article for the *Evergreen Review* about Lowell. I said I would call it "Robert Lowell *as* T. S. Eliot." A while later I said I would change the title to "Robert Lowell as Cassius Clay." I finished up by not writing the article at all. It was not Lowell I was after but the *maître d'hôtel* psychology of literature which Lowell espouses.

In the Jarrell lecture which I published in the *Prairie Schooner*, Jarrell says this of Lowell (I am paraphrasing): Robert Lowell is the poet of shock. His style manages to make even quotations and historical facts a personal possession. "Make it grotesque" could be Lowell's motto. (In the context Jarrell is contrasting Lowell with Richard Wilbur, a poet who makes poems out of the things of life rather than out of life itself.) Jarrell thought that Lowell possessed and wrote out of a life, yet he knew that this life was at least as unreal as Wilbur's life-by-virtue-of-the-things-of-life. Here is a direct quote: "Lowell has always had an astonishing ambition, a willingness to learn what past poetry was and to compete with it on its own terms." My comment is what Jarrell politely implies, that competition is the sole inspiration of such a poet. Jarrell says in a parenthesis that Lowell bullied his early work, but his own vulnerable humanity has been forced in on him (a statement of tremendous humanity and pardon) with a shadow of fear above. Of Lowell's poems he mentions their stubborn toughness, their senseless originality (an expression to conjure with), and their contingency. Some of the poems justify the harshness and violence and what Jarrell calls their barbarous immediacy; he ends by complimenting Lowell, without having convinced us why, for his largeness and grandeur, and throws him a fish in this sentence: "You feel before reading any new poem of his the uneasy expectation of perhaps encountering a masterpiece." In an earlier treatment of Lowell in *Poetry and the Age*, Jarrell wrote: "Cocteau said to poets: *Learn what you can do and then don't do it*; and this is so. . . . As a poet Mr. Lowell sometimes doesn't have enough trust in God and tries to do everything himself; . . . But probably the reader will want to say to me . . . what Lincoln said about the drunkard Grant: 'If I knew his brand I would order my other generals a barrel.' "

Our generation—the generation of Jarrell, Wilbur, myself, Roethke, Lowell, Schwartz, Bishop, Ciardi, Berryman, Kunitz, Nemerov, Whittemore—one is almost inclined to add Merrill, Lynch, Pearce, Fenner, and Smith—our generation lived through more history than most or maybe any. We lived through more history even than Stendhal, who fell, as he says, with Napoleon. We were reared as intellectuals and fought the Second World War before it happened and then again when it did happen. We witnessed the god that failed and helped trip him up. We predicted the Alexandrianism of the age and like everybody else we throve on it. We drove our foreign cars to class to teach. And we bit the hand that fed us, but not very hard, not hard enough. The hand went on signing papers. Once upon a time we were all revolutionaries of one stripe or another, but when we got married and settled down, with tenure, we talked technique instead of overthrow. Half of us stopped rebelling and not because of middle age. The age made it so easy to be a poet, or to survive on lobster, the age gave in so sweetly to our imprecations, the age so needed us to help it hate itself, this spineless age ended by softening the backbone of poetry.

Dylan Thomas was the anti-symbol of our group, that Dylan who died after he saw the faces of mice in the Bristol crystal. It was Thomas who taught poetry to stop thinking, and we resented that! Though we were not all drunks and suicides, we had our goodly share. But all of us felt the rot of institutionalism in our bones. Jarrell got it down in a novel, the kind of novel the age demanded, the exposé of sensibility. Jarrell's novel *Pictures from an Institution* is so brilliant that it defeats itself as a fiction; it becomes a hornbook of avant-gardism, sophisticated to the point of philistinism. Jarrell is misleadingly philistine,

say, about Modern Art of all varieties. It is because he
is impatient with failure or imperfection or goofing around
with the Muse. But this impatience of Jarrell's is also a
veritable lust for perfection; and both the impatience and
the philistinism are what you might call Texan. Jarrell
was a good Texan in the sense that President Johnson is
a bad Texan. *And yet,* what Jarrell does to Gertrude, his
anti-heroine in the novel, is almost beyond belief. Can anyone be that worthy of hatred? One wonders what Gertrude thought when she read her portrait. Gertrude is one
of those savage Southern female novelists who leaves the
world in terror of the art of fiction.

The setting of the novel is Benton, a very expensive
higher education academy only six versts from Sarah
Lawrence or Bennington. Benton's President Robbins
doesn't fare any better than the loathed Gertrude, and
the only lovable character in the book is a German-Jewish
composer-in-residence named Rosenbaum. Jarrell attacks
avant-garde institutionalism and everything it implies by
immolating President Robbins and all his kinfolk in the
way Gertrude might. He attacks dehumanized letters in
his lip-smacking crucifixion of Gertrude. True humanity,
true culture, true wisdom are preserved in the broken-
English Rosenbaums. Jarrell's love of the Good German
led him deep into the Black Forest, deep into German
childhood. I shared with him his love for *Der Rosen-
kavalier,* for Elisabeth Schwarzkopf (who was not a
very kosher German), and even for Mahler. Germany
is the preconscious of Europe, almost all, no, all her
geniuses are maniacs, Germany itself is a maniac, the
bright dangerous offspring of the Western soul. "Must
you learn from your makers how to die?" Jarrell asks the
war spirits in one of so many of his Germany-inspired
poems. In a note to the poem "A Game at Salzburg"
he says that there is a game that Austrians and Germans play with very young children. The child says to the
grownup, *Here I am,* and the grownup answers, *There
you are. Hier bin i': Da bist du.* Then Jarrell says: "It
seemed to me that if there could be a conversation between

the world and God, this would be it." There is an almost
unbearable sorrow in this colloquy, a German-Jewish
sorrow, so to speak. Jarrell lets Dr. Rosenbaum say:
"The people in Hell . . . say nothing but *What?*" To
which Jarrell adds: "Americans in Hell tell each other
how to make martinis."

I am not reviewing the novel, but I give it a central
place in Jarrell's work as a kind of negative plate of the
poetry. The empty intellectualism of America is pin-
pointed at Benton: the author says, "Nowadays Benton
picked and chose: girls who had read Wittgenstein as
high school baby-sitters were rejected because the school's
quota of abnormally intelligent students had already been
filled that year." Jarrell, not quite a Des Esseintes, suffers
from a disillusionment of America which all our best
artists share, suffers from the disappointment at the failure
of the healing-powers of poetry in this nation. Benton—
American higher education—is only a rarer kind of custom-
built Cadillac. One can almost begin to see the coat of
arms emerging on the enameled door. One is already afraid
of who is inside. He says, lapsing into what he thinks: "Is
an institution always a man's shadow shortened in the sun,
the lowest common denominator of everybody in it?" It
is bitter to answer yes, but so it is in the modern Institution. In his anthology of short Russian novels, Jarrell
quotes Turgenev on Tolstoy. Tolstoy "never believed in
people's sincerity. Every spiritual movement seemed to
him false, and with his extraordinarily penetrating eyes he
used to pierce those on whom his suspicion fell." The early
Jarrell published the beginning of a massive attack on
Auden, the most conspicuous idealist of the age. Later he
forgave Auden, ideals and all.

Jarrell's generation, my generation, inherited the question
of Culture, Mass Culture versus True Culture. It is our
pons asinorum and we all had to cross it. Jarrell worried
the problem more than most of us because he could not
take for granted the purely elite aesthetic of Eliot, the
motto of which is High Culture Only: No Foreigners
Allowed. Those of us who grew up with the *Partisan*

Review on our kitchen tables and who wrote for it with
great pride had a slightly altered version of High Culture.
With us it was High Culture plus social revolution. We
won the Second World War but lost the social revolution.
We lost it to what Jarrell called the Medium, the Medium
being a kind of symbol for Mass Culture. In the backwash
of power and prosperity that engulfed America after our
victory, the writers fled to those island citadels called
Institutions. Whether it was Benton or Harvard or
Berkeley, each of these Mont St. Michels harbored its
refugees from the world, from Mass Culture, from the
Medium. Jarrell said the acceptably righteous things
about Mass Culture, that it either corrupts or isolates the
writer, that "true works of art are more and more produced
away from or in opposition to society." And yet he knew
the writer's need for contact with the mass and qualified
his rejections of the Medium. Part of the artist, he said (I
am quoting from *A Sad Heart at the Super-Market*): part
of the artist "wants to be like his kind, is like his kind;
longs to be loved and admired and successful." Part of
Jarrell longed to be accepted by the Medium, but the
thought of that depressed him. He asked, "Is the influence
of what I have called the Medium likely to lead us to
any good life? to make us love and try to attain any real
excellence, beauty, magnanimity? . . ." The answer has to
be no. The middle-aged woman in the supermarket who
buys All and Cheer and Joy for her gleaming washing
machines sees only the image of death staring at her in her
rear-view mirror. Let me read this poem, which in my
mind is already a famous poem.

NEXT DAY

Moving from Cheer to Joy, from Joy to All,
I take a box
And add it to my wild rice, my Cornish game hens.
The slack or shorted, basketed, identical
Food-gathering flocks
Are selves I overlook. Wisdom, said William James,

Is learning what to overlook. And I am wise
If that is wisdom;
Yet somehow, as I buy All from these shelves
And the boy takes it to my station wagon,
What I've become
Troubles me even if I shut my eyes.

When I was young and miserable and pretty
And poor, I'd wish
What all girls wish: to have a husband,
A house and children. Now that I'm old, my wish
Is womanish:
That the boy putting groceries in my car

See me. It bewilders me he doesn't see me.
For so many years
I was good enough to eat: the world looked at me
And its mouth watered. How often they have
    undressed me,
The eyes of strangers!
And, holding their flesh within my flesh, their vile

Imaginings within my imagining,
I too have taken
The chance of life. Now the boy pats my dog
And we start home. Now I am good.
The last mistaken,
Ecstatic, accidental bliss, the blind

Happiness that, bursting, leaves upon the palm
Some soap and water—
It was so long ago, back in some Gay
Twenties, Nineties, I don't know . . . Today I miss
My lovely daughter
Away at school, my sons away at school,

My husband away at work—I wish for them.
The dog, the maid,
And I go through the sure unvarying days
At home in them. As I look at my life,
I am afraid
Only that it will change, as I am changing:

I am afraid, this morning, of my face.
It looks at me

From the rear-view mirror, with the eyes I hate,
The smile I hate. Its plain, lined look
Of gray discovery
Repeats to me: "You're old." That's all, I'm old.

And yet I'm afraid, as I was at the funeral
I went to yesterday.
My friend's cold made-up face, granite among its
*   flowers,*
Her undressed, operated-on, dressed body
Were my face and body.
As I think of her I hear her telling me

How young I seem, I am exceptional,
I think of all I have.
But really no one is exceptional,
No one has anything, I'm anybody,
I stand beside my grave
Confused with my life, that is commonplace and
*   solitary.*

So in that life which is our Way, there is no excellence.
But one wonders, to use Jarrell's pun on the great word
All, if that is really all. When the prophets of High Culture (I called it Hi-Cult in one of my own essays) all died
out, leaving only Dwight Macdonald to rave against the
Medium and Kitsch and Camp and all those once-fashion-
able diseases of the age; when Eliot fell in love and died,
and Pound discovered silence—in short, when the Twenties and Thirties ended, it was already the Sixties, and it
had become hard to say where the Medium ended and
the isolate poet began. How could a specialized study of
the intellectual, say, *Herzog*, be a best-seller? What mass
audience was it that picked that up? Even the woman in
the supermarket quotes William James. The question with
us, with Jarrell, was the probability of accepting the supermarket and its brightly packaged values. Or must one be
an Allen Ginsberg and situate Walt Whitman in the
supermarket, only to say: "See, I told you so! America
has to start over from scratch."

In *Poetry and the Age,* one of the best handbooks of
anti-criticism criticism we have, there is an essay on the
obscurity of the poet. My edition of the book is dated
1955, a fatal year for pronunciamentos about the Audience, the year when some giant beast slouching toward the
City Lights Bookshop gave birth to "Howl." "Tomorrow
morning," Jarrell was saying, "some poet may, like Byron,
wake up to find himself famous—for having written a
novel, for having killed his wife; it will not be for having
written a poem." Jarrell was wrong; the whole generation
was wrong about the Audience and the Poet; "Howl"
gave us the lie. For myself, I was delighted and immediately sent in my resignation to my generation. They
accepted it gingerly but with inquisitorial silence. In the
same essay Jarrell had said, "The general public . . .
has set up a criterion of its own, one by which every form
of contemporary art is condemned." This statement too,
which had for so long been so widely accepted, was already
obsolete. A decade after "Howl"—and I see that poem
as a symptom rather than as a cause—the general public
itself has become the contemporary art audience. There
are very few places in our geography any more which resemble a Nebraska of the spirit; and in any case, philistinism today is no longer spontaneous but organized, political.
Condemnation of the artist today is no longer mere pro-
vincialism; it is, to use a not very old-fashioned term, a
form of fascism. And the general public, whatever that is,
is choosing up sides. The Medium still dominates the
sensory experience of the masses of people, but the Medium itself has become an initiate of Hi-Cult. The Medium
has also had courses in modern poetry and electronic
music.

The Berkeley or California Rebellion, like the Whiskey
Rebellion, was a protest against a central culture. The
California Rebellion struck out at every form of institutionalism it could clap eyes on. This too was a generational
revolt and continues to be world-wide; it is, as most writers
about it have noticed, more a sociological upheaval than

a new motion in the arts. There is no innovation in Beat arts; the poetry stems from traditional rebel poets, Rimbaud, Pound, Whitman, Artaud. And the counterrevolt against Beatism stems from what was left over from the old-guard elite and also from members of Jarrell's generation. Jarrell would not, I believe, commit himself to the new barbarians, as some writers call them. He could not; he was too urbane, too civilized, too much a lover of the perfect. I cannot imagine him favoring for any reason the later phase of Beat art, the jazz-poetry of Bob Dylan and all those electric guitarists who carry their echo chambers with them wherever they go, portable Aeolian winds, and whose motto seems to be Death By Motorcycle. Perhaps finally Jarrell recognized how much of an institution *our* generation had become, how much an institution he had become. I was in more of a position to face the music, the music of the electric guitar, because of my resignation. It was no surprise to me when I published a collection of essays called *In Defense of Ignorance* to receive a letter from a prominent member of our generation that complimented me highly on the book and said how much it was needed, a letter which ended, "but I would appreciate it if you didn't tell anybody." It was of course not Jarrell who penned this. Lowell questioned my adherence to William Carlos Williams. Williams is the godfather of "Howl."

Jarrell's beautiful fable called *The Bat Poet* is, like all true fables, open to various readings. A child can read it as well as a philosopher as well as a poet, each with the same comprehension. A little light-brown bat leaves the pack to go out into the world of daylight to "hang there and think." The real bats don't understand the poet bat, who uses such things as colors in his poems, for the bat poet is a poet. Busy work-a-night bats don't care for color and have no truck with poems. After trying out his poems on such creatures as the mockingbird, who criticizes the bat poet's prosody and complains how hard it is to be a mockingbird; after failing to write a poem about the car-

dinal, who is perhaps too beautiful even for a poem; after
bargaining with the chipmunk, who is the bat poet's most
sympathetic critic (although naturally a poem about the
owl gives the chipmunk the primordial Angst), the bat
poet writes his best poem about, of all things, a mother bat
zigzagging through the night with her baby clinging to
her body. The chipmunk decides that everything the bat
does is upside down. At last the bat poet decides to go
and read his bat poem to the bats themselves, but when he
gets to the barn where the bats collect, he has curiously
forgotten his most important poem and just hangs upside
down and goes to sleep like all the other bats.

Whether to be a bat or a poet: that is the question.
Maybe the poets of Jarrell's and my generation were all
hybrid bat-poets, going back to the institutional barn and
then lighting off in broad sunlight to write poems about
the righteous and dyspeptic mockingbird, the rich-bitch
cardinal, the kindly and existential chipmunk, the Owl who
gets us all indiscriminately in his claws. When I got my
first copy of *The Bat Poet* I couldn't read it. The title
and the drawing bothered me. It was the only thing of
Jarrell's I didn't leap to read, and I gave my copy to a
student. When I went to find a copy I found that my
library at the University of Nebraska had never heard
of it, that no bookstore in my part of the world had ever
heard of it, that nobody I knew within hailing distance
had ever heard of it, except that there was a mint copy
in the state capitol building, which I obtained.

The basic assumption, the basic critical theorem of
our generation was that poetry didn't really *go* in this age,
that the age demanded everything of the artist except his
art, and that the poet was still declassed. Insofar as there
was any truth in the assumption it was a minor truth.
When Jarrell defended Robert Frost in calling attention
to "the other Frost" he was reminding his intellectual
contemporaries that even a popular poet could make the
grade. But Jarrell was really saying about Frost that he was
a poet whose popularity was perhaps accidental. Con-
versely, Dylan Thomas, whom Jarrell thought correctly

one of the most obscure poets of the age, was popular by default. It might be truer to say that Frost and Thomas were not only creative but also performing artists, not only performing artists but artists in action. Frost and Thomas lived their poetry, on stage and off; they were one with it, while our generation tended to hide or to collect in small conspiratorial groups. We barely learned to *read* poetry, because, as we said a little wearily, we *wrote* it. And because we wrote poetry that we were not necessarily committed to read, because we held to the cold North American delivery, we could seldom muster more than a token audience. Even Robert Frost, finally one of our great readers, insisted on the verb *say* for his recitations. Jarrell's bat poet picks up the idiom: he says he is going to *say* a poem to the mockingbird, and so forth. The opposite of *to say* is *to sing,* and even tone-deaf Yeats chanted his works. Pound revived a chant for the *Cantos:* it was one of the qualities that attracted him to the Beats. But the classroom voice and the High Church voice were dominant in the generation of Jarrell. And yet, what else were we to do in America, we argued, in a language which is inflected only in moments of violence? We shift between the nasal monotone and the double spondee. Jarrell is the one poet of my generation who made an art of American speech as it is, who advanced beyond Frost in using not only a contemporary idiom (although in Frost it is necessarily fictitious) but the actual rhythms of our speech. Here Jarrell is unique and technically radical. No other poet of our time has embalmed the common dialogue of Americans with such mastery. And because he caught our bourgeois speech he caught our meaning. Here is part of the marvelous essay-poem about, of all uncapturable things, Woman.

WOMAN

"*All things become thee, being thine,*" *I think
     sometimes
As I think of you. I think: "How many faults*

In thee have seemed a virtue!" While your taste is on
   my tongue

The years return, blessings innumerable
As the breaths that you have quickened, gild my
   flesh.
Lie there in majesty!

                When, like Disraeli, I murmur
That you are more like a mistress than a wife,
More like an angel than a mistress; when, like Satan,
I hiss in your ear some vile suggestion,
Some delectable abomination,
You smile at me indulgently: "Men, men!"

You smile at mankind, recognizing in it
The absurd occasion of your fall.
For men—as your soap operas, as your Home
   Journals,
As your heart's whisper—men are only children.
And you believe them. Truly, you are children.

Should I love you so dearly if you weren't?
If I weren't?
           O morning star,
Each morning my dull heart goes out to you
And rises with the sun, but with the sun
Sets not, but all the long night nests within your
   eyes.

Men's share of grace, of all that can make bearable,
Lovable almost, the apparition, Man,
Has fallen to you. Erect, extraordinary
As a polar bear on roller skates, he passes
On into the Eternal . . .
            From your pedestal, you watch
Admiringly, when you remember to.

Let us form, as Freud has said, "a group of two."
You are the best thing that this world can offer—
He said so. Or I remember that he said so;
If I am mistaken it's a Freudian error,
An error nothing but a man would make.
Women can't bear women. Cunningly engraved
On many an old wife's dead heart is "Women,
Beware women!" And yet it was a man

> *Sick of too much sweetness—of a life*
> *Rich with a mother, wife, three daughters, a wife's*
>   *sister,*
> *An abyss of analysands—who wrote: "I cannot*
> *Escape the notion (though I hesitate*
> *To give it expression) that for women*
> *The level of what is ethically normal*
> *Is different from what it is in men.*
> *Their superego"—he goes on without hesitation—*
> *"Is never so inexorable, so impersonal,*
> *So independent of its emotional*
> *Origins as we require it in a man."*

(It is a long deep poem of a couple of hundred lines such as)

> *You call to me, "Come"; and when I come say, "Go,"*
> *Smiling your soft contrary smile . . .*

two lines packed with as much meaning as "The Death of the Ball-Turret Gunner."

An age's poetry does not purify the dialect, or any of that nonsense which aesthetic moralists believe, but an age's poetry fixes the age for those who care to gaze upon it in another age. Most of the poets of Jarrell's generation, when they were not simply describing, setting up the landscape of the city dump or suburbia or attacking the gleaming machinery of our brilliant kitchens, most of our poets dealt in minor points of ideology, lives of the saints or of boxers, or the symbolism of automobiles. Our technique was irony and nothing but irony, more kinds of irony than the Arabs have words for *camel*. But Jarrell, for all his indirection, spoke directly to the theme and in the direct idiom of our semiliterate educated classes. He listened like a novelist—I have already alluded to his ear— he heard the worst of us as well as the best. Things like iambic pentameter hypnotized him not. He used it as one sits in a Victorian chair in a friend's house, but how well he knew a Victorian chair when he saw one.

No one has ever caught a French writer or a German writer or an English or Irish or Scotch writer asking what a French, German, English, Irish, or Scotch writer is. But

American writers ask practically nothing but What is an American writer? Meaning. What is an American? It is the great theme of American literature and in a sense the "If some day a tourist notices, among the ruins of New York City, a copy of *Leaves of Grass*, and stops and picks it up and reads some lines in it, she will be able to say to herself: How very American! If he and his country had not existed, it would have been impossible to imagine them."

Jarrell is almost as pro-American as Whitman himself. He applauds Marianne Moore's saying about America only one. Jarrell says, for instance, about Walt Whitman that it is not Niagara Falls, the calico horses, and the war-canoe that matter, nor the resources nor the know-how; "it is not the plunder, but 'accessibility to experience.'" He praises her Americanness and makes more famous the famed line about our language: "grassless / linksless, languageless country in which letters are written / not in Spanish, not in Greek, not in Latin, not in shorthand, / but in plain American which cats and dogs can read!"

For *Paterson Book I* Jarrell reserved greater praise, predicting, because it was the most American poem ever, that it might become the "best very long poem that any American has written." *Paterson* didn't pan out that way, for Jarrell or for anyone else, but Williams did. Williams revealed America, New York on its horizon, "a pillar of smoke by day," says Jarrell, "a pillar of fire by night." Williams and Jarrell play with the remark of Henry James that America has no ruins; America is full of ruins, says Jarrell, the ruins of hopes.

M. B. Tolson, the great and practically unsung Negro poet—he too is dead—says somewhere in *Harlem Gallery* that the dilemma of the Negro between the white and the black bourgeoisie is: To be or not to be—a Negro. The Negro has a choice, is what Tolson argues, and he (and I) would rather the Negro become a Negro. But this dilemma does not exist for the paleface American: there is no choice of to be or not to be an American. Once an

American, once an American poet, one can only ask: I am
an American (or an American writer); is there anything I
can do about it? American poets, even as late as Jarrell's
generation, tried to do something about it by remaining
only as American as their passports demanded. A few of
us, following Williams, wore the stars and stripes in
secret, like The Man Without a Country. Jarrell and I
are two of these. The generation of our fathers wore the
flag with the cross of St. George or the flag of the stars
and bars, and some of them sported the ribbon of the
Legion of Honor and one or two the Red, White, and
Black. None of my generation sported the Iron Cross,
which one sees nowadays in dime stores in America for
little boys to play Nazi. But almost all of the generation
of Jarrell at one time or another played Red or Pink.

The value and the quality of poetry, unfortunately or
fortunately, have nothing to do with moral or political
contents. *The Divine Comedy* is banned in Pakistan or
used to be, for religious reasons; modern art and poetry
are or used to be banned in Red Russia, also for religious
reasons. Sad to say, many poets are political or moral
idiots, even among the great. In our own time we have
to fight the tendencies which threaten what is dear to our
own lives and ideologies. But in Jarrell's generation we
were almost to a man humane humanists, and, unlike our
predecessors, were democratic in politics, agnostic in religion, and baroque in literature. Among us only Robert
Lowell and myself could be described as extremists, and
our extremism had different derivations and opposite
goals.

Jarrell suffered deeply through the Stalinist-Franco-
ist-Mussolini-Hitler years, hoping against hope for a better-
ment in the human condition. His first book was called
Blood for a Stranger and was printed in 1942, a war book.
He retained only a few of these poems when thirteen years
later he published his selected poems, but the themes of
war and fascism—war as fascism—were always in his mind.
Jarrell has written more good poems about the wars and

about Jews and Germany, the good Germany perhaps, than anyone else. He has written also the most famous and the best war poem of anyone in the twentieth century, in five lines.

The volume called *Little Friend, Little Friend,* though it has some of his best-made single poems, is a thematic book, a war book in which the poet is personally absent. The title page carries the penetrating explanation of the poem, the pathos of modern war in the code language of flyers: ". . . Then I heard the bomber call me in: 'Little Friend, Little Friend, I got two engines on fire. Can you see me, Little Friend?' I said 'I'm crossing right over you. Let's go home.' "

The anguish of the soldier is shown less in his anonymity, his exile from the human race, than in his emotional, sentimental desperation. The chief symbols—though Jarrell did not write to manipulate symbols qua symbols—are the mother and the cat. It is no Baudelairean cat (woman the destroyer), no T. S. Eliot cat (a kindly figure from the bestiary); Jarrell's cat is the object of love, if not a love-object, a cat who listens. The mother is pure mother who "thinks heavily: My son is grown." That's all; he's grown, therefore he is a soldier. The pilot falling from his plane sees the smoking carrier and its guns as children's toys. For it is true that in the elemental iconography of war everything is stripped down to a child's arithmetic: mother, soldier, cat, gun. There is a salient difference between our war poetry such as Jarrell's and that first great war poetry written in our fathers' war by Wilfred Owen and Sassoon and Rosenberg and Blunden and so on. The British war poets who showed everyone how to write anti-war poetry were themselves all outstanding warriors and heroes. They cried out against war but were as conversant with blood as Lawrence of Arabia. None of my generation were war heroes, that I remember, nor even outstanding soldiers. It says in a note in one of Jarrell's books that he "washed out" as a combat pilot and became a celestial navigator, a much more suitable classification for a poet. In a sense we waited out the war in uniform. Jarrell's ball-turret gunner is also washed out—of the turret with a hose. Unlike the war poets of the First World War, who never recovered from the experience, our generation did. We inherited an historical perspective which was denied our fathers. We foresaw and witnessed the whole world turning into the State. The war was of secondary importance to us even while we were part of it. When we came home there was grass growing on all the highways of the forty-eight states, but not for long. Our army went from demobilization to college or to television school; our poets became the university poets. But the tragedy of our generation—and I believe it is the tragedy—was that our army never melted away. It remained, it grew bigger, it was more and more all over the world. It became the way of life, the state; if not the garrison state itself, then something resembling it mightily. The war never came to a stop; only the protocols of armistice were suspended. Our poetry from the Forties on records the helplessness we felt in the face of the impersonal organism of the age—the Impersonal itself which is always death to poetry.

There is a literary commonplace that American literature is essentially a child literature. That *Moby Dick* is a boy's book—I was given a copy when I was seven—that every American hero is Huckleberry Finn in disguise, that poets are really little girls in mufti, that the artist has to prove his masculinity, and so on. A culture without mythos is forced into ideology. Whitman is an ideologue; his negation of mythology is 100 per cent American. Our poets when they deal in the myths do as Jarrell did, following Rilke and other modern artists, analyze and psychologize Orestes or Orpheus. We understand without belief. This is the opposite of using comparative mythology in order to revive and enforce belief, as Eliot did. Our poetry studies behavior and leads us back to the child. With Jarrell too the child becomes the critic and the center of value. Our mythology is the First Impression, the earliest consciousness; all the big people are giants out of Grimm, and most of them are bad. When a little girl is moving to a new house she thinks:

> *The broody hen*
> *Squawks upside down—her eggs are boiled;*
> *The cat is dragged from the limb.*

She thinks:

> *We are going to live in a new pumpkin*
> *Under a gold star.*

Theodore Roethke was a modern kind of nature poet, a biology poet with the eyes of a microscope. Jarrell was the poet of the *kinder* and the earliest games of the mind and heart. All those wounded soldiers and shot-down men turn back into children, for a wounded man is again a child. In the poem called "The State" the child says:

> *When they killed my mother it made me nervous;*
> *I thought to myself, It was right:*
> *Of course she was crazy, and how she ate!*
> *And she died, after all, in her way, for the State.*
> *But I minded: how queer it was to stare*
> *At one of them not sitting there.*

In his earliest collected work, one of those five-sided anthologies which New Directions invented to launch young poets, Jarrell worried the bone of Romanticism, trying to find a rationale for his departure from what he called Modernism. The crux of the problem of our generation was the Modernism which Eliot and Pound and Joyce represented and which Jarrell said did not apply to him or to us. He pretended that Modernism was dead but knew how well it would flourish in the academies. He catalogues the faults of Modernist poetry as well as has been done: the emphasis on connotation, texture, extreme intensity, forced emotion, violence, obscurity, emphasis on sensation, perceptual nuances, emphasis on the part rather than on the whole, and much more. He even enumerates the Modernist poet's attitudes: anti-scientific (Jarrell was one of the few poets of our age who was not anti-scientific and who understood that Science was not necessarily the intruder in the house); anti-commonsense, and anti-public. He ends this essay, which is very early and very fine, with a touch of the style to come. He has his hypothetical reader ask him a question: ". . . the reader may have thought curiously, 'Does he really suppose he writes the sort of poetry that replaces modernism?' " And he replies with an ambiguous, a diplomatic yes.

It was, say, Eliot, who is yet the most convenient target of attack for new poets, because Eliot erected targets wherever his mind led him; it was Eliot who invented Modernism and had it patented. And it was Auden who first shot at the target and missed. Jarrell took care of Modernism in practice better than in theory, as later he took care of Auden. It became necessary for everyone my age to attack Auden, as sculptors must attack Mount Rushmore. Nevertheless, Auden and Mount Rushmore still stand and probably always will. Jarrell, I think, failed to help establish our generation as a separate force and simply, not so simply, went his way to write some of the most quietly agonizing poetry of our time. His overestimation of Lowell represented a kind of fear that, generationally speaking, we did not exist. He half-feared being ingested by the Lowells. But I am a child, said Jarrell, I am the bat-poet; let me go and I will send you many much juicier poets. I will send you my mother and father and a fat girl in the library and even my cat. When John Ciardi put together an anthology of our generation with self-introductions, Lowell was too busy to write his (as I was too) and Jarrell reprinted his encomium about Lowell for Lowell's introduction. The roster of the generation in that version of it reads: Richard Wilbur, Peter Viereck, Muriel Rukeyser, Theodore Roethke, Karl Shapiro, Winfield Townley Scott, John Frederick Nims, E. L. Mayo, Robert Lowell, Randall Jarrell, John Holmes, Richard Eberhart, John Ciardi, Elizabeth Bishop, and Delmore Schwartz. It is an impressive list, in my view, a loose confederation of states which had no president.

I must say something about Schwartz. Dwight Macdonald wrote a memorial about him in the September 8th

issue of the *New York Review of Books*. In it he said all
the things an editor of the *Partisan Review* should say,
all the hi-cult clichés which the *Partisan Review* takes as
gospel. It is strange, to say the least, that this great publication, one of the great intellectual quarterlies of our century, should always have been so obtuse about poetry, as if
(which I believe was the trouble) they didn't understand
it. They took a Stalinist view of poetry, which is that
poetry should go back where it came from, and then modi-
fied that view with Trotsky's rather nineteenth-century
bohemian view of poetry, which reminds one touchingly
of perhaps Verlaine. They could swallow the *Four Quartets* hook, line, and sinker and turn on the Beat poets like
the OGPU. Macdonald, politically brilliant, a jaded liber-
tarian with the old Marxist leadership principle in his
heart, Macdonald says that Schwartz was killed by America, a statement that wouldn't stand up five minutes in a
provincial psychiatrist's office, any more than that same
college cheer that went: America killed Dylan. Macdonald
says: "Poetry is a dangerous occupation in this country,
as the biographers of too many of our best twentieth-century poets show, from Ezra Pound on, including the recent
deaths of Randall Jarrell and Theodore Roethke. This is
not a new thing . . ." And then Macdonald launches into
Baudelaire on Poe. ("For Poe the United States was
nothing more than a vast prison . . ." and so forth.) This
dismal, sociologically oriented view of poetry (now being
taught in junior high but no further) was shared neither
by Schwartz nor Jarrell nor myself nor by any of the poets
I know of. Whether poetry is a more dangerous occupation in America than tree surgery or insurance salesman-
ship is hard to say. Macdonald points to Delmore
Schwartz's tremendous urge toward self-destruction but
contents himself with the easy out that America got
Delmore. It is one of those facile aesthetic lies which lead
to the formation of poetry committees.

There is this about Schwartz as about Jarrell: both refused that lie, and both were tormented by the strategy
of escaping from the elite committees which survive by

virtue of the lie. Macdonald, discussing his friendship for
Schwartz, cites the Jewish-Gentile difference between them,
as if this were an area of misunderstanding for an editor
of the *Partisan Review* or even *McCall's*. Jarrell, unlike
Schwartz, did not become a part of *PR*, although he
edited poetry and did the poetry reviews for the *Nation*,
a magazine which is intellectually unidentifiable. The
Nation in our time was more congenial to poetry than the
great quarterlies, which always subordinated the poem to
the ideology of the magazine. Jarrell wrote some of his
best critiques for the *Nation*, in that kindly intellectual
morass where one was allowed to Become rather than Be.
In the quarterlies one must have already arrived.

So, after all, Jarrell was hung up, as we all were, by
the sense of common sense, Thomas Paine's or Henry
Ford's or the Scientist's. And after all, Macdonald has
a truth in his craw, that poetry (he meant, I think, *being*
a poet) is dangerous. *In danger* would be a better
phrase, as children are in danger. It comes to the sadness
about us that poets are not loved or are loved in the wrong
way for the right reasons or—whatever that saying is.
It comes to the fact that America the Mother wants to
love her children but is much more successful at killing
them off, or just making them successful. Jarrell had a
brilliant, sure, and subtle mind, and would have been the
greatest poet since whoever the last great poet was, had
he not lacked the sense of power. He lacked it, to his
disaster. It is what you might call a psychological factor,
the psychological factor. He came of a generation that
could not hate Mother America but which was afraid
of her and for her. There is no one of our generation who
betrayed her or who tried to topple the Victorian Statue
of Liberty into the drink. Jarrell was the least anti-American of all of us, and the most. He recoiled from the bore-
dom and the horror and the glory of the day-to-day life.
But what he did in his poetry, which had never really been
done before, was to face the modern scene and to—what
more is there to say—to face it. He faced the music of
the American Way of Life. But the subject wasn't any-

thing that Dwight Macdonald would know about, because
the elites never stoop to the observation of the actual. It
wasn't anything that the power-mad poets would ever see,
because they are so busy climbing Mount Everest that
they don't know what millennium they are in. Jarrell tried
to do the impossible: to observe and make poetry of a
chaos, without being either inside or outside of it. He did
it better than anyone else, better than it can be done. He
did it passionately and with superb control. He did it with
lies and subterfuge and great prose. He did it by hiding
and spying, reporting and keening. I would imagine that he
wept himself to death, out of frustration for the Kafka-like
manias of our time, including those of the intelligentsia;
out of the ambition which he denied himself because he
was more intelligent than any of us; out of the love of the
natural which denies the political. He died, you might say,
because his heart was in the right place and his heart was
even stronger than his intellect. Jarrell was split between
his heart and mind. He was modern, which means hating
being modern. He was born after Humpty-Dumpty fell
off the wall, and he knew that T. S. Eliot Scotch tape
couldn't put anything back together again.

To Revive
Anarchism

Before a presidential election, a gentleman from the Fund
for the Republic asked me for an interview. He was gather-
ing opinions about the coming presidential contest and
wanted the reaction of a poet or two. My first thought was
to beg off. My second was to tell a white lie and give him
the name of one of the two candidates. My third thought
was to tell him the truth. So we made a date for the
interview.

It is not easy to express your honest views to a
stranger, especially if your political ideas happen to be of
an unknown or unpopular variety. I wanted very much
not to be set down in my visitor's mind as a crackpot or
a "fool poet." He had been a Washington correspondent
and was a man of quick perception, charm, and great
knowledge of politics (compared with mine, certainly).
I mumbled and bumbled a good bit before I got out what
I wanted to say. What I told him finally was that I had no
choice of candidates, that I do not vote (except on local
matters), that I am opposed to voting under the "two"-
party system, and that I even attempt to spread a no-
voting propaganda among my friends and students. After
which I tried to make some joke, such as "Pass the
hemlock."

I had a distinct impression that my position, or lack
of it, was quite familiar to my visitor. The word *anarchism*
did not come up in the conversation, but we managed

to discuss it without naming it. There were quotes from
me out of Thoreau and mentions of the *Catholic Worker*,
which I have read for many years. It was a fairly tame,
academic talk, and we parted satisfied and friendly.

As a teacher and writer, I have become increasingly
aware in recent years of the spread of anarchist thought
among the rising generation. They do not call it by that
name or any names; they do not philosophize about the
State of Nonviolence or Disaffiliation, but the interest
is unmistakably there. The Beat movement symbolizes
one extreme of youthful anger against the failure of modern
society and government to keep peace among men. The
Negro equality movement symbolizes a more dramatic
failure of society and government to give the citizen his
due. Throughout the world, the human right of insub-
ordination against industrial society, colonialism, and
militarism and against the entire cult of the Western Tradition (religious, sexual, aesthetic) is making itself felt
in a thousand ways. The governments are losing their
young. The lifeblood of history is flowing away from the
centers of force. Patriotism is having its long-awaited
nervous breakdown.

And not only the young. The generation of the total
war is also abandoning the conventional political thinking
of the past, Left, Right, and Liberal, and is returning to
the example of individual moral force, as the world has so
far known it through Thoreau, Whitman, Tolstoy, Kropotkin, and Gandhi.

At present we are going through the stage of withdrawal
from the old political psychologies of organized governments. And we are witnessing the beginnings of successful
passive resistance movements in America and abroad. But
no appeal has yet been made to the vast American middle
class, the majority class, to detach itself from our competitive industrial insanity. It is indeed our industrial way
of life that lends sanction to militarism and colonialism,
Preparedness and suppression of human rights. Our enemy,
strange as it may sound to American ears, is the Standard
of Living. We worship at the altar of the White Rhinoc-

eros, the American kitchen. Standard of Living is the holy of holies in whose name every other evil is committed. To lower this standard or to equalize it among the peoples of the world is our greatest need. And the first step is to disassociate ourselves from the industrial-scientific madness which rules our lives twenty-four hours a day.

The best government, the anarchists tell us, is the least governing. The worst government is the highly organized and centralized state, such as Franco's Spain or the USSR. The present tendency of the United States toward greater organization and centralization is a peril to every democratic freedom we know. We are drifting toward a totally organized state which is eventually cemented by a secret police, a standing army, an industrial-scientific aristocracy, and a propaganda and communications machine which lies at the very heart of government. The present competitive mania between Russia and the United States in "science" opens the way in our country for every breed of political opportunism. Whether the Eisenhower "diplomatic" Cold War changes into Kennedy's "cultural" Cold War will make little difference to the basic sense of hostility to which the central government is committed. The American people have lost the choice of a peaceful alternative. The switchboard will tell us what to do.

My central point of reference is Gandhi, perhaps the most extraordinary man our age has produced. We are today experiencing the effects of Oriental ideas on our lives to an unprecedented degree. In Gandhi, for instance, we are presented with a new political psychology which is quite foreign to our practical Western minds, as when he says: "It is against my nature to prearrange." Or more striking, when he says of the law of nonviolent resistance "that it is possible for a single individual to defy the whole might of an unjust empire to save his honor, his religion, his soul, and lay the foundation for that empire's fall or regeneration. . . ." Gandhi's belief in the power of right action (Truth) to prevent violence was demonstrated in his lifetime a thousand times over; this is a form of political behavior which is only now beginning to make its way in the West.

Gandhi, of course, was not a provincial Hindu but one who drew on the entire tradition of the literature of peaceful action, mystical and secular. One of his earliest works was a translation of Plato's *Apology* into Gujarati, a bitter irony when we remember Gandhi's own death. He also translated John Ruskin's *Unto This Last*, essays in what Ruskin called First Principles of Political Economy, and of course he was deeply influenced by Thoreau and Tolstoy. The expression "the moral equivalent of war" he took from William James. But the fundamentals of non-violence, noncooperation, and nonresistance are native to the Hindu world. *Dharma*, for instance, is the concept of moral pressure applied to an offending party through sufferings to yourself. To sit *dharma* is to sit mourning. Gandhi's application of *dharma* against British military and legal force constituted a one-man revolution against authority and resulted in the greatest awakening of a nation in modern history. His results range from the abolition of the worst superstitions of his religion, such as untouchability, to the equalization of the rights of Hindus and other dark peoples of South Africa and to national independence itself, a fantastic series of accomplishments almost incomprehensible to the Western mind. The West has so far produced no peaceful revolutionaries of the stature of Gandhi, even including Tolstoy, Godwin, or Kropotkin. The gropings of William James toward such a solution as Gandhi's illustrate the dilemma of the American mind with its predominant images of military force.

James published his pamphlet *The Moral Equivalent of War* in 1910. The work makes rather horrifying apologies to the military and to scientific progress; yet the general drift is impressive. "Pacifists ought to enter more deeply into the aesthetical and ethical point of view of their opponents," says James. "So long as anti-militarists propose no substitute for war's disciplinary function, no *moral equivalent* of war . . . they fail to realize the full inwardness of the situation. The duties, penalties, and sanctions

pictured in the utopias they paint are all too weak and
tame to touch the military-minded." James assumes that
Western pacifism has no language of communication with
our society at large, which is aggressive and ultimately
militaristic. In rather quaint psychology he seeks for some
motive for human action which is as "thrilling" (to use
his word) as bloodshed. Puritanically, he objects to a mere
peace economy on the ground that it may become no more
than a "pleasure-economy." "Martial discipline" in peace
is therefore a necessity. He would have young men "make
war" upon nature—the typical Western fallacy that we
know so well from our scientists; he would send youth
to the "coal and iron mines, to freight trains, to fishing
fleets in December, to dish-washing, clothes-washing, and
window-washing," and so forth. Here we see the cautious
New Englander of the upper crust to whom dish-washing
is almost as much of an epic experience as the charge of
the Light Brigade. But at bottom he is right. "The martial
type of character can be bred without war," says James.
And he ends his essay with the pathetic statement that
Fear is indeed great but Fear is not "the only stimulus
known for awakening the higher ranges of man's spiritual
energy."

James probably supplied no more for Gandhi than the
wonderful catchphrase "the moral equivalent of war." It
was in an obscure work of Ruskin's that Gandhi found the
outline of a practical philosophy. He reduced Ruskin's
message in *Unto This Last* to three principles:

(1) *that the good of the individual is contained in the good
of all;*
(2) *that a lawyer's work has the same value as the barber's
inasmuch as all have the same right of earning their livelihood
from their work; and*
(3) *that a life of labor, i.e., the life of the tiller of the soil
and the handicraftsman, is the life worth living.*

Gandhi says: "The first of these I knew. The second I
had dimly realized. The third had never occurred to me.
Unto This Last made it as clear as day to me that the

second and the third were contained in the first. I arose
with the dawn, ready to reduce these principles to
practice."

The usual objection to Gandhi's ideas is that they are
"Oriental" and do not apply to life in the West, that the
conditions under which Gandhi operated in the Transvaal
and in India cannot possibly apply to civilized Europe
and America. The West has a good deal of fear and loath-
ing for this black little Hindu fakir, as Winston Churchill
so elegantly called him. And the more aristocratic Hindus
themselves, for instance Tagore the Bengali poet, fought
Gandhi at many crucial points. Tagore opposed the
reintroduction of the spinning wheel, the key to a national
economy; he opposed the burning of foreign cloth, which
Gandhi advocated as a method of breaking European
economic slavery. Gandhi plunged to the heart of the
matter when he told Tagore, "I do not draw a . . . distinction between economics and ethics. Economics that hurt
the moral well-being of an individual or a nation are immoral. . . ." Tagore eventually understood and surrendered
the knighthood which the Crown had bestowed upon him.

There is a great deal of extremism in Gandhi's philosophy
which the West will probably never be able to swallow.
His asceticism, his puritanism, his almost violent hatred
for the gains of science, extending even to the science of
medicine, are things we cannot appreciate. "A multiplicity
of hospitals is no test of civilization; it is rather a symptom
of decay," said Gandhi, sounding much like a modern
poet. Gandhi's covering his belly with a band of raw
earth as a cure for dysentery or constipation seems wholly
irrational to us. And yet we cannot dismiss his principle
of the nexus between science, government, and morality.
In the West we are only beginning to examine the irresponsibility of Science, the loading of young minds with
scientific and technological nonsense, the consequences of
which we learn only when it is too late.

In rearing an unarmed army to disengage India from
European rule, Gandhi developed a program of discipline
in which the participant took these vows: Truthfulness

(which is difficult to explain in Western psychology, though it closely resembles our Know Thyself); Nonviolence (which is a synonym for Soul-Force); Celibacy; Control of the Palate; Non-Thieving; Nonpossession; Fearlessness; and *Swadeshi* (encouragement of Home Industry). Most of these vows fall within the scope of our own traditional religions in one form or another. The one that is foreign to us and that may be of the utmost importance in the West is *Swadeshi*, the encouragement of home industries. *Swadeshi*, in fact, may be the nexus between Gandhism and the West.

The East is especially distinguished from the West in its attitude toward the natural world. The Easterner tends to regard himself as part of nature and of the cosmos. (In our view this is considered Fatalism.) The Westerner tends to regard himself as the enemy of nature. We speak of the *conquest* of space or of new lands; we *subdue* the desert and the frontier; we *wipe out* disease. The Oriental, broadly speaking, does not feel combative with the outer world; rather, he regards himself as part of a flux of life in which he is a single element. The Hebrew-Christian Bible begins with the injunction that man shall have *dominion* over every living thing, an idea quite exotic to the Oriental or to the poet like Walt Whitman who says he thinks he could turn and live with animals.

Swadeshi, home industry, does not have to do with government but with self-sustaining. When Gandhi hit upon the idea of the spinning wheel he had his major revelation. It is staggering to think that there was no one in India who knew how to spin (European civilization had destroyed the wheel) and that Gandhi had to search the country from top to bottom to find some old lady who still knew how. In the same way, an English woman had to search the country from end to end to discover the Indian temple dances and revive them. For it is true that mechanization destroys not only the national economy but the arts of nations. Gandhi favored a break with machine industry, followed by a slow and considered assimilation of the machine.

Here is a great lesson for the West. To slow down machine progress, to impede science. To prevent industrialization from becoming the sole way of life. Thoreau says: "Shall we forever resign the pleasure of construction to the carpenter?" He also says: "We are in great haste to construct a magnetic telegraph from Maine to Texas; but Maine and Texas, it may be, have nothing important to communicate." As far as we can tell, Maine and Texas still have nothing important to communicate. In any event, communication in this country is private property, as in Russia it is purely state property. Communication is too valuable to industrial-scientific government to be passed around indiscriminately. It is always the policeman, the industrialist, or the diplomat who controls the wires from Maine to Texas.

True communication is a phenomenon having nothing to do with newspapers, P.A. systems, universal network control, and radar bouncing off the moon. The words of Gandhi were communicated largely by word of mouth throughout India and across the barriers of about twenty languages. Whereas in America it is virtually impossible to find out what is going on in Cuba or in the Congo or in any other place. What is called news in America and probably in Europe as well is what is left of the truth after Communications has masterminded the facts. The very term *artist* in the West has come to mean simply a man who tells the truth. Communications also has the function of controlling the moods of the people. Disaster is the bread and butter of the advertiser, newspaper man, broadcaster, and public relations expert. Little wonder that the Russian ruler visiting the United States had to have a standing army of bodyguards and Secret Service men to keep him from being assassinated. How much better off we would be if everyone boycotted the newspaper, television, advertising, radio, and all other self-styled media of communication.

Any gradual and immediate diminution of our involvement with the industrial system, on any level, would have a direct effect on the peace and well-being of our people.

To remove ourselves from the world of competition is of paramount importance to the individual and to the nation. Competition is the terrible vice of modern society. Competition is the disease of the West and is the source of our violence. Nonviolence means non-competition. Democracy is a nonviolent form of government which is in peril of destruction by the competition of social and economic violence. *Ahimsa,* nonviolence, is a total force and a way of life. It has the power of Christian humility, upon which it is partly based. It is one of the noblest ideas advanced by modern man, and it is destined to spread throughout the world. It cannot be employed by governments because governments are by definition committed to violence. Nonviolence is not a prerogative of governments but of men, even of one man. One nonviolent man, like Gandhi or Christ, can change history. Governments can only keep history on the march. *Ahimsa* can stop history.

Gandhi went so far as to encourage nonviolence to the venomous snakes of India, which take a terrible toll of life every year. You had to overcome this perfectly natural fear of the reptiles. "The rule of not killing venomous reptiles," says Gandhi, "has been practiced for the most part at Phoenix, Tolstoy Farm, and Sabarmati. At each of these places we had to settle on waste lands. We have had, however, no loss of life occasioned by snakebite . . ." And he adds: "Even if it be a superstition to believe that complete immunity from harm for twenty-five years is not a fortuitous accident but a grace of God, I should still hug that superstition."

Without going into this deep and muddy question, we can learn something from this attitude of non-killing. To destroy the enemy was not an aim of Gandhi's; he must be deposed with dignity, without harm, even with honor. This is another concept foreign to Western thought and almost foreign to Christian practice. Non-humiliation of the enemy means to return him to his humanity after a defeat. Vinoba Bhave, the greatest living disciple of Gandhi, who travels throughout India asking for land for the peasantry from the great landlords and receiving it, says: "I desire to humiliate neither the rich nor the poor . . ." This is the opposite of communist expropriation or of capitalist competition. Without a complete bond of love between the giver and the recipient, there can be no permanent guarantee of peace between the possessor and the dispossessed.

The specific issues for which Gandhi fought are generally accomplished in India, but the deeper meaning of his philosophy and his *Politik* may provide an alternative to the ever-mounting states of crisis which are inherent in statesmanship or what passes under that name. Modern competitive society is incapable of keeping the peace. Modern government, committed to a society of competition, is incapable of keeping the peace. Peace can come about only through the nonviolent action of the people themselves. The present tendency of governments to dissolve their empires provides no guarantee of peace. On the contrary, the formation of new countries modeled upon American or Russian economic systems can do nothing but increase the danger of war. As modern government is contingent for its power upon science and industry, there would appear to be no hope of peace except by the voluntary effort of people to place themselves beyond the lure of science and industry. Standard of Living equals Preparedness. Preparedness is always related to scientific warfare. People must, especially in the scientifically advanced countries, act individually to weaken the power of the industrial-scientific oligarchy over their lives. We must "lower" the Standard of Living. We must learn how to sustain ourselves in peace and happiness beyond the influence of the Switchboard. We must do these things without violence and with the high sense of chivalry which Gandhi inculcated in his followers. Instead of class war and hatred as preached by the communists or industrial-scientific competition as preached by us, to survive we must behave nonviolently and in the spirit of love.

A *Malebolge* of Fourteen Hundred Books

From Aristotle to Dante

I spend most of my time under the shadow of a wall of
books, maybe 1,400 volumes, thick and thin. They are arranged for the most part in alphabetical order. Otherwise
I' could never find the one I need for a lecture or a class.
It is not a "library" (odious word when it has domestic
connotations), and if it were it would not be a good library. It is my tool shop, and I rarely ever touch one of
the books unless for work. Yet there are some I have carried round the world with me, some I carried in barracks
bags through a war, some I wrote, and some inscribed by
famous men. On the bottom are books of information; on
the top, books to keep out of the reach of thieves and
admirers. Nearly all 1,400 books are *poetry books* or books
having something to do with poetry. The ones that are
not are books which I have a special fondness or need for
and which I do not want to get lost among the other
bookshelves of the house. I have come to dislike the sight
of books intensely but keep thousands of them out of
habit, inertia, and a horror of empty bookcases. Books also
serve the useful purpose of intimidating your neighbors
and deadening sound. They also save on paint.

As a writer gets older and his skills increase, his horizon narrows. He gets better and better at his craft and is on the verge of becoming a master, if he has not become one already. But unless his range of vision was great to begin with, he may end up with nothing but a handful of shining fragments or only the tools themselves.

I keep a distance between the 1,400 books and myself. They are the tools of my occupation, but they are also the works that have formed and controlled my life. I think they deserve to be talked about not because I have fine or profound things to say about them but because I am what they are. It is the rare privilege of certain people, children, psychotics, lovers, and poets, to talk about themselves without restraint.

It is certainly not fashionable to say so, but I am convinced that one of the highest forms of criticism is criticism in the first person singular. Literary criticism has become an art, one that has pushed poetry aside. But it is precisely because criticism has become so great and proud that it has lost contact with reality. There is no reality of criticism, I say, except the reality of the critic, the *homo criticus*, a man of flesh and blood. When I read criticism I want to meet the author. Come out from behind that filing cabinet, *sir*, I say. The criticism of *This is good* means that this is good for you whether you like it or not. The criticism of *I like it* means that though this may or may not be good, it is good because I like it. The criticism of *This is good* is medicine. The criticism of *I like it* is booze. With psychologists this is called objective versus subjective.

A writer's sensibility and ultimately his life are forged upon this dichotomy, what is without and what is within, the models he is given and his reaction to them. These models may or may not speak to him. Some he will adore; some he will want to smash; some he will be indifferent to. The fault of literary speculation in general is that it wishes to formulate values once and for all; literary speculation fails to take into account the self-betrayals, conversions, reconsiderations, compromises, crises, shady deals,

revelations, and so on, in the sense of values of the particular artist.

I do *not* like the poets I did five or ten years ago. What
is worse, I don't believe in them. Does this distort my
sense of values or of literary propriety or of truth? Not in
the least. It is supposed to be an earthshaking event when
a writer like T. S. Eliot changes his evaluation of such a
poet as John Milton. I must be a far better critic than Mr.
Eliot: I change my opinion of Milton every time I think
of him. The criticism of *This is good* is remorseless and
does not wish to take change into account. The criticism
of *I like it* is based on the reality of change. One deals in
absolutes; the other, in experience.

What better form of criticism can there be than a description of your books, those basilisks that sit year after
year over your head and tell you what you are. I thought
of calling these essays "Fourteen Hundred Books, a Personal *Malebolge*," for after all, those books make a fine
torture chamber for any Inferno.

Now, a formal arrangement of books by alphabet is at
least as rational as the Dewey Decimal System, Roget's
Thesaurus, *Life* magazine, or the *Encyclopaedia Britan-
nica*. Any order is a possible order. Nothing is more arbitrary than a chronological order of works of art, for instance. In school we are constantly beset by calendars,
pretending that cause and effect is a matter of Monday
following Sunday or 1492 following 1491. Artists, at any
rate, are people who disbelieve in calendars and categories.
It matters very little whether Byron and Gottfried Benn
are leaning together. After all, they both begin with B.
Why not a school of criticism based on initials?

My work books have been for so long mixed up with
my pleasure books that I can no longer tell the difference.
All the same the alphabet is forbidding, and in the long
run the aspect of the office has made even my most favorite works slightly untouchable. To really enjoy one of
the books I have to take it out of my study. I have never
been able to *read* in a library. With a book you must be
monogamous, so to speak, for the time being.

We are all of us alphabetized. By some method not unlike fortune-telling or the *I Ching* or the various Uncer-
tainty Theories—astrology, numerology, poetry itself—we
find our modern world arranging itself by irrelevancies.
The artist, unlike people of the Serious World, does not
reject the irrelevant. Rather, he courts it. For whatever it
is worth, when I am done you will have a composite picture of my tastes, opinions, and "sensibilities." And if the
finished job is worthless you will at least have had an
example of a twentieth-century poet who believes in the
relevancy of the accidental. That sounds more pompous
than it is.

A / Aristotle, (Plato), Aiken, Aristophanes, Arnold,
     Auden, Albee, the Apocrypha

Glancing at the introduction to Aristotle's *Poetics*, I
notice first a discussion of Willy Loman, even though this
is the famous Butcher edition with the Greek on the left-
hand page. That's a good example of irrelevance, more or
less. Aristotle, Butcher, John Gassner, and I. The Greek
philosopher was the furthest thing from a poet, the opposite of a poet, but there is no poet who can get by him
without giving a high sign. You keep the *Poetics* around
just in case. In case of what? In case of students, in my
situation.
    Only one thing sticks with me from the *Poetics*, because
my interest in poetic psychology has grown as my interest
in poetics has decreased. Aristotle in a *non sequitur* says
that poetry implies either a happy gift of nature or a
strain of madness. Playing on the Greek words as I make
them out, he says that a poet is either euphoric or manic.
It amazes me that *euphoric* and *manic* are up-to-date,
twentieth-century jargon and that these two views of the
poet were as obvious to the Greeks as to us. But the
philosopher didn't pursue the point, nor have we. Modern
poetic psychology tends to take only the one view, that
the poet is manic. We look upon euphoric poets with

suspicion, unless they redeem themselves by drowning in salt water or wine. Modern poetry has long since committed itself to the manic or mantic view: either mad, divinely or Satanically mad, or divinatory. The romantic view is in disgrace. Euphoria is out.

I have no Plato on my shelves. As far as poets are concerned he is eternally in the Other Room. Plato is our first poetic censor, and all poets as we know them oppose the censor. So much for Aristotle and Plato just now.

I find I am rather short on A: after Aristotle I find only Aiken, Aristophanes, Arnold, and Auden. Conrad Aiken is a modern poet I have waited for and never really read, partly out of a fear that he will disappoint me. It is difficult to explain. Aristophanes, who is almost a "popular classic" today, has not been translated to my satisfaction. Not that I read Greek. I know that there is something there that hasn't come through. A recent translation of the *Lysistrata* by a poet-classics professor at the University of Colorado has the Spartans speaking in an American Southern accent, which he says comes close to "the Doric accent as it affected the Attic ear." The Spartans as great athletes and warriors are of course homosexuals; whether this is a criticism of the American South I cannot fathom.

In the English language in my lifetime W. H. Auden has done most to teach a language and to blueprint a form. As Eliot has struck deepest into the poetic consciousness, Auden has liberated a rhetoric for common use. Possibly, poets in their twenties and thirties cannot understand what happened. If not, they cannot understand why Eliot and Pound went to Europe to live. No matter. And yet I have always had a deep intuitional suspicion that neither Auden nor Eliot is a poet. They may be rhetoricians, writers who have brilliantly kept alive the poetic art of dialogue. As they are linguists, they are teachers. As they are teachers, they are not doers.

Most poetry is a dance of language. And only that. I call this poetry *manqué*. Poetry which refers back to language as the central experience I call inferior poetry. True

poetry in my view is before or after language and uses
language reluctantly. I distinguish between the poetry of
language and the poetry of situation. Almost all modern
poetry is "linguistic poetry." It tries to create new forms
of communication. This is why it detests ordinary forms
of communication. It aspires to universal forms and techniques of intellectual intercourse. It is most expert in
what the schools call Language and Literature. The poetry
of Situation, on the other hand, is a-linguistic and a-
literary. Please understand that I am not trying to patent
a new machine of criticism but merely pressing a couple
of buttons which I have ended up in front of.

The way I grew up with poetry—like Topsy—I had no
tongue until Auden came along. I am not being witty or
cute when I say that I did not understand *Life* magazine
until I read Auden. For, on the one hand, there were
Matthew Arnold and Aristotle and Aristophanes; and on
the other, myself, the street, the radio, the wars, the ad-
vertisements, the great, terrifying sciences, the merchan-
dise of our world. Auden brought all this to a focus in
poem after poem. When I first read him in the black and
exciting days of the Depression, he filled the age with
light, with terrific theatricality and authority. What an
impresario! I remember being puzzled in the Thirties and
disturbed that the King of England presented this communist or Marxist with a King's medal of some kind.
Looking at it that far back, I see this as actual recognition
of merit rather than a political trick, as I thought at the
time. It was as if the King had said: Thank you; we need
you, as monarchies do when they are in trouble. Rather
haughtily, Auden accepted such honors and proceeded
to become an American.

This poet, so perfectly attuned to the English language
and to what the language had said, was singing its elegy.
Auden is the dying swan of the greatest poetry of Europe.
At any rate, that is my picture of him. All the same, he
is a poet of language, one to whom situation is secondary.
He is preeminently adaptable to situations because in his

poetry he is above them. He is the artist as observer, the curator with twenty-twenty vision, the perfect perfectionist. He has brought all the dialects of modern English into line; he has engineered them and taught their uses and generously handed them over to the public domain. After which he has retired into his laboratory.

I find that two paperbacks have slipped over into the *B's*. Next to an *en face* edition of *Beowulf* are the Apocrypha and Albee's *The American Dream*. The Apocrypha I sometimes swipe from when I am writing a poem or teaching "Peter Quince at the Clavier." The Albee is there rather tentatively. American theater at its best has always seemed to me on the level of Clifford Odets. We keep our fingers crossed and hope for something.

B / The Bible, Baudelaire, Blake, *Beowulf*, Browning, Byron

There are twice as many *B*'s as *A*'s per inch. And as quantity is frequently an index to quality, there are some important items, such as the Bible, Baudelaire, Kenneth Burke, Jacques Barzun, Browning, Byron, Jacob Boehme, Blake, Samuel Beckett, and Gottfried Benn. I notice that I have twice as many Blake commentaries as I have Blake texts. This is because I have never been interested in Blake's symbolic and prophetic poems but only in his lyrics and *The Marriage of Heaven and Hell*. I need the commentaries on his commentaries for reference. Hidden meanings irritate me; the poetry of hidden meanings has never been incorporated into my experience. This is a terrible limitation, no doubt. Specifically, what I reject are symbol systems and their techniques of suggestion; even allegory annoys me and with it the allegorical use of culture as we get it in all modern works, which are therefore referred to as Major Poems. The narrowness of my appreciation has formed me into a certain kind of poet and critic; a poet-critic of my generation refers to me as a neo-primitive. I find this designation correct and even flattering. In the Blake songs, whether the innocent or the experienced, I tend to ignore the symbols, taking for granted the obvious ones. If obvious enough I accept them. When the lamb is an actual lamb whose wool can be tugged, I am content. Or even if the lamb is called by the name of the lamb with a capital L, I can accept that. But myth, metaphysics, and mysticism I exclude, rejecting the willing suspension of disbelief for the literal.

Eventually my Blake is edited down to the lyrical rebel Blake. The mystic and homemade philosopher I leave to others. But philosophy, whether it is homespun or professional, seems to me to have no place in poetry or even in poetics. Whole continental glaciers of philosophical poetry have slid from my consciousness into the ocean and melted. As larger and larger areas of poetry have ceased to exist for me, I find my identity threatened by these losses. Simultaneously, philosophy and religion have reappeared and reinstated themselves as discrete and separate kinds of knowledge on my horizon. And ironically and perhaps inevitably I find myself embracing certain forms of existentialism: it is the excitement of the process of starting over that thrills me. Starting over, situating oneself in a Void, breaking out. Henry Miller puts it melodramatically: Break out or die. For years I have wanted to break out of poetry.

But to return to *Beowulf*—I have never read it. Or rather, I have tried from time to time but have only succeeded in adding it to that list of famous works which you never read and never will. Every writer has his own list. (*The Faerie Queene* usually stands at the top.) For centuries Classical Greek was the snob language of European culture. More recently Anglo-Saxon occupied a similar position. But democratic education, even in England, abolished these more or less secret and hieratic tongues. Personally, I propagandize for their revival. The word *pagan* (*paganus* in Latin) meant a yokel; in the

derivative languages it means heathen, and *heathen* itself
means from the heath, a countryman as against a dweller
in the city. Again, it means one who is not a monotheist.
Nature worshipers and polytheists are pagan. What I am
getting at is the double tradition of monotheistic poetry
and pagan poetry. Christianity has provisioned English
poetry from the beginning; even *Beowulf* is said to be
a Christian poem. Needless to say, my interests are in
the poetry of the heath, the vast underground tradition
which defies the urban poetry of God. Robert Graves
has written wildly and well about this "other" poetry.

Looking over my B's, I have decided to say nothing
about Blackmur (whom I do not understand) or Gottfried Benn (who was a "good" Nazi) or Beckett (whom
I like for snobbish reasons) or Kenneth Burke (whose
prose and, I think, common sense fascinate me). This
leaves us with the Bible, Jacques Barzun, Baudelaire,
Boehme (or Behmens, as Blake called him), Browning,
and Byron.

Browning would probably be as dead as Tennyson if it
weren't for Pound. To us, at least. My copies of Browning
are mostly those old, small, too well-printed volumes
which evidently people carried in their pockets on Channel
crossings. Every secondhand bookshop is laden with them.
Generally there is a photo of the poet or a facsimile of
his signature somewhere. I keep on my desk a small bronze
reproduction of two hands, Robert's clasping Elizabeth's,
taken from life (hers has a suggestion of a lace frill). It
is mounted on a small block of white marble and was
given to me by someone whom I do not remember in
San Francisco.

Browning is the pagan poet of the Victorians, or rather
the pseudo-pagan. He is "open my heart and you shall
see engraved inside it Italy" and simultaneously "O to be
in England." Hence the crabbed style so appealing to Ezra
Pound, whose heart is also engraved with Italy but who
cries: O to be in the United States, if the cultural conditions were right. Browning is in fact the ideal twentieth-

century poet, of the prototype of the modern, with his love of the quasi-pagan or baroque. The really baroque poet of his time was Father Hopkins, but Browning had the wealth of nostalgia for the Renaissance which made his contemporaries load up their parlors with junk. I think of him as a great corrupted poet; his sensibilities were richly clouded with the great deeds of books. You never think of him in terms of action; it is no accident that his life was sicklied over by generation after generation of ladies. Browning was a ladies' poet; he went out with fainting.

I seem to recall that Ezra Pound, who is, after all, a first-rate critic, said about Byron that his technique was rotten. It is quite true and also beside the point. You don't read Byron as much as you read about him. The important thing about Byron is not his poetry but the fact that he was Byron, the Satanic lord of the Romantics. This reminds me that Stendhal, whom I admire, wrote in indignation: "What could be more cruel than to pay court, even if only in appearance, to the wretched and abominable hypocrisy which can describe Lord Byron as the leader of the Satanic school of poetry . . . ?" Stendhal, however, tended to romanticize and carp at Byron out of jealousy and his feelings of superiority toward the English. And because of his own sentimental and adolescent theories of love he would fail to see the role Byron played in the European imagination. My knowledge of Byron, however, is extremely limited and is colored by the opinions of Mario Praz, who explains the relationship between Byron as private sadist and Byron as public hero. It is always better to see Byron at his worst. His dandyism, which Stendhal also takes a dim though shallow view of, relates Byron in my mind to all that went badly with the Romantics and with us.

I will skip the Bible, Jacob Boehme, and Jacques Barzun, after all, except to say that Barzun in his Tory phase is a great flop. My real bumbling under *B* concerns Baudelaire.

Though I am no critic or scholar I feel sometimes that I should devote all my energies to writing a book about Baudelaire. There is a point at which all books about a particular author come to an end; there really is such a thing as a definitive study of even the greatest authors. Jean Paul Sartre has written the penultimate study of Charles Baudelaire; but something else remains to be done, something which Sartre, because he is not a poet, would not understand. For Sartre assumes the validity of poetic form and does not examine it. He ignores the dandyism of style and is content to insult Baudelaire's virility and his inability to make the existential choice of freedom.

Baudelaire is modern poetry incarnate, pure pseudo-Satanism. You have to believe in Satan to be a real Satanist. The attraction of Baudelaire is that he is absolutely insincere, pure pose, or what in the jargon is called the dandy. The dandy is a clotheshorse, a skeleton upon which to drape the sensibilities. Baudelaire is a genius, or rather, he is the parody of genius. Stendhal hints at the dandyism of Byron, his beautiful eyes (apparently "luminous" like Poe's), and his perfect teeth (like the vampires of Poe). Stendhal underplays the Byronic Limp: it becomes only a foot turned slightly inward, almost a psychosomatic symptom of Byron's Napoleonic ego. Stendhal adored Byron, while maintaining his jealousy, because Stendhal adored Napoleon. Stendhal, like all political geniuses, judged men by their height. Either they were very tall like basketball players or English dukes, or very short like Corsicans and him.

In the long run you should be a fabulous historian to talk like this. You should be Freud and Gibbon at least. But there are insights better than both and not based on psychology and history. We can see Baudelaire almost in focus. What do we see?

Today we see that the author of *Les Fleurs du Mal* is the central point of reference of modern European poetry. This is not a metaphor but a fact. Baudelaire is the alpha and omega of modern poetry.

We cannot escape Baudelaire without escaping from poetry. He is perfect. For what he believes in least is poetry itself. Poetry is the supreme device of self-assertion. It is the elevation of frustration by the way of beauty. Keats, had he been possessed by the arrogance and asexuality of Baudelaire, might have been the Baudelaire of romantic England. But Keats had had his hands in blood and died of love. Baudelaire could not love; he is, as Sartre says with juristic cruelty, the poet of masturbation. Keats was really aswoon. His love for Fanny was in fact a stake in his heart. Baudelaire could only love his mother and beg her for money to buy more beautiful Effects and black girls and Jewesses, and time to fantasize about Tahiti. He succeeded brilliantly and failed even more brilliantly. He put a curse on poetry that no one so far has been able to exorcise.

Baudelaire is glorious in his banality. He gave us banality as our main theme. He is an absolute devil, which is to say an adolescent.

Eliot places Baudelaire above Huysmans, say, as an artist who saw beyond the mere trappings of Satanism, the Black Mass, and so forth into the problem of good and evil itself. Yet the poems directly addressing good and evil are usually the weakest, the Litanies, for instance. Where Baudelaire really goes into overdrive is not in the poetry of Satan or even of theological ennui and spleen but in his furniture shop. The hair fetish, the jewels, the gamy Negresses and Jewesses, the Russian girl with holes in her dress excited his vacuity. Incapable of surviving at the center of experience, he prepared for experience endlessly. He was an impotent, as was his counterpart Delacroix, who could slaughter thousands of concubines with his brush but whose virility was shamed before one of his models. I detect the same impotence in Berlioz, the Baudelaire of romantic music. The perfect artist of this ilk is, of course, Richard Wagner, whom Mallarmé called a god, as Hitler did. Without trying to match my critical wits with those of T. S. Eliot's, I would argue that the defense of Baudelaire as a poet of good and evil is indefensible; he was no more than a poet of effects, postmortem effects, as Lawrence would say. But with Baudelaire the effects are secondhand and rather shabby at that. Good Will effects. Poe was a true ghoul. Baudelaire was merely ghoulish.

Baudelaire lies at the center of our poetic emptiness. What poet of the twentieth century is not in his debt? He has described a certain psychological void which we all inhabit. Would not Delacroix have enjoyed painting Belsen or Hiroshima? Baudelaire with a Guggenheim would head straight for Hollywood. Berlioz (whom I confess I also love) is the inventor of the sound track and Muzak.

In a non-cultural context, these three are heroes of mine. But in the end they are all geniuses of melancholy; on a shallower level, of an almost justifiable self-pity. Eliot hits the nail on the head when he speaks of Baudelaire's alienation as a contempt for the progressive degradation of Progress—a view which I do not share but which I can understand. But to credit Baudelaire with an insight into the human condition seems to me to be paying him a compliment he does not deserve. I prefer and believe in the attitude of Camus, who says about him:

The dandy creates his own unity by aesthetic means. But it is an aesthetic of singularity and of negation. "To live and die before a mirror": that, according to Baudelaire, was the dandy's slogan. . . . It is a coherent slogan, at any rate. The dandy is, by occupation, always in opposition. He can only exist by defiance. Up till now, man derived his coherence from his Creator. But from the moment that he consecrates his rupture with Him, he finds himself delivered over to the fleeting moment, to the passing days and to wasted sensibility. Therefore he must take himself in hand. The dandy rallies his forces and creates a unity for himself by the very violence of his refusal. Disoriented, like all people without a rule of life, he is coherent as a character. But a character implies a public; the

dandy can only play a part by setting himself up in opposition.
He can only be sure of his own existence by finding it in the
expression of others' faces. Other people are his mirror. A mir-
ror that quickly becomes obscured . . . since human capability
for attention is limited. It must be ceaselessly stimulated,
spurred on by provocation. The dandy is, therefore, always
compelled to astonish. . . . Perpetually incomplete, always on
the margin of things, he compels others to create him, while
denying their values. [*My roman*] . . . *For the dandy, to be*
alone is not to exist. . . .

Camus admits that dandyism expresses a nostalgia for
ethics: it is only honor degraded as a point of honor, and
it inaugurates an aesthetic of solitary creators. Art is the
dandy's ethic. With him begins the age of the directors
of conscience. "When the dandies fail to commit suicide
or do not go mad, they make a career and pursue
prosperity."

I am not looking for a formula for the modern poet,
but I think Camus has unwittingly given us a good one.
Baudelaire is the model for what we think of and designate
as the modern poet. He is the zero who becomes a quantity
by demanding that others create him while he denies the
value of their existence. He denies his environment, first
of all. He denies or repudiates the idea of progress of any
kind. There are only two possible directions of his mind:
toward the past, personal or mythic; and toward the
Ideal. The Ideal may be religious, mystical, occult, simply
aesthetic, or some combination of these things.

The Ideal is invariably an escape from Progress and
Contentment. The attraction of Eliot and the attraction
of Eliot's attraction to Baudelaire reside in an almost
Oriental death wish to deny life because life denies them.
At the age of seventeen or so Eliot was already creating
himself, vis-à-vis Others, as the Old Man. Baudelaire (and
even Rimbaud) are most alive with hatred in the presence
of mother. Rimbaud had his one moment of love when
the kindly nuns were picking the lice out of his hair. Even
then, as he reported in a beautiful poem, he could not

cry, but he had an intense desire to. Woman-hating is characteristic of modern poetry, whether it is outright hatred of the female or the homosexual love-hate of the mother. It is not too farfetched to say that American poetry has become dominant in the modern world because America is athletically female. The modern prejudices against Romantic poetry are generally directed against youthful "heterosexual" love. This kind of love implies biology, progress; it is therefore "bourgeois." The modern poet is biologically recessive and wishes, sometimes articulately, to be the end of his line. Aesthetically, it is fairly common to find the modern writer constructing the "last" novel or the "last" poem. That too is an ideal—to escape the round of life, beatify yourself.

In Baudelaire there is an immense and resonant whimper. It echoes into our lives more than a century later. His superb and, as I think, brutal artistry provides almost the last *raison d'être* for poetry we have. The *fact* of Baudelaire makes modern poetry possible. But whether poetry should still be possible is another question.

The Flowers of Evil is the original and the final flower of modern poetry, one of those inventions, like the Gutenberg Bible, which can never be surpassed no matter how refined the techniques of printing or poetry become. And this too is as if Baudelaire had put an end to the progress of poetry.

And yet his work says nothing, unless it says that Beautiful Poetry is dead. It says that life is unendurable (the typical adolescent slogan which, if exaggerated, leads to suicide). And finally, in a failure of imagination, it falls back on the Sunday School doctrine of Original Sin, which explains everything and nothing. People end up arguing whether Baudelaire was a Christian and, if so, whether he was a good one or a bad one. This is something like debating whether Trotsky was a good Trotskyite or a bad one, for it appears to me that Baudelaire invented a religion of his own.

C / Cummings, Coleridge, Cavafy, Catullus, Chaucer,
  Carroll, (Dickens), Crane, (Thomas), Corso

This brings me, by the logic of the alphabet, to E. E.
Cummings. My personal feelings about his work are highly
positive. He is a domesticated Baudelaire refined by
generations of Bohemia and by Harvard. This is the worst
possible background for an artist. In Cummings there is
the beginning of happiness, but it is carefully guarded
lest the yeast spoil the beer. All good modern poetry is
French-cooked, as against English indigestion. France,
after all, is the antidote to England, in poetry as in
everything; American poetry began to grow up when it
ditched England and went to Paris. English poetry happens to be the greatest poetry of Europe; yet somehow
English poetry more or less comes to Britannia-ruling-
the-poetic-waves, and all the great navies of English poetry
come back to that precious stone set in the silver sea.

The American Academy of Arts and Sciences, which was
chartered in Boston in 1780, and which included the
Adamses, John Hancock, etc., wanted to give the new
country of America "the air of France rather than that
of England." That is a quotation. It is applicable to
Cummings.

To have ". . . the air of France"—what is that? It was
and is, we hope, to be more rational than other Europeans. To be clear. To be (if we are speaking of the
eighteenth century, which was their climax and ours) *free*.
To allow Rousseau and the Marquis de Sade, although
France didn't in actuality allow either. But we have them.
They weren't burned at the stake. The French have con-
tributed three great areas of vocabulary to the world:
the vocabularies of eating, loving, and revolting. They
have left the terminology of music to the Italians and the
terminology of philosophy to the Germans. But the languages of food and drink are French, as are the languages
of bed and the barricades.

A Bostonian like Cummings, with the multiplex back-

ground of a "high" American; with the pride of England,
which he was honor-bound to reject as an American; with
the pride of a Bostonian aristocrat or eccentric, which
he cherished; with the anger of the poet exposed to New
York; self-protected, hypersensitive, sentimental, furious,
controlled—he is the American, as most of us are, to
whom France is heaven itself. Or the place of asylum.

Cummings was essentially a happy man who developed
unhappinesses when he walked down the street. This
mirror dawdling down the lane cracked itself daily into a
million lovely postcards. Every poem he wrote is a concession to a housebroken Baudelaire. For Cummings just
didn't believe in Original Sin (consequently he is a "minor
poet"). Everyone, especially newspapers, expects the poet
to invent a new religion if he can't join up with an old
one. Cummings didn't.

There are two extremes of honeybee Cummings, sweet-
ness and anger. But the sweet is sometimes saccharine;
the anger, uncentered. Cummings' anger is momentary, a
getting-even with modern ugliness. The anger of a Rimbaud is magnificent and lethal—it is lethal still as an
example of the destructive—while the anger of Cummings
is polite outrage. It leaves us in want. Much of the poetry
of his generation of anger had to be written, and the best
men wrote it. All the same you feel that much of the
poetry of this negative sensibility is a mannerism, a carry-
over from a deeper and more virulent bohemianism. It is
satire and specifically anti-American middle class. Eliot
summed up this kind of anger and reproach in the line
"Chicago Semite Viennese." Kipling had described the
citizens of Chicago as savages. To the expatriates the
parvenu American abroad incorporated all the vices of the
Shylockian Jew or the pachydermatous Midwesterner plus,
I suppose, the brummagem of Viennese architecture and
pastry. The expatriate poet was embarrassed by his countrymen, to say the least. And back in New York after the
stock market crash had made literary expatriation impossible, the writer raged against the national image.

Luckily, the bulk of Cummings' poems are *objets d'art*, if you can use that expression in a complimentary sense, as I intend. They represent what is left of the poetry of pleasure, poetry for the joy of improvisation. Cummings has not yet been taken as seriously as he should be because he did in fact *play*. Whereas the poets who were carving out monumental niches for themselves *worked*. Cummings and even Wallace Stevens were regarded as slight, not serious enough. The poetry of the Serious World, which has dominated literature for half a century, is not quite sure whether to accept Cummings. Serious Criticism looks upon him as frivolous. Most of his books are called such things as *And* or *Is 5* or *One×One*, signifying that the whole is greater than the sum of its parts and showing his patronizing faith in connections. Even a title like *No Thanks* suggests acceptance in its idiomatic courtesy. He puts the title translated "rejoice" into Greek as if to say that joy is nowadays a Dionysian rite. In fact, Cummings had to lead the life of a happy anchorite in order to enjoy his vocation. This is sad.

My beautiful title "From Aristotle to Dante" has alchemically changed to "From Aristotle to E. E. Cummings." That's what I call poetic justice. And this is right. I have really been writing about Baudelaire, and I did not know I was going to do this. My method seems to be paying off, for I still feel honest.

I was once stationed at a resort hotel in Australia during the war with the Japanese or somebody. I had never run a telephone switchboard, and the one I was assigned to operate carried phone calls between generals and headquarters and nurses and dates as well as personal Red Cross–type emergencies and just phone calls. I never really mastered the thing, although the idea intrigued me. One afternoon, toward a weekend, the board was loaded with battles and assignments and assignations and nonsense and ennui; suddenly I got mixed up and in either panic or disgust or both, I grabbed armfuls of rubber snakes, the red and the black, and yanked them all out of their respective holes. I didn't have long to wait. Sergeants and colonels, nurses and people came roaring into the room, demanding to have their connections fixed. I was immediately removed from the switchboard and shortly after transferred to New Guinea. You might say I have been in New Guinea ever since.

From Coleridge to Eliot

I am a modern poet who has always been unhappy with modern poetry. I believe that modern poetry is linguistically centered when it should be situational. I am not talking about Engagement. Engagement is necessary but is not the end of poetry. The reason why I talk about the poet rather than the poem is that poetry is most of the time only a postponement of reality. Poetry is most of the time a delaying action or a wish. Modern poetry has done a great thing in defining a stratagem; our poetry plans and sometimes achieves a unification of being. But it stops there. Planned poetry is like planned parenthood and ends up in stanzaic boxes in a moral suburbia where all action is directed from outside. The praise I give any poem is praise for the man of situation and not the stylist. The artist who unlearns a style is the interesting one, the live one. If he seems a vandal or a criminal that is because we are looking at him from inside the box. There are certain dominant concepts which I would like to get rid of: genuis, masterpiece, major and minor, taste, vulgarity, obscenity, et al. You know the list.

I was in an art gallery and heard two curators discussing a large new canvas with paint in some places an inch thick. They were discussing the cost of saving this new painting which the artist had painted in such a way that it would disintegrate in a year or so. That was the artist's intention and he was right. But culture was out to trick him. Culture is always out to trick the artist into immortality and permanence. Ninety-nine times out of a hundred it succeeds. It is the hundredth artist, the one who escapes culture, who serves the world best. He serves the world by

entering it and leaving it. If you follow my observations
about the fate of poems and poets, you will see that I am
propounding the survival of the artist as a man, not as
a divinity or an oracle.

Coleridge was a favorite of mine in my youth, but
eventually my taste whittled him down to his two most
famous poems. Even the *Biographia* was a favorite with
me, the beauties and defects of Wordsworth's poetry
especially. Coleridge's theory of the imagination never interested me. Once I developed an interpretation of "The
Ancient Mariner," after I had read Robert Penn Warren's
brilliant analysis of the poem. In my interpretation it is
a poem that rids the poet of religion.

I prefer the poetry of the commonplace to that of the
dream. Poetically speaking, I don't believe in dreams and
dislike intensely to hear the poet referred to as a dreamer.
Between the poetry of language or symbol and that of
situation, I chose the situation. There is mystery enough
in common experience without compounding it. One of
the virtues of modern poetry is that it can be and sometimes is situational, factual. This may sound like
Gradgrindism.

For example, the poetry of the modern Greek Cavafy,
which is practically in a class by itself. Cavafy writes two
kinds of poem: the love poem and the poetry of his past,
the past of his race and culture. It is something more than
artistry which makes Cavafy succeed where more preten-
tious poets have failed. It is a gift for identification with
his past, not simply an intellectual wish to be so identified.
Cavafy was known as an amateur historian, so to say;
he really knew the past in that cold, rational way. Yet he
could read through history to the past itself; he had the
faculty of becoming the past. He was Tiresias himself. I
read him in English only, but I can discern that his success is based upon the clarity we associate with the best
prose. But what he saw in those incidents and anecdotes
of the past is unlike what anyone else had seen; and he
did not invent anything. He revealed.

As against the use of history in Pound's *Cantos*, which is sometimes done brilliantly, sometimes not, there is history purely assimilated in Cavafy. I think that Cavafy would not have bothered at all to be a "historical" poet if he had not felt natural in the historical role. Pound's history is arrived at, and he seldom does anything with it except quote it. Now and then, as in the imaginary angry letter of Mozart to the Archbishop of Salzburg, he will interpret. Generally, Pound will juxtapose the factual with the mythic, an extremely uneasy combination of values, although exciting. Eliot in his use of myth projects and evaluates; essentially he despises history and uses it with contempt. But to Cavafy the past is literally present, not as a device but as something staring him in the face. One of his "key" poems concerns a god who comes to earth at times to visit the lowest quarters of the city and debauch himself. It is an exquisite and luminous poem which says more about the psychology of the ancients (and of Cavafy) than Gibbon himself. But mostly he deals with specific characters of antiquity, great and small. Or ones he introduces as walk-ons to make a point. Intermixed with all that are the love poems, which are, you might say, a repudiation of Baudelaire. Cavafy was always at the center of experience as Baudelaire was on the outskirts.

Cavafy in my address book suggests Catullus. The difference between Cavafy and Catullus (another of my favorite poets) is temper. Catullus goes crazy with love or hate or lust or anger. Cavafy is sage, not because he is cautious but because he knows he is an old toad. In Alexandria they called him the Old Poet. He chewed his cud over a long period of his life. Catullus evidently wrote at white heat, a bad practice for poets who want to be remembered for more than ten years. So far he has been remembered for two thousand.

Here I will quote Horace Gregory, who has done a very readable translation of the poems and has written a handsome introduction. Gregory says of this young two-thousand-year-old poet:

The characters who live within the story remain untouched by middle age; none has lived long enough to bore his sons and daughters with the memoirs of how wicked he once was; none is afflicted with palsy or arthritis; none suffers the slow mind and speech and the quick irrational rage of dipsomania; none lies awake counting a slow pulse beat and with it all the fears of hypochondria. None lectures on what he might have been. The charm of the brief story is its immediacy, and associated as it is with the poems of Catullus, the youthful characters even today live in the present tense. I suspect that Catullus and his friends . . . had made a cult of youth, and that within that circle, sex and madness, art, beauty, grief, guilt, slander, even murder were accepted as the order of the day or night.

I like that passage. Aside from its literary wisdom it touches on certain profundities that are abysses. One is that poetry is the business of youth. Another is that because of poetry, anything goes. What, then, is poetry? Obviously, if it is merely a cult of youth it is worthless to adults except as evidence. If the Greek anthology or the *Oxford Book of English Verse* are kindergarten readers —but Freud said all that.

Chaucer spoke the best bad English. Having to memorize the prologue to *The Canterbury Tales* in Middle English when I was in a Virginia high school gave me my first poetic jolt. Not that this glorious set of couplets determined me on a career or even made me "love" poetry, as the saying goes. But I suddenly knew that there was such a thing and even what it was. Here was a great-hearted language that didn't sound like any other language. It was as if music had been translated into meaning. It was an excuse for meaning; it redeemed speech. It was a place to go. I don't think we had to memorize the whole 860 lines, but I like to think we did. The teacher was one of those kindly, horse-faced spinsters who really came alive with poetry. She was the spitting image of Edna Mae Oliver playing Betsy Trotwood and had the same make-believe severity. Consequently, I associate my love of Chaucer with Dickens, which isn't much of a jump at that.

When I look at the Skeat edition of Chaucer, which I have from a Chaucer seminar but didn't stay with (it didn't seem the same as the old horse-faced Chaucer), I marvel at the prodigiousness of nature. I once wrote and published a very bad sonnet about Shakespeare which I sent to William Carlos Williams (it was part of a youthful book), and he replied in anger about the vastness of Shakespeare. Not anger really but impatience with himself. Dr. Williams was as busy as Chaucer and wrote so well because he was so daily occupied, like Chaucer. Work has neither dignity nor holiness but is liberating. The right work, at any rate, which has nothing to do with aspirations but which suits the worker, whether a diplomat and FBI agent like Chaucer or Doc Williams delivering slum babies by the thousands. Poetry comes from occupation or contact with life. Williams was the editor of a magazine called *Contact*, which meant just that. The poet who is out of contact with the quotidian life is dead. The pure artist lives in deep freeze.

As you get older the past comes closer. This is a phenomenon I have never seen discussed. When I was a child the First World War seemed something that had happened in remote antiquity, though it had just ended. Today I feel as though I took part in the Civil War or the Revolution—I mean this literally—and can situate myself within almost any event of the past. (Otherwise, I feel fine.) Possibly, this is what is meant by the curious term *wisdom:* the faculty for abolishing time. Thus, if I skip from an aside about Chaucer to Lewis Carroll, the five hundred years between mean nothing in themselves.

What was it like in the days of the Empire? In England in the nineteenth century there were almost no prophets, political or otherwise, among the poets. There were a few protestors, social reformers, and expatriates; but because England had never lived through the crises of the street barricade, which is almost a daily occurrence in France, England tended never to face reality. Dickens could make jokes about missionaries and Arnold mourn the twilight of the spirit. Byron remained a scandal of

society practically until our time. England produced no
seers reveling in the derangement of the senses, and even
the famous Outcasts were men of the Establishment, like
· Byron, Shelley, Wilde, and Swinburne. With the deaths
of Byron and Shelley, England fell into a political sleep
as far as the arts were concerned. No one could hear in
the Tennysonian droning of innumerable bees the coming
of the Luftwaffe. The French child-poet Rimbaud had
more political acumen than all the English Victorians
put together.

I don't mean politics in the common meaning, but
simply intellectual awareness of the world's business. No
writer, no matter how realistic, could hold a mirror up to
that world; and the only one who did held it up with
a malicious grin. Even then, he told what he saw to children, for no one else would understand. Lewis Carroll's
novels were, in fact, for children (not quite children;
perhaps Victorian Lolitas of a kind), but his message
spread like wildfire through the half-conscious mind of
adulthood. For what Alice dreamed was aboveground, and
what book her sister was reading when Alice fell down
the rabbit hole we can be sure was not only exotic but
"uplifting."

As we approach our own time the forms of fiction are
driven to deeper and deeper depths of organization in
order to deal with experience at all. Hence the prevalence
of the dream and the employment of child heroes or
"pathological" adolescents, whose pathology reflects us.
Carroll, as someone has put it, was a left-handed genius
in a right-handed world. And as a first-rate mathematician
and a puzzle-maker he could prove that you can get to
the top of a mountain fastest by running in the opposite
direction from where it stands.

Where Alice goes all symbols are alive. Words turn
into beings, mostly of the ridiculous variety. Beings turn
into other beings. The metamorphosis from babe in arms
to piglet is almost too natural to be noticed. Everything
exists in an element of surprise—for Alice. Only for Alice,
who is symbolically always against the grain. Nature is

natural, and the only unnatural thing is man. Alice is human-trained, but she is young enough to be more natural than human. At the end of *Wonderland,* the Empire reverts to a pack of playing cards and then leafmeal. At the end of *Through the Looking Glass,* when Alice is also Queen Alice, she seizes the banquet cloth and yanks it off the table, "and plates, dishes, guests, and candles [come] crashing down together in a heap on the floor." Both books—and this is not at all incidental—end in Victorian apologies of the most saccharine variety. *Wonderland* ends with a kind of prayer for Alice by the older sister that she shall keep through her riper years "the simple and loving heart of her childhood"; *Looking Glass* concludes with one of Carroll's serious parodies of Victorian poetry in tercets, ending in the almost unbelievable slogan: "Life, what is it but a dream." To Carroll the greatest crime of mankind was to become a member of the adult world. It is probably not very original to say that this eccentric Oxford reverend and don was the Rimbaud of England, a seer and a rebel down to the marrow of his bones.

I have mentioned Dickens in passing. When I first became caught up in the life of reading, Dickens was my architect of coziness. Even today I resent the allusion to that "David Copperfield kind of crap," though I know it is true. Salinger has killed Dickens for at least one generation of young people. The Alices of the twentieth century no longer disguise their enmity for authority, even though they have not progressed very far beyond vandalism and are not even very good at that. What fascinated me about Dickens was that he pictured a world (I believe it was the real Victorian world) in which one neighborhood did not recognize the existence of another. That is, an escaped child or runaway from the workhouse or a cruel guardian had only to make the perilous journey through the No-Man's-Land of crime and evil in order to arrive at the Bedroom Beauteous with its white lace curtains overlooking the Never Fading Flower Beds. The good men and good women were strong but never showed their strength; the very existence of their strength would precipitate the downfall of the villain. The higher order of bourgeois exuded a moral radiance which put to shame the cad, the tyrant, and the thief. Dickens was not so much a reformer as the vicar of the bourgeoisie. It was from Dickens that I learned that England is the most beautiful country in the world. I have never been in England. Nor do I have Dickens among my books. I have a lover's quarrel with him; all writers do. All the same I have a different and deeper version of Dickens. Not the Victorian or the latter-day platitudinous Shakespeare of types. Not the social reformer. Not the Hollywood Dickens or the history-of-the-novel Dickens. But rather the *absurd* Dickens which made all these others possible. The Dickens of *La Comédie Humaine* of England which, like the Alice books, sinks the Precious Stone into the Silver Sea. Dickens, unlike the poets who were his contemporaries, undoubtedly heard the buzzing of the buzz bomb. Or so I like to imagine.

But in our time you had to wait for A *Passage to India* to begin to understand England and Dickens' bourgeois heroes. And real clarity was not possible until such writers as Orwell dropped the disguise of fiction and recited the realities without literary style.

Where plain speech is possible, the imaginative forms of literature begin to wither. The poetic drama begins to constrict when the novel appears. The novel begins to weaken as other protocols of evasion become less necessary. Ultimately, the great literary forms are threatened by their own inability to present the truth. Poetry in our century has spent most of its time trying to find a rationale for its existence. This is what modern poetry is about.

After the anti-novel, what? What happens after a thing like *Journey to the End of Night*, where all values are erased, political, moral, and aesthetic?

Camus says (if I may repeat it) that with our age the artist takes on the role of the director of conscience. Yet with an author like Céline or Henry Miller, conscience ceases to exist. You might call it a form of Buddhistic insanity or psychological seventh heaven. I sympathize strongly with this persuasion myself, having arrived at it through a series of disillusionments with the world of Seriousness.

Maybe I should call these essays "Shapiro in Wonderland," for I suddenly find myself confronted with Hart Crane.

What's the matter with Hart Crane? That is a question that poets and other writers have been asking for forty years. As a longtime editor of Little Magazines, I know that there are two poets who have outdistanced all others in acquiring elegies about themselves: Hart Crane and Dylan Thomas. Crane had a headstart on death and will probably keep the elegiac lead.

There are obvious reasons for this awe and amorousness for both poets: violent death and suicide provide a catharsis for the myth lovers. The violent end of a more or less young poet is like the meaningless shot that assassinates some inane archduke in some forgotten hole in the Balkans but starts people all over the world annihilating each other. I remember reading in a Baltimore paper one time about a man who murdered another in a bar over the question of how to spell the word *psychology*. It was a sensible though apparently drunken argument, such as Christopher Marlowe might have been engaged in when he was murdered.

Suicide and murder may on occasion be impersonal acts. A purely passional murder or suicide is of little consequence. Thomas' "suicide," I believe, had no social implications whatever; his miseries were apparently all his own. Myth lovers try to make something of Thomas' death, but it doesn't wash. He was a poor boy who won the sweepstakes and couldn't wait to get rid of the winnings so he could talk about the time he was rich. Fame played the dirtiest trick on him that it can on any poet: it came to him when he was unprepared for it. Consequently, Fame destroyed him. And it came to him in the worst place in the world for fame, America. In America, success is the calling card of the undertaker.

Thomas resented Fame. Hart Crane demanded it. Crane

got the opposite and is still getting it. With Hart Crane
the insistence upon poetic recognition is rather elevated.
It is impersonal and infuriated and naive. His earliest
critics referred to him as a naïf, which was true in more
ways than one. As a naïf he appeals (say, in the way the
non-English poets appeal to me). He was trying to invent
a language of the right depth, something akin to the
poetry of Samuel Greenberg, which he purloined. But he
failed. Crane fell into the worst kind of rhetoric ever
invented: advertising. He advertised Love. What is worse,
he advertised it in a Shakespearean format.

Yet the great thing about Crane is his "foreignness,"
but in his case the foreign land is his own America. He
saw quite clearly the impossibility of poetry in America
and went to the poetic soapbox, much like Vachel Lindsay, to stump for it. He would have liked to be illiterate
but was only uneducated. He was, like nearly all American poets, cursed with a touch of the poison of culture,
wanting to be cured and wanting another bite.

Crane is American because he is a bottomless pit of
insatiable appetite for everything. The Allness of Whitman is tempered by humor and a shrewdness for the safety
of his sacred hide. The Allness of Hart Crane is as senseless as the man who goes over Niagara Falls in a barrel.
Crane is therefore heroic. Whitman is only a saint, by
now a great aromatic neuter god, an Elohim, around
whom a religion of America revolves. Hart Crane has left
us the image of himself walking off into the twilight
holding Walt's hand. It's pure calendar art. I prefer
Lorca's image of Whitman with his beard full of
butterflies.

I will close the file on the letter C with a remark about
Gregory Corso. He has a Bomb poem which is probably
the best of all Bomb poems. I wrote the first A-bomb
poem when the first bomb was dropped, the day it was
announced. Mine appeared in the *New Yorker* magazine
and was about Faust. It is a very literary poem, but I
claim a patent on the invention.

The Corso Bomb has a structural flaw which practically

invalidates it. It is printed in a book with normal turnover leaves; the bomb poem is a fold-out. It exfoliates three leaves when it should six, because at the bottom of the third fold it says in bourgeois italics in parentheses: (*continued—over*). This wouldn't matter except that the poem is a *carmen figuratum*, figuring the mushroom cloud, and should have been allowed to unroll its length (as perhaps it did in another editing, which I have not seen). Hart Crane, had he seen this poem, would not have jumped off the SS *Orizaba*. He would have jumped on this poem.

It is a poem as good as "The Waste Land" or "The Ode to the Confederate Dead," with the difference that it is learned without knowing anything. For cultural reference it is one up on Ezra Pound. It is exactly like *Life* magazine, if Henry Luce could write a poem. It is literature learning from sub-literature and pre-literature, and therefore I think it has great value. Not as a work of art, for works of art have long ceased to exist on this level. But as a further dig into the archaeology of the modern poem. In this kind of poem the poet makes the initial concession to failure (that is where Hart Crane made a fool of himself) and then improvises. It is the poem that goes for broke.

Crane lived only several years before this kind of breakthrough. He had the talent and the temperament for invention and certainly the ambition. But he was always falling back into the arms of literature, and fell back into the sea. He had not the opportunity to learn contempt. He was a babe in the poetic woods. It was part of his time to revere the poem. Whatever he knew of Rimbaud and those other blasphemers of the poem, he never learned to spit. He was a perfect sacrifice to the textbook.

The Corso poem, as corny as the typographic device may be, is a better breakthrough than *The Bridge*—to calligraphy. A poem should be written in handwriting, like a genuine hand-painted oil painting. I was in some library recently where they had a collection of Hart Crane manuscripts. I wanted to see his handwriting and what the

manuscript of *The Bridge* looked like. I saw mostly typewriter. The personal letters written by hand were interesting, but I could date the handwriting by the style. It
was not distinctive.

The picture-written poem is primitive and good. All
prosody is calligraphy. Poets should describe their poems
in writing or painting or illumination, whether it is the
initial lettering of medieval monks, Rimbaud stealing the
technique of cheap book illustration, the comics, Japanese
artists turning a word into a painting, or Kenneth Patchen
scrawling out his poems like handbills or Torahs. Modern
poetry has this genius: showing the poem as you read it.
You know what it is before you read it. "The Waste Land"
has this beauty and Pound's *Cantos* splendidly; they celebrate the printing press, whatever else they do. This is the
domain of the modern poet very eminently.

D / Dahlberg, Dowson, (Swinburne), Dante, Donne

Now I come to Edward Dahlberg. For many years I
kept him in the Other Room, but he is now in the *malebolge*. When I had discovered almost ten years ago that
I had bored all the way through poetry and come out on
the other side, I knew I could not get back into the
painted paradise and didn't want to. I lost my nostalgia
for poetry, which is something like giving up the idea of
Good and Evil. Now what seemed poetry to me was what
other people called prose. The Edwardian novelist used
the word *God* as a poetic metaphor, so that one day one
of them asked: What is the *prose* for God? Myself, I can
no longer find a differential between prose and poetry, and
what is obviously poetry irritates me.

Dahlberg writes like an "Old Testament." For many
years I couldn't read him because I didn't want to be
thundered at, but I gradually transported him to my cell
for sound effects. His books, all beautifully printed and
illustrated, are priapic and baleful sermons in the wilderness. In a book on writers he says: "In almost a hundred

years of American Literature we do not have one feeding,
breeding, sexual male, not one suffering, bed-pining Manon
Lescaut or a Shulamite. There are no ripe women here.
Writes the poet William Carlos Williams . . . , 'Emily
Dickinson, starving of passion in her father's garden, is
the very nearest we have ever been—starving.' "

Or again: "Heine sang of Nordsee maids; Dostoevski
ached for the Foot of woman; Melville, in rapt, torn
paeans, warbled the festal founts of the teats and the anus
of the whale!"

Or yet again: "To damn sensuality, laughter, and
irony, Cotton Mather had turned woman into a witch; Poe
took the infernal witch, begot by Mather, and buried her
alive. Melville exorcised her! Lady Dickinson hid in
Christ's bosom."

And once more, about Walt Whitman: "An obese,
prophetic, fragrant man, with heavy-lidded eyes, pink,
gospular face, and gaudy swollen pieties—as Thomas
Eakins had painted him—announced, 'I am the true
Bread.' Out of Jesus' mouth he took his most equivocal
parable—'For my flesh is meat indeed, and my blood dwell-
eth in me and I in him' and made of it a seminal New
Testament."

This is about as much poetry as people of our time
can stomach; for it is criticism as recited by an Othello,
it is biblical exegesis by a riverboat medicine man, the
style is as phony as Shakespeare's and as expensive, and
every word he says is jagged and deep and festered down to
the bone. Dahlberg is a gentle man who cannot bear to
look into the flames but who does anyhow, out of necessity, and then apologizes for what he has seen. He is
a very American writer because he is both a Stylist and a
Believer. He believes passionately that all is dead with us;
he is generally convincing.

What is missing in American literature, maybe all our
arts, as Dahlberg intimates, is sensuality. A people without
sensuality is a prurient people, a people of dry lust. Crea-
tively speaking, we are the Unfulfilled. Dahlberg is a
Mediterranean *manqué*. His last book, called appropriately

Because I Was Flesh, is a brilliant and baroque decla-
mation on the subject of his illegitimacy. He is in fact as
well as in his books the perfect symbol of the American
writer: he is a bastard. Bastards in real life are easy to
come by but hard to recognize. This poet answers his
own roll call. He cries out from his Sinai in the great
American air-conditioned desert for a Karamazovean sensuality, not for the dessicated lusts of the bureaucracy or
the burlesque. He is no voyeur.

Lewis Carroll has just introduced me to Ernest Dowson.
We are back in 1890. English poetry ran out of gas when
it ran out of virgin territory. I am not a Marxist, or maybe
I am, but I recognize a clear correlation between English
greatness in literature and Britannia ruling the waves.
When the idea of England the Supreme fell into dis-
favor with her poets and other artists, the arts fell. The
dismal produce of English poetry from 1901 on is summed
up in such a poet as Ernest Dowson, Lionel Johnson,
Bridges, Masefield, or Edward Thomas. An unbelievable
vacuum, a hole in the fabric, was suddenly visible to the
heirs of the greatest poetry of Europe. English poets gave
way to Irish, Welsh, and American.

The time of the greatest upheavals and revisions of
poetry was in the last century and took place, naturally,
in France. England didn't hear a whisper of it. Swinburne
had an elegy for Baudelaire, but it didn't amount to much,
even as Swinburnean verse. Swinburne finds Baudelaire
strange and mysterious. (I don't know how many times
the word *strange* recurs in his elegy.) But there is nothing
strange or mysterious about Baudelaire to us. Swinburne
is quite aware of the fetishes of Baudelaire, remarking
on the symbols of sterility frequently and even offering
the Frenchman a lock of his hair.

You must say about Swinburne as Lawrence said about
Poe: *Poor Swinburne.*

But none of this took hold in England. English poetry
muddled through Victoria and grew shabbier and shabbier
until it hit bottom with Oscar Wilde and Ernest Dowson

and Francis Thompson and those sad peripherals who felt that because they versified they were aristocrats. Edith Sitwell, in a recent edition of Swinburne, considerably bowdlerized—as if you have to bowdlerize *him*—talks about Swinburne as an aristocrat. English critics have done this for a long time, as if to prove that because Algernon was really of the Establishment, his little aberrations or whatever you call them were superior amusements.

I am fascinated by Dowson, a minuscule Swinburne but an honest victim of the obsession of poetry. The titles of his poems go: "Benedictio Domini," "Flos Lunae," "Vanitas," "Spleen," "In Tempore Senectutis," "Chansons Sans Parol," "My Lady April," not to mention long ones like the "Non Sum Qualis Eram Bonae . . . ," which is in a way the last poem in English. It is perfectly just that from this poem came the title of a novel called *Gone With the Wind* and a dance tune called "I'm Always True to You Darling . . . in My Fashion." Dowson expresses to perfection in *parvo* the bankruptcy of English poetry. Ezra Pound brushed him off with a dirty line that read: "Dowson found harlots cheaper than hotels," and then proceeded to linguify English poetry as it hadn't been done since Milton. Pound did a spectacular thing: he grabbed the deck of cards that Lewis Carroll had thrown in the air as a protest against Victoria and proceeded to tell fortunes. Eliot got the message and bought himself a set of Tarot cards. Modern poetry was born that way. Rather gently Pound, who knew French, whatever else he didn't know, and Eliot took English poetry by the hand and led it back to the continent, to France and Italy, which had fertilized the greatest poetry of England. Pound discovered Italia for the twentieth century. Both discovered the Dante we know.

I have nothing to say about Dante. I can't read Italian, and in English he is pure nonsense. It delighted me once to read in a Pakistani newspaper that he had just been banned in a new English translation for Moslem countries.

I fight censorship in this country, but I am definitely in
favor of banning Dante in Pakistan. Literary imperialism
holds no attractions for me.

So with John Donne, who was invented for our age
by T. S. Eliot. I grew up on Donne, the profane Donne,
not the religious pastor who tolled the bell. Someone
should, if they haven't, make a study of poets who repented
their profanities and became God-struck. Donne is a good
example. English poetry never quite made it across the
barrier to a free art but always crept back into the asylum
of the Church. Eliot is the modern Donne. Why should
poets be buried in Westminster Abbey? Potter's field
would be more decent. Or the burning ghats. Religion is
such a poor substitute for poetry that only the lame,
the halt, and the blind should resort to it. I would suppose that there are more English poets who staggered
backward into religion than any other. Even the rakehell
Earl of Rochester had a deathbed conversion, if we are to
believe the accounts. And Herrick. The nicest example is
Christopher Smart, a beautiful poet whose religious psychosis landed him many times in the laughing academy
because he blocked traffic trying to get passersby in the
street to kneel down and pray with him.

The American republic, by demanding freedom from
religion (this is what I think was meant by our revolutionaries, not a free-for-all religious orgy), opened the gates
for a religious Disneyland. So far we have managed to keep
the concessions numerous enough to bewilder each other to
a standstill. I am in favor of any religion that gets strong
enough to become a threat to any other. I would like to
see mosques and stupas rising all over the country and
people throwing down prayer rugs at five o'clock on Fifth
Avenue. John Donne lived at a time when poetry had
already lost its mana, its magic, when literary men were
turning to prose and the novel. Poetry sensed freedom
and was afraid. John Bunyan knew more about the uses of
literature than Donne. Milton wrote the final epic for our
tongue, a great nonsense that backfired into melancholy
and handsome Satans: Fatal Men, Byrons and Swin-

burnes, whose ultimate fame rested on *noblesse oblige*. English poetry is so clearly a poetry of aristocracy and pretenders that, in a sense, it never came to know what poetry is. It is, I have reiterated, the greatest body of poetry of Europe, but how much of it is poetry still remains to be seen.

E / Eliot

The letter *E* apparently is not pushy in the library catalog. I find I am stuck with Emerson, Eliot, Empson, Euripides, and Paul Engle. But the only *E* I have anything to say about is Eliot. Emerson, whom I agree with (insofar as I know what there is to agree with), I find impossible to read. He has a corrupt, euphuistic style of prose which turns my stomach. His poetry style is, on the other hand, quite interesting, and someone should look it up sometime and give it a place in life.

Allen Tate, introducing Eliot in Minneapolis some years ago, described him with painful accuracy as "the most eminent man of letters in the world [today] and the greatest living poet."

No one denies either title to fame. They are matters of fact. A man is eminent in his art when he is so acknowledged by his contemporaries and his elders; the more so when he and his juniors give in to their seniors and go along with the tide. The evidence is also all on the side of Eliot in the matter of being the greatest living poet. Insofar as we have an idea of "great" and an idea of "poet," no one can dispute with Eliot for the heavyweight title. Nor are there other ways of assessing the values. Eliot and his reputation are as solid as Fort Knox or the Vatican.

I will offer my own interpretation of the Eliot phenomenon, of the man who left the fringe culture of America to become a Britisher and an aristocrat, a high member of the Establishment, and who ended by becoming the *most popular poet in the twentieth century*. Poetic Justice caught up with this fellow.

Eliot probably never knew what hit him. A man steeped in the riches of European literature, philosophy, and theology, unaware of the historical upheavals going on around him, opposed to change even in free verse, which he did not really like; a poet who wrote only a handful of poems (as few as any famous poet who ever lived); a critic who really took the bull of culture by the horns; a mediocre playwright but a first-rate church pageantist; a dandy of the English high middle class; a man who reintroduced religion to the intellectuals; a political Puritan who held back from fascism because of its primitivist vulgarity—he is not an easy figure to cope with. And yet no one can deny his preeminence as the greatest poet of the twentieth century in all countries or, a larger provenance, the most eminent man of letters of our time. It is so. The age gets the heroes it deserves. And Eliot in poetry and cultural criticism is the hero. How can this be?

My explanation is simplistic. Poetry had died in England around 1900. It had never been born in America. A pair of more or less English poets from the colonies came to raise the ghost. In American fashion they saw there was work to be done: buttressing up the tradition, stimulating the sense of appreciation for the past, and providing a formula for the present. Pound kept in close contact with *Poetry* magazine until he didn't need it any longer. Eliot as cultural diplomat introduced England to the poetry of France, which apparently England didn't know existed. True, people like James Elroy Flecker had translated Verlaine, but Verlaine to England was something like the golden journey to Samarkand.

The Eliot phenomenon was that of shoring up the ruins of a vast, beautiful, and extinct culture. This he did with the aplomb and dedication of a Doctor Schweitzer. Eliot became a witch doctor for English poetry, pretending or believing that he could bring it back to life. The whole world stood by in admiration and disbelief.

It was the gesture rather than the results that mattered. Nothing happened except that the *man* became more and more famous, a hero of culture, a one-man operation in a jungle of despair. In fact, it was heroic, as Pound was heroic; everyone must admire this fantastic organizational know-how, the efficiency, the planning, the foresight, the marketing of these two young American go-getters.

A world that had lost "poetry" on the lowest stratum could only begin to reaccept it on the highest. Eliot demanded that poetry be "integrated" into society once more. He "integrated" it first with the literati, then with the critics, then with the professors, and finally (undoubtedly to his dismay) with the American public itself.

There were two forces working that helped produce Modern Poetry. One was a poetic vacuum of the democratic masses in England, America, and elsewhere. The other was a vital intellectual aristocracy, which Eliot joined. The poets of this elite could not but relate themselves to the monstrosity of illiterate democracy. Pound in his early years of expatriation wrote: "The thought of what America would be like if the classics had a wide circulation, troubles my sleep." People have written a long time about what a classic is. Pound and Eliot knew. To them a classic was the point of reference itself, no matter how they tried to democratize the past by trying to smuggle it into the present. One who uses such a term as *a classic* is perforce a dogmatist, an absolutist. Pound with his Booklist, Eliot with his revisionist curriculum of great books—it comes to the same thing.

It comes to the notion of saving civilization. Which is to say, saving the capital. The capital is the fulcrum and depository of culture. It is what is invested. To such poets as Pound and Eliot poetry has always been ancillary to, secondary to, culture. Culture represents an element in which ideas can perform experiments.

What I am trying to say is that both Eliot and Pound and all such directors of conscience are always the most horrified at their own successes. *They did not mean to be taken literally.* This is why they indulge in definition, the sweeping statement, and employ the voice of authority, on the one hand, and withdraw from the application of their ideas, on the other. Eliot's endless humility or Pound's retractions show a fundamental irresponsibility. "I didn't mean to be that anti-semitic or anti-democratic," says Eliot. "I was only looking for an ideal society." Pound is amazed when they put him in jail for aiding and comforting the fascists with whom his country is at war. "I was only being a good Jeffersonian," says Pound.

I believe Eliot to be a minor poet, in my sense of the word. This is not meant as an insult, if anybody should care. I know from experience that anyone can learn to write poetry which under certain circumstances may be acclaimed as great or immortal. On the other hand, I think that Pound in the *Cantos* has made poetry possible for the modern world (to paraphrase a remark of Eliot's about Joyce). Poets in the past decade or two have discovered Pound. Nobody has discovered Eliot as a teacher or master, only as a philosopher. Pound is a poet, an artist, who has made a language in which poets can speak, sing, or yell. Eliot has made poetry respectable again; that is probably all he has done. Pound's followers are beatniks. This is in his favor. Eliot's are professors.

Eliot must have sensed the danger of popularity from his earliest beginnings; he was always taking away what he had given. Pound plowed on and on with his big poem, his archaeological Dig, shedding fresh earth in all directions. If, toward the end, he says that he really didn't discover Troy, he is merely suffering the same kind of guilt that American authors always do when they blow their brains out or jump off boats or drink toilet Lysol. It's old Protestant-Mosaic law: you can look into the Promised Land but you can't go there.

Modern Poetry has given us Pisgah sights of culture which would take even Lewis Carroll's breath away. We should be grateful. Despite the shady or misguided motives of those poets of culture, they have given us a new definition of the organization of life. This new definition is *disorganization*. I am beginning after a decade of swatting the tsetse and subverting Pound to appreciate their gift to us. I am only just beginning to give in to the *Four Quartets* as a model from which to go into production. And the vast and glorious junkyard of the *Cantos* is, I confess, my favorite promenade, my arboretum, so to speak.

From Frost to Lawrence

I ought to remind you that I have a plan and not only the ABC's. Man is the monkey who sat at the typewriter and wrote all those books. There was nothing at the beginning but an alphabet, and nothing at the end. To most men of letters most books have died at one time or another; literature is an endless and very ancient cemetery which is still being used. There's always a little more room. But the writer can never live among those monuments; he has to build his own. As soon as a man publishes a book he is out of its range. The poet notices with curiosity that someone is reading him. Ha, says the poet to himself, he *thinks* he's reading me. But the last book is never right and the poet starts a new one. Is there any end to this? Does the writer ever pack up and go home? And where is home? One day William Shakespeare said goodbye to all those plays and went up to the country. We never heard from him again except for a rather angry epitaph: Good friend for Jesus' sake forebear to dig the dust enclosed here. He put a curse on bone-movers. Did he have Westminster Abbey in mind? He had the sense of finality, not immortality.

I go through my alphabet to see what is still present, what still speaks to me. Each generation must make a total revaluation of the past. All we can teach the young is what we believed in, but the young are under no obligation to us whatever. I sometimes feel a twinge of conscience about this, insofar as I have one: I have spent many years opening every door I saw to the young. I tell them: Loot the past, don't arrange it. Take what you want; it's all free. Those are artifacts, not gods. Only have the decency not to smash things unless you really mean it. Iconoclasm is okay but not as a way of life. If

I seem to be knocking around a few idols it's only to make it easier for others to erect new ones. The greatest thing about the Victory of Samothrace is the missing head. And so forth. I belong to the anti-discipline discipline.

F / Frost, (Bradstreet), (Dickinson), (Robinson)

Robert Frost, I read somewhere, is a descendant of Anne Bradstreet or a member of her clan. Anne Bradstreet was a good housewife poet and a Puritan of the seventeenth century. Poetry in her time and place could be tolerated if it served God and Calvin. "In Adam's Fall We Sinned All" said the best and most primitive New England poem. New England isn't exactly the Tahiti of Baudelaire, but it is beautiful in a grudging kind of way. Anne was careful not to see too much beauty in it, as was her counterpart Emily Dickinson, who insulated herself from the sight of man and played a kind of correspondence chess with God and Nature. Both women were thoroughly domesticated. New England was God's kitchen garden, and that was good enough for them.

They were bitter women who resented Spring, as Eliot did or Robert Frost. Their joy existed in the ambiguous satisfactions of a dangerous existence. A recent writer has described Frost as an existentialist. The idea makes a certain amount of sense.

The name Robert comes from Robert E. Lee. Frost's father was a sympathizer with the Confederacy. Robert was born in California. His mother was born in Scotland. He is about as much of a New Englander as I am.

I don't think of him as an American poet at all but as the last Colonial, the end of the line of the great English poets. It was England that recognized him from beginning to end. Frost was the center of the English country poets who called themselves Georgians. He felt at home with them, within the continuum of the English tradition, and antagonistic to everything new in art or poetry or society. After England had first acclaimed him (it is true, through

the good offices of Ezra Pound) he returned to America
and invented New England. Frost probably could not
differentiate between New and Old England. He always
thought of America as a colony, at least a colony of the
Tradition. He was never an Establishmentarian poet or a
culture racketeer, but both England and America finally
brought him to book as a member of the Establishment.
Oxford, Cambridge, and the Senate of the United States
gave him their highest honors. It took time, but it happened. And yet politically, philosophically, aesthetically,
Frost had no direction. He was simply a poet who appren-
ticed himself to the art and rose to become a master of
it. He is even more conventional than his master Edwin
Arlington Robinson, a poet who is equally a master but
a master of dullness. Frost is not dull. He is hard and
bright, shrewd and cautious and cynical, but clear in
the head and surprisingly honest. Most of his poems are
analyses of platitudes or elaborations of them. He lacks
originality in every way but maintains a massive and heroic
disbelief in man's fate. He knows literature and has probably read it all, but he himself is not Literary. In his work
you run across Lucretius and Horace and Theocritus, but
although he was a contemporary of the Symbolists, you
would think he had never heard of them. And he had unlimited ambition—but for what?

Frost suffered all his life from popularity. Or at least
after the age of forty, when England had made him
famous and the Americans adopted him. Literary criticism
despised him for this; present literary criticism is trying
to convince the public that they don't really understand
Frost and should take a course at the university or maybe
even a seminar. Literary criticism, despite the fact that
Frost is the most traditional and conventional poet since
the Victorians, resents his disinterest in ideologies. Frost
himself wrote no criticism. He is practically the only
modern poet who hasn't.

What he wrote were poems in the most presentable
definition of the word. Every Frost poem is hand-tooled
and worth the price, whether it is a narrative, a ballad,

a lyric, a sonnet, a masque, or a bit of blank verse. His teacher Edwin Arlington Robinson wrote blank verse that would put whole universities to sleep. But Frost works like the maker of precision instruments, within the line and within the poem. His expertise is so far in advance of what he can do with it that you are left with thousands of examples of master craftsmanship that only seem to lie around the shop. What is missing in this great artist is passion.

In a sense, the accusation against Frost's popularity is meaningful. The poems are something like Steuben glass or Cartier Fifth Avenue diamonds: costly, well-set, and, except as conspicuous consumption, worthless. They are Georgian poetry aspiring to the Poet Laureateship, a title which Frost would undoubtedly have earned had he remained in England. Toward the end of his life Frost was referred to by American journalists as our Poet Laureate. Which he was. I would like to remind my countrymen that the office of Poet Laureate is unconstitutional. Pound got him launched. Eliot turned his back on him, as he did on all Mannerists. The critics watched him with a deadly eye: they were always trying to convince themselves that all of Frost's poems were just a variorum edition of Joyce Kilmer's "Trees." After all, Frost is constantly saying that only God can make New England, which is probably true. Anne Bradstreet had the same idea. The only breath of fresh air New England ever had was when Emerson and Thoreau were around. Emerson as a poet, even as a craftsman, was more interesting than Frost. If Frost learned anything from Emerson it was of little consequence. But Emerson was a stuffed shirt, for all his Hinduism and Unitarianism.

We are left with Frost, who is left out of practically everything. He is not really English, not really American, not really New England, not really modern (whatever that is), not really a *poète maudit*, not a poet of the academy or of the body politic, not really popular, though his books have a vast circulation. He is something like the Wandering Jew of the Tradition. He will wander all over the world for a thousand years or so, wondering what he did that made him so isolated and insular. Should he have written free verse or novels or discussed the Role of the Artist in Modern Society? In his way he was doing these things all the time. What is missing from Frost? What is it that all that excellence withholds? Passion. Instead of which he gave us thrift: narratives of New England farmers, sonnets with involuted and perfected stanzas about woodchoppers and ants and white, dimpled spiders. Frost is in the tradition of Henry Ford, Thomas Edison, and Conrad Hilton. He was a one-man success who was going to make the going concern sit up and take notice. He manufactured Georgian *objets d'art*.

By standards of production and value, Frost can stand up against any poet in the fantastic English tradition. He can write rings around John Donne. His sonnets make Shakespeare's look like a schoolboy's. He can construct stanzas better than Keats. His blank verse makes the nineteenth-century excursionists look like used-car dealers. His lyrics are as exquisitely balanced and mellifluous as Blake's or Walter Savage Landor's or *The Shropshire Lad*. Beyond question he is a poet who will always be looked at for one reason or another, long after the English language is dead. People will go to him as we go to Theocritus and will say how damned good he was.

I started to write an academic explication of the famous sonnet called "Design," a more than perfect sonnet in which a white, fat spider and a white satin moth are all whitened up together on a silver loom of a spider web, and somewhere in the Mozartian sestet Frost begins to ask his "why" questions: Why these things are beautiful; why they are out to kill each other; and whether Design, with a capital *D*, would stoop to such lowly insectivora. Possibly he is playing in his way with the Argument from Design by designing the argument. A sonnet is a form of insect life, among literary phyla: why not the sonnet, says Frost.

Why not. For William Carlos Williams said that all sonnets express the same thing—nothing. A sonnet is a beautiful nothing. So is a white moth, Frost says. The contradictions within the sonnet are not, after all, different from a spider web decorated with a white moth and white spider, the whole impaled on a white flower.

In the twentieth century, if poetry has done anything it has questioned what poetry can do. And so far it hasn't come up with any answer, except academic compromises, theoretical pedagogy, and vague notions of the refinement of sensibility or of cultural responsibility. The writers themselves—I exclude poets—have adhered to an uneasy support of poetry without actually supporting it. The modern writer supports the Poet because he is one of their guild; poetry itself we do not find being shored up by our novelists or playwrights (those who hundreds of years ago abandoned poetry). Poetry is kept alive with us by critics and critics alone. Critics have achieved their highest place in our age, an age that will undoubtedly raise statues to them, because they have gone to the barricades for the Poet. Without poets, what would critics do?

Probably society wants poetry to survive. Society needs poetry badly. Without poetry with a capital P, society with a capital S would have to invent it. It always does.

Now and then in Paris there are farmers' riots. All produce in the quite tiny country of France flows into Paris, which is exactly like the New York Lorca describes with unadulterated hate:

> They butcher each day in New York
> four million ducks,
> five million hogs,
> two thousand doves, to a dying man's pleasure;
> one million cows,
> one million lambs,
> two million roosters
> that splinter all heaven to rubble . . .

Lorca in his Iberian way is like Robert Frost: the belly of the city is without bottom and consumes Nature. The City is always in an Alexandrian state, waiting for the barbarians who always take too long to come. The man in the country tries farming a little and reads his books and is eventually consumed either by a Farmers' Co-op or by a Revolution. If he is fortunate enough to live with a peasantry he can survive intellectually by nostalgia and rancor.

Now this is all so but is very old hat and behindhand. Robert Frost was a sulky farmer, a pretender to the countryside, as Cummings was a city-sulker, pretending to be of the city that slaughtered all those doves and hogs at dawn. And neither was of the city or of the country. And both had a thing in common (many things really) but mainly their wish to keep things as they were. Both poets hated (to use another capital S) Science and (capital T) Technology. So did D. H. Lawrence and many of my favorite poets, though my favoritism balks at this point. I love Technology to the point of hating poetry.

Doc Williams had a formula which I like. He formulated two great categories: Botany and Litany. He is Botany. Litany is formal society. I like to spread the definitions to Biology and Culture. That is, there is what grows or happens and what is done to what happens. Jungles and gardens. Junkyards or museums. I prefer junkyards. Rubble as against Versailles.

We who are rubble-mongers are usually classified as some kind of Decadents or degenerates, pseudo-primitives or persons of jaded tastes, Huysmans characters whose nerves are so limp that only a major electric shock can make us feel anything. All the modern arts are populous with such types; some of them are among the greatest men. And there is a hyper-insensitivity among young writers and artists, an aesthetic brutalism, which I think is magnificent. It is based on the natural agnosticism of the young in matters of art, but it is beefed up by an immunity to illusion—the illusion of Good Taste and Excellence—which has been shot into their veins for generations. We have amongst us a generation of old young men in the arts who have the hides of dinosaurs and the antennae of luna moths. They are preconscious and super-conscious at the same time.

G / Ginsberg, Graves, Goethe, Goodman, Gray. *Bhaga-*
vad-Gita

Ginsberg is not a poet but an overthrower of poets.
He is one of a long line of Dandies and railroad dyna-
miters, like A. E. Housman (who didn't really blow up
any trains), who lyricized about the death of song. As
Baudelaire hated street lamps in Paris and made *gas* an
infernal symbol, as Housman hated Queen Victoria's
twenty-one-gun salutes, Ginsberg hates sleep. In one of
his poems he describes flying over the United States at
night and imagines all the people down there copulating
or fornicating, as the case may be. This is a very theocentric
psychology. What he really resents is that people are
asleep or having fun when he is passing over, like the
angel of death.

There is a great virtue in this poet, which Williams
grasped before anyone else. He is the angel of death to
poetry. *Angel* is one of their love names; he is a self-
invented toxin, a bacterial smut. He is closer to what
Baudelaire hoped to be than the Frenchman ever was.
The difference is that Ginsberg wants to be good where
Baudelaire wanted to be evil. The flaw in Ginsberg may
be that he is a Jew and Jews have no sense of evil but
only a sense of right and wrong.

I understand quite well why a poet like Allen Ginsberg,
a queer, a dope advertiser, a professional Jew-American-
Marxist, a master of self-advertising, a San Francisco
Shelley, a Hindu-Whitman Transcendentalist, a Salvador
Dali of his own familial entrails, should be one of the
favored poets of our time. We are just beginning to come
into the time when Negro poets will really let us have this
kind of thing. (My one and only prediction.) Negroes
are even more literal than Jews, who have a lot of law
behind them and who in a way invented it. When Negro
poetry lets loose it will probably sweep all European poetry
so far away that it will take centuries before it is
rediscovered.

Poetry, as we know it, has always been the spices of
the East, hard to come by, achieved by heroes amidst
great conflicts of nations, the occasion of magnificent
revelations of other lands and glorious kings.

The difference between Frost and Ginsberg is only the
difference between *F* and *G*. One is the function of the
other. One is all order; the other, all chaos. The orderly
one doesn't really believe chaos exists and is eternally
propitiating Design or Providence or even, in a slack
moment, God. The disorderly one sees nothing but Chaos
and "the best minds of his generation" being destroyed by
capitalists and squares and heterosexual suburbanites.

Frost really did believe in Design, like a Thomist. Ginsberg believes in God as the cosmic finger painter. Dylan
Thomas was part Frost, part Ginsberg. This made him
a metaphysical poet.

I hoped to put in a good word for Goethe, who always
needs it, Robert Graves, Paul Goodman, Thomas Gray,
and the *Bhagavad-Gita*. It is time to move. But in passing
I should make a mandala of those *G's*: Goethe, the great
bourgeois deity (Henry Miller's sobriquet) and author
of Romanticism. Gray, the Robert Frost of his time.
Robert Graves, the one-man Resistance Movement against
modern Classicism. Paul Goodman, a Goethe of New
York, the type of the crucified intellectual of our time
who believes in both poetry and direct action, lyricism
and soup kitchens, orgone therapy and economic utopia.
A wonderful figure. And then the *Gita*, which hovers over
America like an ectoplasm: Thou art That; I am the
slayer and the slain; and all that sort of New England
"philosophy."

H / Huxley, Hopkins, Homer, Herrick, Hardy, Huysmans,
    Herbert

Every age invents its own pharmacopoeia and subsequent
mysticism. Nowadays, there are writers like Graves, Aldous

Huxley, Alan Watts, and so on who have provided an unexpected substantiation for religion through brain chemistry. They suggest, in one way or another, that the bases of all religions reside in the prehistoric drug rituals, some of which still survive in out of the way places like Texas. Mere plants growing in the desert have been superseded by pure acids in the laboratory: certain of these produce in the mind either madness, sometimes incurable, or a perception of unity "with God," as it were. Aldous Huxley's description of the hilarity of the colors of automobiles in Hollywood is identical to the reaction that Dylan Thomas had driving past a million-car parking lot in Chicago. A perception of absolute unity in nonsense. Beauty by default. The mystical nun rolling on the ground, hysterically intoning "The Love, the Love" is experiencing the same thing as the poet or the person with a dose of LSD in his bloodstream or, according to old wives' talk, the dying man's vision of unity. I submit in all seriousness and possibly with no great originality that poetry, like religion, is an attempt to regain this psychological plateau where Unity is (why, I don't know) Bliss. Poetry is a stratagem of unification, as religion, any or every religion, is a stratagem to regain the paradisal state of oneness. That is why I say that such experiments substantiate religion, why perhaps poetry is at bottom "religious," and why religion is at best a poetic technique.

Yet Freud was accurate when he described religion as a socially acceptable psychosis. And I think I am correct when I describe poetry the same way. The forms of poetry and of religion are "insane." The goals, however, are worth the risk.

But One-ism, Monism, quickly festers when it becomes an end in itself. Whether in politics or in psychology or in art or in religion or in the quotidian life, to exalt Oneness above Many-ness leads to disaster. It leads to Dandyism and Napoleon, Hitler and the Master Race, the Chosen People, the theory of genius, and the cult of personality. The cleverer religions are always polytheistic while denying it. In a durable religion you do not have one God but a godhead, out of whom flows at least two others. Or you have the Hindu Great Being which emits gods and demigods and saints by the trillions.

People have been writing in the past few years about an apparent split (dichotomy is the trade name) between the arts and sciences. Eliot, perhaps, gave this debate a platform when he invented the expression "dissociation of sensibility." Most of this journalism has come from England. It is picked up in America mostly because we have a vast army of professors in ivy-covered towers who believe that they are medieval monks protecting Latin and Greek and algebra. Aldous Huxley's last book was on that subject. Huxley had lived at least half his life in Hollywood, a nephew of the great Thomas Huxley, a fine satirist of our age, a man with a deep fear of technological irresponsibility, and a man with a true love of what he once described as his expensive education. So Huxley never escaped from this old-fashioned Victorian formula of Science versus Art or religion. He saw all the evil results of technology, instead of splitting his sides laughing, but seldom saw anything evil about poetry. Poetry to Huxley probably represented beauty recollected in tranquility, a kind of rich man's view. Art is for leisure. He never quite understood that poetry is a forward motion of sensibility, an explosion. In his excellent anthology of mystical writings he doesn't even include Gerard Manley Hopkins, a "natural" for his purposes and for his own tastes. *The Perennial Philosophy*, as he calls it, is one of the best thesauruses of its kind. But Huxley fails to see the nexus between poetry and philosophical mysticism; he does not see that the stratagems are correspondent, that poetry is nothing more than a method, another method, for achieving unity. He would rather keep poetry in a room of its own, for the cocktail hour or for the darkened mansion of Taste. I was once an admirer of Huxley's poetry, which I doubt if any of you have ever seen. His were well-made poems, with translations of such poems of Baudelaire's as "The Damned Women" and "The Lesbians." Huxley, like his master D. H. Lawrence, might have been a first-

rate poet had he gone that way. Possibly he did better not
to. He is in the great tradition of Defoe and Swift and the
science fictionism of our day. He was a good man who
knew his own gifts but whose contribution, after all, was
his awareness of the possibilities of science to throw light
upon insensate relationships.

Aldous Huxley was a shy poet. And Hopkins was a rich
one. Hopkins was in many ways the type of modern poet,
which may be why he was not accepted until Auden resurrected him. Hopkins was an English Protestant who
became a Jesuit, suffered in Ireland and Wales, and
doomed himself to obscurity and God knows what. The
nonrecognition of Hopkins is very precious to us who
accept his worth as a poet and his personal, maybe hilarious
attitude toward it. Hopkins was an unquestionable believer.
He existentially chose Roman Catholicism, which is the
most beautiful and intelligent religion in the shop window;
he chose it to punish himself and poetry. He did both.
He punched the hell out of poetry. When he got through
with it poetry looked like the day after Mardi Gras. It
was, you might say, a Pyrrhic victory.

But, disappointingly, in the long run Hopkins also ends
up in the anthology, which to poetry is a fate worse than
death because it is death itself. Hopkins is really what
Robert Bridges thought: a Victorian eccentric, like Coven-
try Patmore. The inscapes turn into Russian Easter Eggs,
which are museum pieces, shipwrecks carved into crystal
or nutshells, or the Lord's Prayer etched on the point of
a needle. But there he is, the perfect counterpart of
Emily Dickinson. I have been trying to marry Emily
Dickinson off for a long time. First to Whitman. Hopkins
would have made a better husband.

Poetry is "Unitarian." Science is "Unitarian." Inscape
or quantum physics or Brahma exhalation-inhalations or
the Perennial Philosophy or Zen or W. B. Yeats or the
Zohar or Hasidism or Ginsberg-Ferlinghetti—aside from
matters of vocabulary and sophistication there are few
differences.

Writers have tried various methods for explaining the

poetic loss of interest in our time. No one has ever quite succeeded in explaining, for one thing, why poets give up or die young or jump off boats and, concomitantly, why grown people give up the enjoyment of poetry, even when they retain their love of literature. There hangs over poetry a kind of stigma of youth. It reminds you of Bernard Shaw's remark: Why should beauty be wasted on the young? A few years ago an anthologist asked me to pick out a favorite poem which I had written and comment on it. I picked one written in prose and asked how long grown men and women could listen to rhymes and meters. I had reached a point at which even the greatest poetry in rhyme and meter seemed to me a childish evasion. At best I could appreciate the classics only by putting them in a class of things which belonged to some childhood of culture.

I place Homer and Horace and Herrick in the childhood of time bracket. H. D. and T. E. Hulme are reference books when something comes up about Imagism or Classicism. Haiku also. Thomas Hardy as a poet I keep handy as a novelist who anachronistically felt that he must revert to the poem. His poems, always given a place of honor in the modern anthology, are strictly amateur affairs; that is their charm. He was a Sunday poet who would with delightful naiveté interlard his curious stanzas and strange idiomatic sayings with whole undigested chunks of philosophy. He would take a term like Immanent Will and capitalize it. It is like an illuminated manuscript of the Middle Ages and is very appealing.

The novels of Huysmans I keep for theoretical substantiation of some of the things that happened to poetry just before our time. And George Herbert I have because I used to memorize him before I heard of the Metaphysical resurrection many years ago. He seems the least precious and self-conscious of his group, the one who actually believed what he was saying, one who neither took poetry too seriously nor faked the condition of his soul.

But most of these authors are dead to me, and the ones that aren't are generally those who have avoided the forms and the special rhetoric of the poem. This is why I prefer poetry in translation today: I don't have to suffer through metrical tricks and the idiotics of rhyme and that special holier-than-thou flavor of poetic diction. The pretentiousness of poetry, which I once thought of as its nobility, I see through. And I see, or think I see, as well the neurosis anxieties of the poets themselves. It has been said that rhyme is a symptom of the schizophrenic; I would not know whether that is true, though I certainly agree with Whitman's observation about rhyme that it is essentially a *comic* or humorous decoration. I would amend this to read: Rhyme is comic and funny except in musical poetry, where sound drowns out sense. And sound poetry, as Ezra Pound observed, is the least translatable. Music cannot be translated, only transposed. Those funny little couplets at the end of roaring Shakespearean speeches always give us a start. We can think of them as a cue, perhaps to the audience, that something of consequence has come to an end. They are also a recall to artificiality.

The prosodic niceties and protective devices had apparently all been abandoned in the early years of the century, but in general they were only scotched, not killed. There is more rhyme and rhythm today than there was in the eighteenth century. True, they are used humoristically and with a different dimension of meaning, but nevertheless they are back in vogue. Unless you are a stylist, as nearly all poets are today, you must search for a reason to go to poetry at all.

J / Jonson, Jeffers, Juvenal, (Pindar), Jones, Jarrell, Joyce

I haven't been able to read Ben Jonson for years, except to teach. Nor Robinson Jeffers. Jeffers seems a humorless ass whose psychological isolation is unbelievable and boring. He is a dilettante of the touch-me-not school of poetry, who took his book-earned German pessimism literally and who knew as little of what was going on in the twentieth century as any writer of note I have ever heard of. Yet, curiously, he had given up the poetic decor, perhaps only superficially, for he certainly hung on to the tragic formulae and even the Freudian melodrama. You might ask: What is it I would have Jeffers do? But that is never a question another man can answer. What he did do, however, lies cold on my bookcase.

I have Juvenal in English, which is so good that I have no desire to read him in Latin. There are Roman poets you cannot read in English with any appreciation: Propertius, for one. Catullus is for the Latin, though he makes a great splash in English. Pindar is supposed to be another poet whose language contains him utterly. I have never found anything worth lingering over in English Pindar, and I can't read his Greek. But I have been convinced by many people for years that Pindar is one reason why you must know Greek.

There is obviously poetry which devolves upon language for its total value. This is a limited form of the art, I think. And at the other extreme there is the poetry in which the perceptions and revelations are of primary importance. In between there are many combinations and nuances of the extremes. My guess is that poetry begins to approach its true and "natural" state when it departs from a special language and the styles which we associate with it. It then approaches prose and eventually becomes prose.

I notice I have jotted down the name of David Jones, the contemporary British poet much acclaimed by T. S. Eliot and W. H. Auden, next to the name of Randall Jarrell. Jones happens to use a style which he adapted from the *Cantos* and "The Waste Land," footnotes and all, and which on the surface seems "free" from the usual mannerisms. But underneath the free style we have a new manner, the mythic-encyclopedia style of the modern learned poet, the poet of history and Culture. His avoidance of the common prosody is certainly in his favor, and his poetics are a great advance over those of the pre-Eliot poets; yet his clerical and God-centered subject matter and argument leave me with no more than a technical admiration for his work.

Jarrell is one of the poets I most prefer. He is curiously not appreciated by his contemporaries, possibly because we are in the midst of an Alexandrian or baroque or neo-classical revival of verse. He writes the best "slack" verse line of anyone in our time, with assurance and with a sensitive knowledge of the rhythms of our kind of speech and writing. He is conversant with tones of speech and gradations of meaning which his fellow poets are unable to cope with; those who insist on the metrical constrictions necessarily limit their acquaintance with living language. Further, he is devoted or addicted to the poetic slant of perception, so that in a sense none of his poems are failures. He will apparently write a poem only when he has perceived. He is consequently what I call a Happy Poet, one who has patience instead of insistence.

The great Jay of our time, the centerpiece of the total modern anthology, is James Joyce. Joyce miraculously embodies in his work the dangerously split character of contemporary artistic man. He is a writer who invents blind alleys down which all writers rush with eyes closed. There are no exits. The world is over. Everything ends in a confusion of sleep, and except that this creature of myths and symbols begins where he ends, there is no escape.

Joyce takes monstrous revenge on history and on literature. He closes all books. When T. S. Eliot first discovered *Ulysses* it seemed to him that Joyce had re-opened the paths to literature for the modern world. Yet the opposite was the case. Joyce was simply reciting the funeral march of the earth, much as in that dirge that Laforge had done. All was over except a solemn procession of magnificent suns. The great book of sleep, which is *Finnegan's Wake*, tells us nothing; it told Joyce's generation everything. Possibly it helped send Eliot to church.

As poetry goes, Joyce is unsurpassed in our century. He is hardly a novelist in any known sense of the word. He writes by syllable, by letter, not by word or phrase or paragraph. He is *par excellence* the poet of our day, and it is in Joyce that the failure of poetry as an art is most brilliantly established. Taking a somewhat Satanic view of his work, you can see in it the most thorough exposé of the insipidity of linguistic poetry that has ever been written. Not a device of ancient or modern rhetoric which is not mercilessly parodied and put in its place; not a literary form or symbol which is not fixed wriggling on a pin; not a language or hero or famous *magnum opus* which is not ticketed and catalogued for the stacks.

Joyce is one of the marvels of the twentieth century, like a skyscraper. He is a feat of engineering.

K / Keats, Kees

I have several well-marked copies of Keats, which I marked up myself about the age of nineteen, when I carried him in my pocket. At a glance at him I see that certain passages, such as the opening of "Endymion," still ring true. I find myself surprised at how much Keats talks about food—apparently he never got enough cream as a child—but mostly I turn away from his mooniness and can't quite believe some of it:

> *thou was the glen:*
> *Thou was the mountain-top—the sage's pen—*
> *The poet's harp—the voice of friends—the sun;*
> *Thou wast the river—thou wast glory won;*
> *Thou wast my clarion's blast—thou wast my steed—*
> *My goblet full of wine—my topmost deed:—*
> *Thou wast the charm of women, lovely Moon!*

And yet there are the great agonized odes and at least one of the greatest English sonnets and Keats's supreme poem, "La Belle Dame Sans Merci," which stands in relation to his other works like "The Ancient Mariner" to Coleridge's. Keats, after all, is a lover's poet and perhaps can only be understood or felt by the young, though

I doubt if the young of this generation carry Keats in the glove compartment. Allow me to recommend it. But Keats is perennially young and perennially dying; he came of a time when death and youth were intimates. In our time the very idea produces rage and indignation. Even my remark about Keats's cream was a kind of twentieth-century reaction about his tuberculosis. Romantic poets loved life and died young, or so we think of them. Modern poets destroy themselves fast or slow in one way or another.

Opening at random the poems of Weldon Kees, a modern poet whose city I lived in and who apparently leaped from the Golden Gate Bridge, I read:

> The surgical mask, the rubber teat
> Are singed, give off an evil smell.
> You seem to weep more now that heat
> Spreads everywhere we look.
> It says here none of us is well.

It must have been Baudelaire or some theologian who said that the whole world is a hospital, a curse that has been ricocheting off the consciousness of poetry for at least a hundred years. I myself have never understood the suicidal impulse, being too Keatsian perhaps. And between the Romantic dream of continuity and the modern nightmare of self-destruction modern poetry has decided for the latter. Possibly the difference is one of attention. The Romantic poet attended to Nature or what he thought of as Nature. The modern poet has only contempt for Nature—anyhow he can't be bothered with such trivia—and an even greater contempt for Man, with a capital M. Modern poetry, as any paperback textbook will tell you, is anti-humanistic and at the same time urban. This means that the poets are city dwellers who live in the city only because the countryside is worse. Ours, as it has been said in many ways, is a poetry of sensibility, a poetry in which art emotion has superseded ordinary emotion and feeling.

I have been lugging this subject in from time to time; it is an old obsession of mine. Once upon a time I blamed the poets for not being able to see beyond their poems, for taking all the stereotypes of the Symbolists and the *poètes maudits* and using them as rubber stamps. Today I see many more sides to the question. One is the psychological inability of the poet to find a place in the modern world and the underlying suspicion he has that poetry is obsolete. It is interesting that both Eliot and Pound hated jazz and modern painting at the time when they were planning their *démarche* upon twentieth-century poetry. What Anglo-American poetry lacked that the other arts didn't was a sense of liberation. The Pound-Eliot philosophy is one of high achievement, hierarchies of value, and strategies of education. While seeming to be avant-garde they were so only for purposes of maneuver or through a true perception of the failure of forms, which might have frightened them. It is significant that Eliot abandoned all experimentation in poetry, though not in philosophy and other matters, after "The Waste Land" and never cared to understand what William Carlos Williams was up to. Pound, who was always farther out on a limb, kept close contact with Williams, as if to find an excuse for his own radicalism.

It is certainly true that other arts, especially painting, have adopted an aesthetic of art emotion over whatever art emotion is over and that suicide is not unknown to the modern painter either. My feeling as a "layman" in painting, however, is that painting is in touch with the street. I mean that the street accepts the painting. It does not accept the poem. A painter is a better insurance risk than a poet.

And everyone knows that music, even of the most abstract or scientific or intellectual variety, has achieved the sense of freedom. If it is laughed at it is no longer beaten to death. The same can be said of the most *outré*, far-out, farfetched, obscene, or whatever novel. And none of this can be said for poetry.

If I seem to be arguing for the death of poetry that is not it. I am presenting what I think to be certain facts. Poetry seems to be killing itself off, and poets as well.

Or what has for so long sailed under the name of poetry.

I could describe poetry as it is as a set of stock poetic responses infinitely refined and buttressed up by an immense and traditional prestige. Why is it that the poets have failed to respond to their own predicament?

Poetic death is the rule rather than the exception. The poetry of death, the death of poets, the hospital view of the world—some of this is too true to be mentioned. But it is such a limited and ill-considered truth that you are sometimes tempted to place poetry in the category of phrenology and numerology. Though even there—if only poetry were interested in what science ignores and fears, such as the fact of individuation, it would give itself some life. But there is the modern poem, outraged at science, turning its back on contemporary middle-class life (which is the majority rule in most of the Western world), inventing new labels for the old containers, immortally rewriting the same six poems. I am probably not the first skeptic to say that modern poetry is an industry, an industry that refuses the use of real money but which has a value all its own, which in turn does have a certain market value, not for groceries, but for cultural institutionalism.

And yet there are no people with whom I feel more natural than poets. They are the tribe that speaks my language. With a poet either it is not necessary to speak or speech is all nonsensical happiness. Poets in the most limited definition are those who have the highest sensitivity to speech. A poet can tell more about a stranger by the few words he says than a psychologist can in a year. Words are what he knows the world and others by. Rather, knowledge to him is musical verbiage. I don't want to produce more epigrammatic rabbits out of empty hats, but I am trying to say something about the limits of the artist. Other people, Serious People, have varieties of techniques for knowledge and communication. The artist generally has only one, his particular medium.

I saw films that Weldon Kees made. They were good. And they were deadly. They were transcriptions of the

modern poem, his poems and all of our poems. Scenes
that were almost stills of the dumps and backyards of
San Francisco. There was never a living thing except once
a bird on a garbage can. I understand that despair perfectly without being able to join in it to the death. I
know it and believe it, and I see no other idiom if you
are so directed. But I reject it. Stylized despair is not
enough. But no one can be so cruel as to call it that for
a man who takes his life. I can only conclude that I do
not understand the suicide of poetry.

L / Lawrence

My *L*'s are formidable. There is a whole shelf of D. H.
Lawrence, half of it worthless commentaries, but anything
with the name of Lawrence on it is immediately put under
my personal lock and key. There are also Leopardi and
Lautréamont and Edward Lear, each more terrifying at
one time or another than the next. There are Robert
Lowell and a couple of his ancestors. And there are William Ellery Leonard, another suicide, and Garcia Lorca.
It's enough to start a religion based on letters, as many
religions must have been. There is also one item left over
from my childhood, a once beautiful white and gold "Hiawatha" which came from the library of the lady who wrote
Little Lord Fauntleroy (I think it was a lady). "Hiawatha"
has always given me a feeling of sadness; it is such a *wrong*
poem and it should have been something else, God knows
what. Maybe before long someone will discover that it is
the great anti-poem of the nineteenth century.

Lawrence has no reputation as a twentieth-century
poet. Or so I gather from the anthologies and from what
criticism of him I have read. Or he is someone who wrote
powerful, "seminal" novels and diatribes and who dabbled
in poetry. I disagree with this view and think of him as
perhaps the best poet of the twentieth century in our
language. This shows where my criteria are and perhaps
explains the simplicity of my poetics. Not all of his poetry

appeals to me; the early "Georgian" lyrics are as good as anybody in England was writing in the early years of the century and had a good deal more meat on their bones, but they were mannered according to the mode. Lawrence was trying to break out of the portion of society he was imprisoned in and played the game for a while. But the minute he had the bit in his teeth he was gone forever from polite literature. That is my view of him, a man who was suspicious of literature and the Life Literary, as he was of patriots and coal-mine landlords.

One reason why I think of Lawrence as the best poet of the twentieth century was that he was not a *great* poet. He never wanted to be. If I read him correctly he thought great poets were pompous idiots whose sense of values were those of fashion designers or politicians. All of that miserable and self-important bickering about forms and symbols and correcting taste would have made him retch. Lawrence was not a literary chap but a prophet and an ancient mariner. Having mastered the art of writing at a fairly early age, he dropped it. He was an anti-artist in full bloom. His escape from England was as much an escape from English literature as it was from the climate and the middle class.

Lawrence's ideas are not interesting. Or rather, the interesting thing about them is that they freed him from the art world and left him alone to observe from without. All the same he is a poet, having stripped down the poem to its nudity. What he did was to deny it as art and to employ it as a tool for his particular kind of evangelism. Insofar as any modern writer has been able to do this, Lawrence refashioned the poem into a Stone Age ax. I believe that his Stone Age-ism was sincere and not a device of the sophisticate. Although he is a poet of negation, which makes him belong to our time, he is not concerned with sabotage for its own sake: Lawrence is really trying to clear the way for the human condition by getting rid of its monuments and roadblocks.

The brilliant thing about his poems (that is, the ones I like) is that he perceives beauty in terms of function.

This is why poets like Eliot were afraid of him. Instead of a hierarchy of functions or a bestiary in which Nature existed for the edification of Man (the Fundamentalist theology of most modern poetry), Lawrence saw the meaning of the particularity of beauty. There is no other poet in the modern canon who can look at a fig tree or a kangaroo or a bat, at a horse or the cross in the shell of a turtle, at eagles and of course goats, at grapes and cyclamens, and at the Evangelistic Beasts and see them! Them —the things themselves. When Lawrence looked at a peach he saw what was there. Then he gave it to someone.

> *Why the groove?*
> *Why the lovely, bivalve roundness?*
> *Why the ripple down the sphere?*
> *Why the suggestion of incision?*

Man is not superior to the animal, nor woman to a peach. Quite the contrary. Woman is that which uncontrollably exfoliates. Beauty is a by-product of nature, not an end result, not certainly a function of the intellect. Lawrence struck terror into the hearts of the literati. Culture to him was the pap of self-consciousness, the detritus of intellectual landowners, the festering carbuncle of civilization. Lawrence, I think, recognized the ridiculous romanticism of his gesture; but he had no alternative. He did in fact feel at one with the sub-mental function of grasses and elephants and runaway gypsies. He had the healthy instincts of the animal to get away from foulness, and now and then to return to his vomit. Lawrence's hatreds are sometimes childish, sometimes prissy and effeminate, sometimes mere vanity; but on the whole they are hatreds grounded in pure physical revulsion for the horror of human conceit, cruelty, and savagery. He was not an exoticist, though he was something of an idealist, a man who, had he been involved in politics, would have lent himself to disastrous world enterprises. He flirted with fascism in Australia.

Mostly, Lawrence is concerned with the avoirdupois of things. Living things. This is part of his mysticism. He perceives the balances of forms of life, literal forms, in motion. Nothing is static, as with Robert Frost, whose handsome bestiaries always doubt the value of the function. Frost will admire a mosquito only if its intelligence impresses him as commensurable with human intelligence. Lawrence has no such spectrum of intelligence. He will play around with the sound and gestures of the mosquito and compare the thing to a Frenchman, for instance, but in the end he gives in and demands equal rights for the insect. But Lawrence has the power of the *sauvage* to become mosquito or turtle or elephant; he has the power of mimicry which is not parody and outsidedness but the gift of identification. Or rather, of propitiation. Lawrence hated a thing to become not-itself. And because he demanded this selfness from Lawrence, he recognized it in all things. Consequently, he could perceive the outlines of the other. And he could perceive the outlines of the genera of poems, nearly all of which he rejected as feeble emanations of human cultural conceit. Lawrence has little or nothing to say about English poetry, except the evangelistic sections of the Bible. Shakespeare he sweeps away *in toto*, with his left hand. Knocking off Shakespeare in a pettish little poem seems as childlike as Shelley demolishing God. Except that what Lawrence says about Shakespeare is true in every sense. The poem is a bad, doggerel poem; what other form could it take? Its import is that of an unreconstructed primitivist.

I have not said what I wanted about Lawrence. This seems to be the case with Lawrence admirers. And I have been remarking only about a handful of his poems. The poems called "Nettles" and "Pansies" are as important to me *as poetry* as anything he wrote. These are little catty slurs about politics and persons and objects within his momentary view, marginalia. Yet they satisfy the provenance of the poem to me. They are like a one-man Greek Anthology, small fragments of poetry gouged into the ugly plastic of the modern consciousness. It was Lawrence who saw modern man as robot, woman as gutta-percha sunning her synthetic flesh on the beaches. And it was Lawrence who resurrected Christ in the symbol of sex. The beautiful parable or novel called *The Man Who Died* is not only a poem of blasphemy against the religion of restraint, nor is it merely modern intellectual priapism. It is rather another of the great cries of triumph of the Dionysian artist of our time: Whitman as against Poe and Baudelaire; Rimbaud as against Eliot; Lautréamont as against Yeats; Lorca as against Frost. In *The Man Who Died* the resurrection is the erection. It is God made *flesh.*

From Lautréamont to Robert W. Service

Something reminds me of a major omission in my roll call: the name of William Gaddis. I had forgotten him because I give away each copy of his novel *The Recognitions* I get my hands on; I force it on people. And my forgetting was a little traumatic: some time ago I was in the process of publishing a special issue of the magazine I edited devoted to Gaddis. There was so much material that I thought of two issues. Writers, critics, and scholars from all over the world were going to contribute to the resurrection of this gigantic, all but unknown American masterpiece of a novel. Its theme is counterfeiting, the spiritual counterfeiting of our time and place. Unfortunately, I lost the editorship of my publication. Or rather I resigned as editor after a few local smut-hounds, fundamentalists, and administrators banned some story I had accepted for publication. I went on the radio and read the story and so published it, in the old-fashioned sense. Everyone was disappointed that it wasn't obscene, irreverent, and in bad taste, which is what a local newspaper called me. Gaddis got lost in the shuffle. The novel is published by Harcourt.

L / Lautréamont, Lorca, Lear

Lautréamont (whose name really begins with a D),
Lorca, and Lear make a trio. Lorca was murdered by
Franco's men. Lautréamont, who died in 1870, is said to
have been murdered under similar circumstances by agents
of the French government and because of the fact that
he was a Socialist. Edward Lear, an English contemporary
of Lautréamont, was a kind of court jester to certain
nobility and lived to a ripe old age. What they have in
common is Nonsense.

As everyone knows who has ever thought about it, there
is no such thing as nonsense. There are only efforts in
that direction. In poetry, successful nonsense is almost
always a triumph over Seriousness. Nonsense has one
virtue which great poetry lacks: it clears the mind. It de-
flates. The moment a nonsensical poet makes his appearance, he is in danger. Lautréamont, with his great
glob of blasphemy against the dignity of institutions and
sacred cows, is still being lynched in effigy. Lear, with his
purely absurd version of Victorian society, is also suspect.
Like all such writers, Lewis Carroll or Mark Twain, he
is kept in mothballs by the cautionary insistence that he
is a nursery poet. The Mother Goose rhymes are also
said to be for the nursery. They are and they aren't.
Mother Goose is a poet of such cunning and brutality
and inanity that she has been virtually banned in America
for many years. A rational people will tolerate no such
baby-sitter. You have probably seen the bowdlerized
Mother Goose in which you don't take the old man by
his left leg and throw him downstairs but you take his
right hand and kiss him.

Lorca, who was assassinated by the police orthodoxy of
Europe within this generation, was in love with nonsense.
For Lorca it was the tongue of fury and of glorification
of his death-ridden country. Sometimes there is no other
course for the poet but the nonsensical. This may be such
a time. I use the term with or without quotes; it may
mean "obscure" or "surreal" or "primitive." Spain has

given us Gongorism, Picasso, Lorca, and the best of surrealism. Lawrence hated the death-compulsiveness of Spain; so did the great Spanish artists. There is the Spain consecrated to the endless death of the spirit and the Spain of its half-demented artists and poets. There is only one Goya, one Cervantes, one El Greco, all artists of distortion. Lorca himself is Spanish baroque like the Escorial, which hypnotized Gerard Manley Hopkins and helped him discover his style. Lorca too is a nursery poet. The innocent ballad or not so innocent of the *gitano* he turned into weapons to torture the Church and the State. He was a marked man. Spain has its Civil Guard again and its priests, but its great martyrs and exiles have helped revolutionize all the arts of the modern world.

M / MacNeice, Melville, Mallarmé, Mencken, Mailer

The alphabet is bisected by the *M. M* is a big letter and means a thousand. It also stands for Mother. I imagine that poets who are *M*'s have certain things in common: Mickiewicz, Milton, Mencken, Melville, Malinowski, who is the poet of the savage, Mallarmé, Marianne Moore, and Norman Mailer. *M*'s seem to run toward Romanticism, even when like Mallarmé they run it into the ground. One of my favorite twentieth-century poets is Louis MacNeice, who managed in an extraordinary way to remain outside the ideological arenas. He is an exception to *M*. If, a thousand years from now, you were looking for a poet who had captured the tincture of the twentieth century, MacNeice would probably be the best example or guide. While all his fellow *M*'s run toward millennialism, MacNeice was content to celebrate the perfections and contentments of our world and of himself. Possibly his worldliness saved him from the idealism of his fellows.

Before the Fall man lived in the Trobriand Islands. The Islanders believed, as Adam did, that man had no part in the procreation of man. Eve had laboriously to explain the facts of life to her husband. It says this on

page one of the Bible. Milton, as generations of poets
and critics have pointed out, was dissatisfied with the
rules of order of Paradise and reveled in the Fall. Almost
all the true poetry in his epic is pagan or Satanic; the
theological stuff is deadly. It was Milton's good-looking
Satan who brought into the world all the Byrons and Don
Giovannis of our modern age: those who would save the
world through Sin and those who die for the liberation
of new worlds. As we tend to view the Islanders as inhabitants of Eden, so do we romantically wish to destroy
their paradises, and do. All paradises are destroyed by the
romantic millennialists because they know there is a
better paradise the next time. Mickiewicz was the nineteenth-century Polish poet who invented Romanticism
for his country. He is their Byron, Whitman, and Goethe.
The M's are nature worshipers and believe in many gods
and in the godliness of mankind. They are also mystical
without being mystics. Each constructs a mystique, to use
the popular word of our time. Mallarmé mysticized poetry
into something like a religion. Poetry was, he discovered,
l'explication orphique de la terre. Poetry explication probably begins with the remark. And while there are no
noble savages in Mallarmé there are plenty of fauns and
satyrs and ice-cold priestesses. But Melville knew the
Gardens of Eden of Polynesia at firsthand; but true American that he was, he set out to hunt down the primitive
consciousness of the whale. 'The awful and infuriated
whale turns upon the ship, symbol of this civilized world
of ours," as Lawrence puts it. "She sank, taking with her
Negro and Indian and Polynesian, Asiatic and Quaker
and good, businesslike Yankees and Ishmael; she sank all
the lot of them." Melville had his revenge on the evil
white consciousness of the modern world. But he knew
that white consciousness had triumphed after all. Polynesia was a boyhood dream.

In our time the road to Paradise is reached by way of
the soapbox. There is a larger literature of protest today
than ever before, and it is all (to use a current vulgarism)
utopia-directed. What political view the protestor takes is

beside the point, for in general the protest is not construc-
tive but aims at abolishing our bourgeois way of life. In
scuttling middle-class values you must go either up or
down: down to the dream of the noble savage or up to
some ideal of static order.

I grew up, as a Baltimorean, much under the influence
of H. L. Mencken. Mencken was the highest type of
journalist, which is the lowest type of writer. He was
also a humorist. What Mencken's spectrum of values
was is almost impossible to say; he was a kind of Nie-
tzschean of the turn of the century variety. His atheism was
of the fashionable sort which serves the purpose of calling
attention to your other activities; it was bait for what he
called the Booboisie. He retained also a vestigial German-
ism, even with a flavor of militarism, though Mencken
was no Junker. He discovered certain writers among his
contemporaries, such as Sinclair Lewis, but he also claimed
to find genius in Hergesheimer and James Branch Cabell.
What really kept him going was a kind of good-natured
anger, frequently fake. He burlesqued every aspect of
democracy without ever pausing to consider the alternatives. Possibly my own tendency to take the other side of
almost any argument came from my early exposure to
Mencken and the fact that he outraged all right-thinking
people. It was from Mencken that I first learned how to
shock the Squares. In the long run Mencken might have
had a wider effect on a couple of generations of writers
than is suspected. But at bottom you must consider him
as stodgy and unimaginative as the clumsiest, beer-swill-
ing burgher. He saw nothing in poetry, for instance, not
because he had worked his way beyond it but because
he did not understand that it was one of the subtler
dimensions of language.

The name of Norman Mailer (who has certain things
in common with Mencken) strikes the same terror into
the hearts of this generation of bourgeoisie as Mencken's
did in his time. But the differences are vast. In the first
place Mailer is a creative artist of a very high order;
second, he has an organizing as well as an analytical mind;

and third, Mailer is personally as well as intellectually infuriated by the world around him. Mailer is much more deeply offensive than Mencken, who was simply a gadfly and a Middle Atlantic Till Eulenspiegel. American intellectualism has come a long way since the Twenties. For one thing it has absorbed and frequently rejected the great ideologies of our age: Marxism, Freudianism, fascism, Scientism, Buddhism in various forms, expatriatism, bohemianism, and so forth. Mailer is glib, brilliant, and apparently capable of juggling any number of ideologies without making a fool of himself. If he writes poetry that sets the teeth of "professional" poets on edge, that is both his privilege and his form of protest at the moment. If he is violent in action he is simply taking literally his own existential philosophy. *The Naked and the Dead* may be a *tour de force*, but it is also a satire on war fiction and something of a burlesque of the Great American Novel. Mailer is a critic, an encyclopedist in the old sense. He alphabetizes and editorializes every American act and event, no matter how trivial. He is obsessed by our violence and determined to track down its sources. He fights fire with fire. "Our time," he says, "is obsessed with sex as blood, as murder, as adultery, orgy, and rape." But a few sentences later he adds: "Talk of pornography ought to begin at the modern root: advertising." America is out of joint with Nature and has dehumanized itself by putting the cart before the horse; or in Mailer's powerfully unlovely language: ". . . and if we die too soon with too little, our senses lost before our leaving, no one to mourn us but that three-hundred-horsepower chromium cunt in the cement-brick garage—well, death is better for the race than consciousness, . . . for with consciousness might come a cataclysm of history, a shift from the manipulator to his human material, and then, all horror of the void, what can eternity offer to a defeated power?"

To the modern artist like Mailer it is almost better for the race to die by its own hand, as it seems to be doing, than to continue counterfeiting life. Mailer has raised the monotonous howl of protest to its greatest volume. As a technique, noise has long superseded argument. Even so, he can modulate his tone; in fact, as a craftsman he is in the category of Joyce. The excess of artistry sometimes seems gratuitous. And I prefer the essay style to the fiction. The poems (if they are poems) also seem to have a self-value as well as a nuisance value.

N / Nin, Nietzsche, Neruda, Nerval, Neill

N is the refinement of *M*, and without stacking the index, I find Nietzsche, Pablo Neruda, Anäis Nin, Gerard de Nerval, and Alexander Neill. In my youth, under the influence of Mencken, I read Nietzsche's *The Anti-Christ* in Mencken's translation. I have always had a copy of *Zarathustra* in every inner sanctum of my own and if I knew German would probably try to translate it myself. I admire as well *The Birth of Tragedy*, his first work. All the Dionysians, including the world-destroyers, center around Nietzsche.

The works of Anäis Nin, still an unknown, original genius (as the Russians used to say) and of our own time and place, well, they baffle description. They are poetry of the kind that has been discovered by a growing number of modern writers, the poetry of self which surpasses fiction and revolutionizes it. It would seem to others that hers is the work of a purely feminine sensibility, a kind of modern Jane Austen, but I think not. Technically surrealist, she is one of those writers who erased the line between poetry and fiction.

Pablo Neruda is a surrealist of viciousness, a gaucho of communism, a Stalinist of the bedroom, a Lorca without children. "Unfortunately," he says, "I have nothing to give you but fingernails or eyelashes or melted pianos." You would have thought all the pianos had melted long ago, all the urns of ashes dumped, but in South America there is still, as in Spain, much blood dying to be spilled. In a way it is optimistic poetry because it still believes in revolution, with the worldly *Paradiso* at the end.

Nerval's real name began with an L, but what difference does that make? He chose N. Before he settled on
N, he tried R, G, F, P, B, and E but finally named himself after a field and the Emperor Nerva, adding a *de* to
separate himself from the bourgeoisie. He clowned in the
best bohemian manner of a century or so ago, fell in love
with actresses, drank wine out of skulls, went to the
Orient where he purchased a Javanese girl whom he
tried to give away because she ate onions in bed, and
eventually hanged himself. Nerval was hallucinated or
what we call schizophrenic. He could perceive experience
outside of time, and it is this that endears him to us.
He was a Dionysian Dandy. He can imagine Notre Dame
cathedral in ruins, like an ox reduced to a massive skeleton by a wolf, and in the same second watch its recon-
struction in the imagination of future tourists.

"Next slide." Alexander Neill is a Scotsman who gave
up a professorship in English Literature to help destroy
the whole idea of cultural discipline. He is today a very
old man whose school called Summerhill in Sussex is the
most radical experiment in education ever attempted
anywhere. The students need learn nothing. You can
spend the years from kindergarten to college age without
ever learning to read or write. Others, if they so wish,
become doctors or writers or waiters or engineers or ditch-
diggers. The only thing forbidden in this world is Thou
Shalt Not. It is a world in which taboo itself has been
exorcised. Neill is a kind of Kropotkin anarchist who believes and knows that people living in groups come to one
another's aid out of natural impulse. Boys and girls live
together, and if there is freedom of love there is little
incidence of pregnancy, perhaps Neill's one concession to
England. The whole philosophy is based on education
without fear. Children or young adults coming from the
outside world may take months or years to recover from
past disciplines. All of them eventually do to a greater or
lesser degree. There is no regard for "manners" or "morals"
or religious dogma or faith or ethics. Yet the Royal Com-
mission of Education, which examines the school from

time to time, gives it a good rating as an educational institution. That is amusing.

O / Ovid, Olsen, Ortega, Orwell

O is for Ovid, Ortega, Charles Olsen, and George Orwell. Ovid is a big O, as much for his book on the rites of love, which every poet wants to write and in one way or another succeeds in writing, as for his exile and his metamorphoses. The pagan recognition of the sympathies and antipathies of the higher forces is in a sense the biggest step poetry has so far taken. Pagan poetry like modern physics knew that the fine line between subject and object was a wavy, variable line. The gods can be persuaded. With the pantheon pagan man had more than diplomatic relations. Man was a power whose only defect was mortality. Or rather, mortality was the greatest gift of the gods. Man had something the gods had not: he could die. Who then was the god?

Charles Olsen is a disciple of Pound, and I like him for that. Pound in the long run is the best modern master, if you need masters.

Ortega, or what I know of him, is another Spanish revolutionist and an intellectual anti-intellectual. He says that the intellectual barely lives. "It is undeniable," says Ortega, "that a large part of science and literature has . . . been produced in a somnambulistic trance; that is to say, by creatures who are not at all intelligent." I don't know of any other writer in our century who has hit this particularly important nail on the head. The key word is *somnambulistic*, a word not unknown to modern literature as one of the symbols of our age.

Literary and scientific somnambulism has given birth to our world of comforting devices: our hospitals, which are combinations of the movie house and concentration camp. Our schools, which are combinations of federal penitentiary and the Chamber of Commerce. Our laboratories, where men dress in white and enact laws which make murder respectable on the military and hygienic levels. Our publishing industries, where all human action is reduced to a sentimental foulness and *faisandage*, where even Bibles are turned into dirt. Our religions, which compete with the art museum and the psychoanalyst's den. Our factories, which are more brilliant than palaces, whose executives go to the tops of mountains to study Aristotle. By courtesy of the Ford Foundation.

Somnambulism has become a universal way of life in the Western world, led by America, where sleep may be the national industry. Or rather sleepwalking. The one cry of American writers and artists (those more or less not asleep) has been from the beginning: Wake up! To arms, citizens! Which in this country means: Have a cup of coffee. The way I see modern somnambulistic society is this: there are only two classes of people in the United States, the bourgeoisie and the artists. Between them there is no communication. Not that these two classes are at war, as they were in the past; on the contrary. The bourgeoisie—that is, everybody except artists—no longer hate the painter and the poet; rather, they dreamily accept the artist and even his work. And this acceptance drives the artist to invent louder and louder alarm clocks. But the bourgeoisie slumber on.

I have a deep and uninvolved respect for George Orwell, who is in some ways the perfection of the modern intellectual and artist. Orwell as an Englishman had that extraordinary discipline of the man who knows that he is nothing but part of an Order. He loathed the Order, though it had molded him. He was a hard, gem-like flame with tuberculosis. He was not a hater. Neither was he a lover. Lawrence escaped from the realistic horrors of the English working class and middle class by kidnaping the bosomy and titled Frieda von Richtofen. Errol Flynn couldn't have been more dashing. Frieda's bosoms are plastered all over Lawrence's books. Lawrence, like Keats, needed that heavenly rise and fall. Not Orwell. Orwell was an Englishman who would never have drowsed into the question: Do I love England? Or even, Do I love life? Orwell was a man, by which I mean that he was conscious of his hide and considered it part of his homo sapiens. He was without self-defense and therefore without cultural poise. He was Orwell. (His real name, incidentally, was Eric Blair, which was enough to turn anybody into a writer. Eric Blair is the name of a small boy in a ruff.) George Orwell is a noncommittal, anonymous name, like Winston Smith, a name you might take for the Secret Service. It is, in any case, the name of a man who knows that there is no point in loving yourself. Orwell is of that superior type of modern man whose disillusionments lie deeper than bitterness. He is funny without gaiety, absurd without hope. This is why he failed to understand the laughter of Henry Miller, or rather why he was perhaps in awe of it. Orwell is a poet of misery. Suffering lies next door to happiness or insanity. To Miller, misery is merely a matter of bad luck; he can shrug it off. But in his confidence that misery is only a symptom of stupidity, Miller faces the deeper condition of suffering and can see into the abyss.

There is a radical difference between the American writer and the English of our time. The English tend to be political in their sensibility, which is to say that they work within the framework of a tradition. There has probably not been an English revolutionary writer since Godwin (unless Alexander Neill is an example). The British revolutionary Marxists of the Thirties were all considered bourgeois by Moscow, as in fact they were. Orwell took the only course open to the English writer with a political orientation and became a sympathizer with the anarchists.

The British writer may loathe government by politics, but he observes that English power is a moral or cultural force and can forgive the blindness or greed of the political man. The American writer cannot regard American power as anything but what it is, power perpetuated by the Marines. The absence of any urbanity in American political behavior, to put it gently, further alienates the American artist, who always tends to see the sellout and the prostitution of values in our political life rather than anything favorable. This is true even in the popular imagination, in movies and musical comedies and popular fiction in which the politician is always represented either as a bona fide procurer or petty thief or as a kind of Dostoevskyan idiot who makes good. Abraham Lincoln is always pictured as the latter, as is George Washington. They were heroes because their hearts were pure. Thomas Jefferson never figures as a hero of the American myth because Jefferson was cold and proud and above all an intellectual, a *philosophe*. *Philosophes* don't throw silver dollars across the Potomac or tell earthy jokes to get elected.

William Carlos Williams, in one of his early books, tried to write an American history beginning with Eric the Red. It is unknown except by a few students and writers. American writers in general grow hysterical when they think of the realities of our history and our present ignorance of it. Ezra Pound is a good example.

P / Poe, Pope, Perse, Pound

Pound brings us to P: St. John Perse (really an L), Edgar Allan Poe, Péguy, Alexander Pope, and Ezra Pound.

Poe is the great ambiguity of American letters, our first and strangely our most influential writer, even today, if we credit such things as science fiction, modern poetry, and spook puzzles. I don't feel I have anything to say about him; everything has been said and said perhaps too well by such writers as Lawrence and Eliot and Tate. For Poe is less a literary figure than a force. In every way he epitomizes the poet and his opposite, the man of reason. Ratiocination, to use his word; for Poe could not reason in any common sense of the word. He was a born martyr and the first American dandy, a histrio, a gentleman and a death's-head of the aristocratic. As auspices go, it is a bad omen that he is our first man of creative genius. The speed with which he was imported into France is alarming. England has still not heard of his tintinnabulations.

Alexander Pope is too close to modern Academic poetry, which he helped found, for me to be articulate about. Not that I dislike Pope; on the contrary. But it is many years since I have opened his well-wrought books. When I do I am startled by their kind of excellence, *excellentia in vacuo,* if that's Latin.

Perse is a modern Frenchman whose early books I admire deeply and whose late ones I admire, when I follow them, in a different way. French poetry is so proud of itself that it makes me want to laugh; it certainly has a right to be proud, but you would like it someday to get off its high horse. This is very unlikely to happen.

P is for Pound. For many years I wrote articles and reviews trying to bring Pound to book. He has been an obsession of mine ever since I learned to read modern poetry. I would say today that he is still the most interesting artist of poetry of our time, the one who had both the best insights about contemporary poetry and the best solutions to its problems.

I am not concerned about making these remarks consistent with any I have made in the past, in the event that anyone should go to the trouble of comparing them.

Pound occupies a strange chair in poetic history. He is a great inventor who is his own capitalist. Or rather— and I mean this in a way which I would like to be construed charitably—he is a Henry Ford, a man who got the bugs out of the poem and who mass-produced his invention. As Henry Ford wished to put every American on wheels and did, Ezra Pound wanted to saturate America with great poetry of every clime and age. And in a way he too succeeded. Pound as much as any man has been responsible for the wide circulation of the classics in this country, though he professed to be horrified at such a thing.

Pound has a low opinion of the drama and a high opinion of the epic. He has a low opinion of Whitman and a high opinion of Dante. Without religion he seeks a metaphysic in Confucius. He is very Palladian, a Jeffersonian gone to seed. He knows, as all American poets do, that poetry is sissy and he has to learn to play rough. One way to do this is to play politics, *realpolitik*. To get his country off the dead surface of the stereotyped political images he goes to the absolute extreme without actually breaking off relations.

Pound was also a declared anti-semite. The word is now obsolete, though the thing is not. Pound's anti-semitism has a date on it. All American writers of his generation are anti-semitic, anti-Negro, anti-Asiatic, and so forth. Eliot and Pound are not alone. Williams, if you read his fiction, was the same. Cummings also. Wallace Stevens, Fitzgerald, Dreiser, Mencken—you can't name a writer of the early twentieth century who wouldn't answer to the accusation. This anti-semitism was grounded not in fear or in religious belief but in cultural embarrassment, snobbishness. The modern American resented being identified with the foreigner, the melting-pot immigrant, or what the European called our mongrel race. Pound left this country so long ago, as did Eliot, that their anti-semitism can only be considered provincial. For it is only in the last generation that Americans have given up ridicule of foreigners as a way of asserting their equality with them.

I have never read anything about Pound that made more than fragmentary sense, and I have never read anything about him that was not true. To put this in more basic English: no one has seen anything whole about Pound because this is impossible. For one thing, when you say "Pound" you mean both the man and his writings. Criticism tries to help him along to the stacks by asserting that his works are the man, that he is above his acts, good, bad, and indifferent. He is his personae. And this too is true and is part of the trouble. Pound could never make a clear distinction between life and poetry and ended up having poetry at the expense of life. He is possibly the most addicted *littérateur* of our age, comparable to Flaubert of the last century in his amazement that people

outside the life of art can demonstrate any sense of value.
(This was the antithetical attraction between Doc Williams and Pound: you suppose that Pound would have had
difficulty in tying his shoes, while Williams was tying
all those umbilical cords among the slums of New Jersey.)

My feeling for Pound's *Cantos* has grown with the years,
as much for their excellence as for their inevitability.
Pound, though he is sociologically dated as an American
animal (species 1910 or thereabouts), is quintessentially
an American poet. If the *Cantos* are not the Great American Poem, there will never be one.

Juxtaposition is old stuff in modern literature, but in
Pound (and this is what is typical) the past is always
contrasted with the present, to the detriment of the present. This is nothing new: if there is one law of Modern
Poetry, whether in Poe or Baudelaire or the "Cornbelt
Metaphysicals," it is that the present either gets it in the
neck or suffers a cultural snub. I have wished for years
to write a book about or simply make a list of the great,
fine, noble, liberating, heroic deeds, acts, artifacts, and
men of our age. Yet you postpone this praise, for it would
be certain to be debased by creatures and powers who
defame praise and associate it with softening of the brain.
If a young poet should ask me what to do I would tell
him: Praise something, anything. It does sound like
Pollyanna.

Critics differentiate between the American *révolté* and
the European *révolté*. The American man who revolts is
always considered an adolescent; the European in revolt
can be and commonly is an intellectual. Everyone under
the age of twenty in America is expected to kick over the
traces. After that, if he doesn't give in he is an "artist,"
which is a form of late adolescence and for which there are
specified places, asylums and skid rows and creative writing
classes. The American artist cannot recapitulate the artistic
gesture of the declassed artist of Europe because here
the artist is no longer declassed; only the *révolté* is. No
country in the world has given the artist more oppor-
tunities than the United States since the Renaissance.

One Pound critic, a good one, in an essay called "The Revolt of Ezra Pound," says that "Pound stands a much better chance of being understood by Europeans than by us. . . . We lack the *révolté* tradition and . . . the day may come when we are not even capable of imagining it. . . . *Révolté* is un-American."

Would it be too much to say that all Pound wanted was to be a poet? That is what he wanted. But the country he came from didn't want poets and certainly not A POET. Insofar as the American mentality—I won't use the word *sensibility*—goes, when it sees the word *poet*, it responds: Poet, go home. And poets go home. And where is home? Europe. Not because Europe loves poets; it has killed most of them. But because in Europe the individual can pursue his private aberration, which is against the law in the United States of America.

So the cultural orientation of American poetry is always a drive to the East. To the East Coast of the United States, thence to Europe, eventually to the Orient. But the world is round and has no frontier, and you end up in California. Pound stopped in the best place in the world for artists, which is a cross between California and England and antiquity and the East.

I would nominate Pound as the poet of the greatest poem (lower case) of our time because he throws in Homer and Cavalcanti and Rihaku and the kitchen sink and lets order take care of itself. It is the formlessness of the *Cantos* that makes them possible.

R / Rilke, Rimbaud, Ramakrishna, Roethke, Ransom, Rexroth

I have more Rilke books than I know what to do with; about as many Rimbaud: Roethke; a bona fide Ramakrishna bible sent me by an American convert; Herbert Read, the anarchist baronet; a bit of Edwin Arlington Robinson; and as rational renegades, I. A. Richards and Racine.

It is a long time since I fell out of love with Rilke. Nowadays I don't know what it is that bound me to him when other poets my age were addicted to Eliot or Hart Crane. Rilke is so much the poet of the perfect poem who in the long run is *too* recessive, too guilty, too sensitive. Of all the exiles from modern life, he is the sweetest, the most reflective, this puppy of minor princesses, like Lawrence, who is a rabid tiger beside Rilke. I would imagine that Rilke is the Keats of our time, murdered, as one valentine legend has it, by a rose. Or a castle. Or a unicorn. Like Ezra Pound, Rilke lived poetry after turning away from what poetry is made of. He watched life always at the edge of the crowd, always more in front of the painting than in it. At the end there was the great burst of the *Elegies* and the *Sonnets,* a mixture of a not very convincing angelology and a mystique of the sensual. Rilke had the Slavic sensuality; that was what he was good at and why I adored him for many years. His One-Feeling (*Einfühlung*) was a cut above the common sentimentality of English poetry; yet in the long run it is also the poetry of I feel, therefore I am. Which is never quite enough for the poet. Perhaps he is the final narcissist of the modern poem.

Rimbaud is comprehended only by the brightest neurotics in this country, to whom he is a god, a child-god, who abdicated shortly after he had run the gamut of poetry. The greatness of Rimbaud is his abandonment of art. He did it without a flourish, without dotting an *i* or crossing a *t*. He did it because he saw that the road had ended. He left Verlaine with his pistol smoking, blubbering on his way to jail, "pawing the rosary," as Rimbaud, the great yokel, crudely put it. What a fool he was not to come to America instead of going to Abyssinia or wherever it was he went to destroy himself. In America he would have been a great movie producer or a Vladimir Nabokov or a J. P. Morgan. Rimbaud was not really adventurous. He went where he would be punished and was, in gravel pits, in climates that even imperialism had forgotten. He was a born conscript.

Still, he is the prototype of the *révolté*, the rebel who will never surrender to the evil women of his family who destroyed the boy. Long before he died he had forgotten that he had ever been a poet. His nausea for poetry is his greatest legacy to us.

Theodore Roethke was a child of Rimbaud who held to poetry to the end. But as an American he was also a child of Modern Poetry, which is to say Yeats, Eliot, and the whole canon of right-thinking literature. Roethke found a stratagem for remaining a poet, a lucky accident: his childhood in a greenhouse in Michigan; his Germanic background in the same place. His poetry is a running battle between this organic mythology and the profession of letters. Strange and wonderful distortions of the poem and the man result.

After glancing at my Ramakrishna I have decided that anything I can say about it will be foolish. My knowledge of Ramakrishna's mysticism (but this is not so much a question of knowledge as one of belief) was never anything worth mentioning, but I have had an intuitive feeling for the psychology of godhead or absorption, which is what Ramakrishna is about. Hinduism is an uncomfortable philosophy; it allows for every horror of life and death, perpetuating the evils which can only be eradicated by spiritual perfection. Spiritual perfection is, on the other hand, a device of self-destruction. India is at the mercy of her philosophy and lies eternally on the altar of history, as it does today. What is the solution to this?

I find I have forgotten John Crowe Ransom and Kenneth Rexroth, strange bedfellows. Rexroth is a regular R; Ransom is an exception that proves the rule. Ransom is a poet as excellent as any in the English anthology. Hence he seems an anachronism to our time, when the perfect exists as imperfection.

S / Service, Shakespeare, Sandburg, Stevens, Spender

Coming to the end of this unalphabetical alphabet, I face the enormity of S. Shakespeare, Sandburg, Wallace Stevens, Spender, Spencer, Sitwell, Swinburne, Sophocles, Swedenborg, Delmore Schwartz, Stendhal, Schiller, Gertrude Stein, St. Beuve, and Robert W. Service. I think I am most qualified to talk about Robert W. Service, who was the first poet I ever heard of after Oscar Wilde. Wilde was my introduction to poetry. My father was a traveling salesman and kept a limp scarlet leather collection of Wilde's poetry on a table in the living room. The pages were edged in bright gold, like a naughty Bible.

I have never looked at a poem of Service since I was a young child. Lately I received a copy of a book called *The Best of Robert Service,* and I found two or three of his finest chestnuts in printed type: "The Spell of the Yukon," "Sam McGee," "Dan McGrew." A thing that fascinated me about this paperback book was that it had no introduction and no biographical poop, even on the back of the jacket. Shakespeare himself can hardly claim more fame. An index of first lines at the back is further testimony to the deep fame of the book.

Leafing through the poems, hoping to find that there were others as memorable as the ones I had mentioned, I shut it hastily and returned it to the shelf, not to be opened until my grandchildren find it.

A poet like R. W. Service raises questions deeper than those raised by Yeats. He is not merely a good bad poet like Kipling, as Orwell described the Englishman. Nor is he a bad bad poet. Nor is he a poetaster. He is definitely a poet, a superlative poet on the lowest possible level. He is evidently immortal. Quite likely he is an unintentional poet. He is a natural: sublimely unoriginal, uninventive, and unintelligent. (For many years it was assumed by millions of people that Service was dead, until not long ago it transpired that he was living on the French Riviera, a millionaire, apparently rich from his poems.) Service represents—if he represents—what is the remainder of the

poetic language among the folk, if there is a folk. The
sludge of the tradition rests in him as in the lyric tradition
of Broadway and Hollywood. What I am saying is that
such poetry is neither good nor bad; whether it is poetry
at all is an academic question. To me Service is as much
poetry as *Hamlet* or "The Rape of the Lock" or the "Ballad of Reading Gaol." "The Shooting of Dan McGrew"
is neither better nor worse than "The Raven" and was
apparently written in the same mood. I began with Lautréamont and end with the author of "The Spell of the
Yukon." I will stop before Shakespeare. I have left the
beloved Rilke behind and am out in the cold with Orwell
and Mailer and all the anarchists, existentialists, and
anti-disciplinarians. I might quote Henry Miller: I have
no money, no hopes, no prospects; I am the happiest
man in the world.

To have reached the point of disengaged engagement is
such a delirious experience that you could roll on the
ground like St. Theresa, or whoever it was, intoning "The
Love, the Love!" To which I would add: the nonsensical,
the hilarious, the obscene!

From Shakespeare to Yeats

Sunday is Shakespeare's birthday. You could make fifty
volumes of Robert W. Service out of Shakespeare. Shakespeare when bad is worse than any poet in history. For
sheer dreariness and phoniness and hot air, the Bard
takes all honors. But then he compensates for all that in his
less wheezy passages. I will say that I feel about Shakespeare an intimacy which I cannot define. I feel an almost
proprietary knowledge of him. This is partly because I
grew up on him, read every word he wrote, thousands of
them, a hundred times, memorized long and short passages out of context, and knew him like a primer. And
now when I ask myself why I did this the only answer
I can summon is that I was drunk on language. Had I
been a literary seer like D. H. Lawrence I would have

seen through all that at an early age. It's all language, said Lawrence, beautiful as the dyes from gas-tar. Supposedly, everything great happens up there on that stage and on those battlements. I wonder now if anything did happen up there on those battlements. Shakespeare is the play doctor, probably the best that ever existed. Shakespeare is the improvisator, beyond the reach of any other anywhere at any time. He is peculiarly *modern* in this respect. He takes what is handed him and fixes it. And being an actor himself, undoubtedly a brilliant one, a lover of voice, he runs in his baroque improvisations until the audience is language-drunk. Universally speaking, there are only two or three writers from any time and everywhere who fall into Shakespeare's class. Homer is the only one I can think of offhand. Not even Dante, who is still banned in Islam, fits this class of artist.

Possibly Ezra Pound is right to try to bring down the great Elizabethan balloon. Shakespeare is always on stage, which is why nobody will ever know who he was. Beyond doubt the greatest on-stager in history, he immortalized Gesture. The Gesture of language preeminently. But also the Gesture of gesture. In Shakespeare no act is trivial, as long as it is on stage. "Pray thee, undo this button." This is a favorite line for intimidating sophomores. Why? Because this is supposed to prove that kings have buttons. Which is a Big Deal. Or Hamlet. "O what a noble mind is here o'erthrown." Has anybody anywhere ever found anything in Hamlet, either the play or the man, that was *noble?* Can anyone be less noble than Hamlet, this cowardly, churlish, bombastic, ill-bred prep school boy? What an opportunity for the great Elizabethan who was doing his best to pull the rug out from under the nobility, which he always does. Why are the bodies piled deeper than Austerlitz at the end of *Hamlet* and God knows how many other plays? Because the Revolutions were coming and Shakespeare knew it. What blood lust Shakespeare had for the aristocracy; he was insatiable.

But all on stage. The Puritans were coming too to cut off that kind of fooling around.

The eternal attraction of Shakespeare is that of the
absence from life. He lives only up there. He comes from
nowhere. He goes back to nowhere. He leaves a curse
on his tombstone. There is no jotting of his handwriting.
Every year people write books about whether he ever
existed. It is all song, the song of language, which Shakespeare made into the most beautiful language of all. All
song, all gesture, all absence from life. In the four hundred
years since then there has been no poetic drama. Shakespeare took it with him. Shakespeare killed poetry for the
stage by glorifying language above every other form of
human experience. I think that is what Lawrence was
getting at or Mark Twain or Tolstoy or any writer who
finally admits that the greatness of Shakespeare is forever
contained in the English of Shakespeare, beyond which is
only what he himself called the "insubstantial pageant."

One characteristic of the twentieth century which is ours
alone is that we can have two such poets as Carl Sandburg
and Wallace Stevens, who are contemporaries and oppo-
sites. They are both poets with an equal claim to their
own value; they are in conflict (neither one respected the
other); and yet both are products of the same age. This
kind of thing could not have happened in another century.
Both claim to be the culmination of their own kind of
avant-gardism, and are. Both are experimenters. Both are
the flower of their experimentation. I would like to relate
them.

If instead of applying a valuistic yardstick, trying to
determine that Carl is better than Wallace, or vice versa,
we tried to understand two such poets in relation to one
another, we might find out something. What, I am not
sure. We should know something about ourselves and
about the parochialism of modern culture, its factionalism,
for instance.

If we had had no twentieth-century poet since Whitman, Sandburg would perhaps be the greatest poet of the
twentieth century. As it is he is small fry. The same is true
of Stevens, one of the most consummate artists of poetry
any nation has produced in our time. But Stevens is prob-

ably as little known in Europe as he is here. Rather, only those who "specialize" in poetry would know. Thus, on both ends of the poetry spectrum there is no response. Sandburg made a kind of cult of crudeness and succeeded in attracting attention to his Americanism not so much by his poetry, which is far superior to what we like to think, as by his amateur forays into folklore, American jokes, and singing. Stevens underwent an endless refinement of sensibility, clarifying his tones and symbols until everything he did turned into music or painting. Everything except his philosophy, which clouds over most of his later work.

My guess would be that Sandburg spent a large part of his life wondering why he was rejected as a poet by his literary colleagues and possibly wondering why he had accumulated a mass audience of nitwits. Quite surely he knew that his mass audience was the television audience, a cut above or a cut below; what he thought of the others we know from such poems as "The Abracadabra Boys," in which he boils people like Eliot and Pound and others whom he not very gracefully designates as fairies.

What interests me is that Sandburg, a long time ago, made an intellectual decision to abdicate from intellectualism, while Stevens made the decision to become an aesthete. And I suggest that we might find a better resolution to our understanding of modern poetry, in this country anyway, if we saw that Stevens is part of Sandburg and Sandburg part of Stevens. "The Emperor of Ice Cream" is as consciously crude as "Chicago"; both poems have more or less the same thing to say. The only "refinement" is in Stevens' presentation of raw beauty as a metaphorical puzzle. Yet praise of Chicago at its worst is the same. The salient difference between Sandburg and Stevens is patience. Stevens can address Mozart during a time of poverty and say: Be seated, thou—till the sad time is past. Sandburg is corny enough to talk about spiders making their webs in helmets or the barrels of rifles. But neither poet ever comes to terms with the life of the age and what it means either to boast about smoking chimneys or to condemn them. Neither poet found a way to put into one the aesthetic sensibility and the blind dynamics of the modern machine world.

Ever since poets became the directors of conscience they have wanted to be the directors of the economy or of the state as well. And to a certain extent they have succeeded in impressing the statists and even politicians about their superiority of moral fiber and even about their intellect in practical affairs. After all, Ezra Pound's economic theories are no less intelligent and just than those that are at present in operation.

It is sad to remember that poets like Auden and Spender could hold the machine in reverence only when the machine was in disuse. When it was polished up again and purring they saw only that it was used for killing and plunder. Poetry has not yet advanced beyond this superstition. Usury, exploitation, colonialism, wage slavery—the poets can see no farther than these stock attitudes.

There were periods at the beginning of this century when poets looked with a fresh eye on invention, not only their own but every kind. Whitman had tried to make something of cables and steamrollers; Hart Crane, of bridges and airships. All of this was immediately put away by criticism as child literature or Jules Verne. The poetic formula insisted that the use of the machine, especially the automatic machine, destroyed man's place in the world. Baudelaire didn't invent the hatred of the street lamp; he popularized it. I persist in thinking that modern poetry is still acting like those eccentrics who refuse to bring electricity into the house or those who think it is evil to enter an airplane because God didn't intend man to fly.

When poetry got off the Shakespeare stage, where was it? It began to ask itself: What am I to do now; what am I to think and dream? Modern poetry is jostled in the traffic; it has tried many escapes and many departures but always ends up with a new eviction notice from the ivory tower and is back on the sidewalk where it belongs.

Instead of playing with words, poetry should be playing, as Sandburg started to, with machines and men. Poetry must give in to the machine; it must learn that the machine is part of man's own biological condition. I must sound like an old-fashioned Futurist, those people who used to say that a speeding automobile is more beautiful than the Victory of Samothrace. I fear for the biological survival of the poet; he may become as extinct as the dodo because he exists in another rhythm from the modern world around him.

If tomorrow you put on a desert island a painter, a sculptor, a musician, a novelist, a dancer, and a poet, having to fend for themselves, you can bet that the poet would be the first to succumb. Not only do painters and sculptors know how to use their hands and can lift things, but they probably also know metals, woods, and plastics and what they are made of and how they can be assembled and disassembled. They would probably know the difference between mushrooms and toadstools, methyl alcohol and scotch. A musician would know less of the *materia silvae*, if I may invent some silvan Latin; yet he too would probably have the hand skills which would help him last the first twenty-four hours. In any case he could probably tell a ship's horn from a hippopotamus. A novelist might be the handiest of all, with his random knowledge of so many irrelevancies and chicaneries. The dancer would be the second fatality after the poet.

Now I will contradict myself. During the First World War, at least in the British Army, there was an extraordinary number of poets who were decorated for extraordinary bravery. There were probably more in the Second. This fact, on the other hand, may bear out my point: namely, that the poet has no sense of survival.

That poets make good soldiers is a horrible paradox. But they do. Well, all I am trying to do is to get the poet back in the world. I don't mean that he has to sit in a foundry or make gooey sounds when he sees a dynamo but that he should be as much on the frontier of outer consciousness as any scientist or technician or soldier on the firing line. Is poetry itself going to fall asleep? Has it been bitten by the tsetse once too often?

T / Terence, Tennyson, Tzara, Tolstoy, Thoreau, Thomas

Terence, Tate, Thoreau, Dylan Thomas, Tolstoy, Tolson, Tristan Tzara, *Tristan and Isolde,* and Tennyson. Here my alphabet goes to pieces.

Once I could read Terence in Latin and like it. It was crude stuff, metrically and otherwise, but savory.

Tennyson is one of those poets who always turn up in decorated bindings; that is his fate. Critics will always battle over him and wonder how such a man of genius could publish so much drivel. Intellectually he is weak and frightened; lyrically, whatever that means, he is unsurpassed. I have never read anything of any scope that dealt with him objectively and intelligently. Tennyson has the gift of rubbing people the wrong way, making them either coo idiotically or snarl and show their teeth. My private opinion is that Tennyson knew that poetry was moribund and was rocking it to sleep.

Whenever I go into an art gallery, big or little, I immediately head for the bright colors, like a child. The dark and oiled masterpieces are not for me, unless there is something as wild as Uccello or Giotto with those three-dimensional eyes; all primitives I understand, I feel. Otherwise I seek out the light-blazing, transparent, or opaque thicknesses of every modern artist. Thus, on my bookshelf Tristan Tzara is more important to me than most books I have, though he himself did nothing but undo everything. Dada has never died and probably never will as long as we have academies and blue ribbons. I keep by me for my soul's sake a copy of Tolstoy's *What Is Art?* wherein all masterworks are dragged over the coals and through the ashes in a one-man massacre of cultural standards which still shocks readers. Thoreau is a Tolstoyan of our own place, a man yet to be reckoned with not as a writer but as a man of defiance. Thoreau's style is scratchy and unpleasant, but it could hardly be otherwise. With certain writers, such as Tristan Tzara and Thoreau, it is never how they do something that counts but that they have stared us in the eye.

Dylan Thomas is hard to be objective about. People

of my age knew him at his best and worst, loved him and envied him. I discovered him for myself long before he was known to the public but when he had already written most of the poems which later he made famous by reading them in his great basso voice, a natural organ refined by the BBC Third Program, as he himself joked. His poetry and his fame were two unrelated things. The poetry contained enough explosive to blow several lesser poets to bits; but it contained Thomas, as Donne's poetry contained Donne or Hopkins' contained him. Thomas' poems are powder kegs without fuses; the public unfortunately supplied the fuses. What interests me now is that the public, which did not ordinarily detect anything about any poetry, sensed the firepower in Thomas' lyrics, which sent them into an orgy of destruction.

Thomas is in fact something of the martyr that Rexroth and others made him out to be, but not in that sociological way that twentieth-century poets like to think. Thomas was martyred in a different way: this is going to sound farfetched but here goes.

Thomas came at the end of the ancient tradition in English poetry—metaphysical poetry, if you like—in which the total emotional force of being is formulated into precise, symmetrical structures. As he was a purely personal poet, the person was what the poetry held. The imagery and symbolism with such a poet in our time, who was a sophisticate and somewhat avant-garde, grew more and more tangled and coiled upon itself, never actually losing itself and its connections with the man. With such poets the eventual outcome is insanity or suicide. Thomas did not take either course but chose to remain himself. But the audience knew that he was trapped and cried for him to break out, to be free of the poem. He could not break out any more than the spirit of a tree can break loose. He did not even try. If anything, he tried to stay where he was, and in the last analysis he did. The orgy of shouting around him was for his liberation but only drove him deeper into the tree, where he died, crucified from within.

U / Unamuno, Ungaretti, Upanishads

Passing over Theocritus without meaning to except that I didn't see it, for I place him with poets like Chaucer and Juvenal, though probably no one else would, I find a triad of U's: Unamuno, Ungaretti, and the Upanishads. Hindu mysticism is at once brilliantly releasing and revolting. The Thou art That is at once beyond comprehension and too patently true to be bothered about. You are too busy going about your business to agree that I am the slayer and the slain. It's one or the other. And seeing infinity in a grain of sand is not as profound, I think, as seeing geology in a piece of chalk.

V / Vergil, Valéry

V is for Vergil and for Paul Valéry. Modern poetry and criticism brought me up to believe that Vergil is only something to fall asleep over. Robert Graves has the last word on this poet, as far as I am concerned. Vergil was the official poet *par excellence,* one who has the excellence of taste to leave instructions to have the masterpiece burned after he is quite sure that it won't be. Poets are worse book burners than Hitler, theoretically.

Intelligence is the last stratagem of poetry. It is the first noticeable characteristic of ours. When poetry has nothing else to do it turns intelligent. It examines both itself and its reason for being. I take this to be the sense of Valéry. There is the tragedy of the fate of poetry implicit in this phase: all is over and done with except our consideration of it.

W / Whitman, Williams

With Whitman, Williams, and Edmund Wilson (and many small w's in between) the alphabet comes to an end. It is held up by Yeats as the Great Bookend.

After a lifetime of protest in favor of certain authors, you give up the fight. Or rather, you recognize the inefficacy of argument. There are some authors, and even poets, whom people believe in or not, as the case may be, and no amount of persuasion or passion or logic or learning or comparison is going to make a bit of difference. It is as if there were Whitman people and non-Whitman people, two races who do not understand one another's languages. I have always found this to be so.

With Whitman there is a further inducement to stop talking Whitman: he is one of those poets who create the kind of following that embarrasses even their admirers. Whether Whitman would have objected to his loyal misinterpreters I rather doubt. As a poet who had no audience but only fanatical and mystical disciples, he probably would have welcomed the worst audience as better than nothing. But the central irony of Whitman remains: he is the first American poet and very possibly the last, one who demonstrates in one lifetime the beginning and end of an art. If there is anything that Whitman leaves us with it is the conviction that American poetry is what America does not want. America wants poetry, no doubt, but the kind that perpetuates and recapitulates the misery of the human condition. America wants and has the poetry of captivity and enslavement, the poetry of the trap, the poem entombed in its forms. Whitman offered to liberate poetry from all that, but we did not want it. Instead we invented the mythopoeic poem of the Western Tradition, the poem in which everything could be put back, as Pound once referred to the *Cantos*, into a ragbag.

When I speak this way I am not in any way criticizing the skills and perfections of the contemporary poem. Our poetry is so well made, I think, because it has no inherent values, only traditional value, value which we adhere to not because we believe in it but because someone once did.

The best of American literature (what I call best) is bound to appear childish or childlike to Europeans.

Thoreau, Mark Twain, Melville, and Whitman are children in every sense of the word. They resist what psychologists call maturity because to be mature in the
childhood of our time and place is nonsense. It is not
entirely mock innocence, though there is an element
of corruption among our child writers. Are not Hemingway and Fitzgerald children? What a travesty it was
for Hemingway to go from his boyishness to the image
of Papa. Nobody ever took the Papa seriously; if there was
one thing Hemingway did not have and could not have,
it was what the fathers call maturity. Wisdom he had
not.

Whitman was acting naturally and within his time and
place when he tossed out the old creeds and the events
of the past. There is much of this refreshing childishness
in Pound, although with Pound there is also the odor
of culture or corruption. Whitman truly believed, and
was conscious of, self-conscious of, the fact that the
American had the possibility and the right to be a new
man. Make it new, Pound intoned over and over again,
but unfortunately lost sight of the thing to be made new.
It was not poetry but man that needed renewal.

Why can't we understand William Carlos Williams'
rage at Eliot, whether we believe Williams or not? It is
important: Williams knew that Eliot had betrayed American literature by giving poetry back to poetry just at the
moment when it had spread its wings. Poetry was snared
again. From the time of Whitman to the early years
of this century there had been a breathing spell, as if
we were hesitating to make the decision whether we
should or should not have poetry. Then the new poetry
suddenly appeared—Sandburg, Lindsay, Masters, Fletcher,
Pound, H. D.; I no longer can recite the roster. But just
as suddenly the counterreformation set in, and in the
space of about ten years we were back in the Anglo-American trap. Poetry was once again in the tradition, no matter
how wild Eliot appeared to be in his early work. He took
infinite pains, the pains of genius and generalship, to
convince his elders that all should be well and that the
American nag could be held in check. And it was.

Irony upon irony: had Pound remained in America this might all have been different. But Pound could no more remain in America than a fish can remain in the sky. So for Pound the American poem was destined to remain a blueprint, a theory, a crazy masterpiece cross-fertilized by Michelangelo and Grandma Moses.

Williams, when you look back on it, had a larger measure of self-control than he was entitled to. Especially in his poems, where he lays it on the line time after time that the poem in the old sense is dead. The measure of speech is the measure of life, he demanded over and over, until he sounded like a nut. He was the furthest thing from a nut or a genius. Williams did not believe in genius. Genius was academic.

The limbo that Williams occupies is not unlike the one where Whitman lives. It is a locale without dates (though Williams flirted with Poundian culture off and on, never really catching Culture's eye). All Williams' work is a kind of immense footnote to *Leaves of Grass* (as are the *Cantos* and "The Waste Land" in their way). But with Williams it is the American poem vis-à-vis *Leaves of Grass*, which is so far the only poem we have to go by. When Whitman says in his Hallmark Card diction that whoever touches his book touches a man he is saying everything he has to say, a thing that no European had ever been able to say, that Boileau could not say when he inscribed the epigram that the style is the man. Who touches this touches a man, in my translation means that there is no such thing as a poem. With Williams it might mean more shrilly that poetry is dead, dead, dead. With Whitman it means: No matter; let's take our shoes off and wiggle our toes and see God, okay, boys? Only Whitman has the charm and elegance (he is damned elegant) of a poet like John Clare or Christopher Smart, poets of the asylum.

> That I walk up my stoop [*says* Whitman]
> I pause to consider if it really be.

This has always struck me as one of the most marvelous *détentes* in poetry. It is a gesture, of course, even a con-

cession to Valérian consciousness, but it is so bright-eyed
and bushy-tailed and gorgeously simpleminded that only a
mystic or a great scoundrel (as Hopkins called Whitman)
could say it. I compare it with Clare's "I left the little
birds / And sweet lowing of the herds / and went to find
out words / —do you see?"

That *do you see?* and Whitman's *I pause to consider if
it really be* are really the same thing. Though *do you see*
is both sad and funny and Whitman is being pompous-ass-
funny and also pointing his finger at you.

Williams is full of that (I am going to invent a new
French form of poetry) *poésie de détente,* which is probably bad French, as I don't know French or even English.
The *poésie de détente* is the poetry of the Relaxation
of International Tension. It is the poetry of the Ignoring
of Nations. I see no difference between Whitman's *Alle
menschen,* etc., and Williams' anti-Europeanism. Williams, like most good American artists, was also so anti-
American that he was run out of the Library of Congress.
This means that he was fanatically American, like Pound,
to the point of martyrdom. Pound and Williams and
Whitman are American fundamentalists: they actually
believe that the Bill of Rights is in effect. Consequently
they run into the law, all three of them.

And all three were trying to abolish nations and to
retain places. Whitman constantly chanting about things
in place: the moth eggs are in place; the stars are in
place; he was in his place. (This was the opposite of the
English mannerism of pointing out that you should *stay*
in your place—the difference between Culture and Nature.) Williams made an obsession of the thing being
the thing, no matter how disgusting, and, more important, being in its place. It enchanted Williams to see
that no one had removed a rotting apple from the
porch rail or to see a huge brown paper rolling down a filthy
New Jersey street in front of a car, looking perhaps like a
fallen body. Williams wrote deeply in prose and in his
poems about the displacement of nations, Negroes, whites
from the South, Mediterraneans, Jews; he wrote viciously,

like a harassed baby-deliverer who was also trying to be a poet, trying to discover why you should so be. He had to recoil from Europe, especially from England (it doesn't help to say that his father was English); he recoiled from Europe because he was an American.

I would put it this way: The American does not believe in Europe, but the European idealizes the American. The American cannot believe in Europe because that is where he came from. Williams, in his first good book of essays called *In the American Grain*, tried to abolish every vestige of Europeanism from his heroes who landed and settled and explored and colonized, and then tried to wipe them out, as America wipes everything off the slate. The book doesn't get anywhere, like us. It gets everywhere, like us. Americans don't play the game and are universally love-hated (there is probably a word for it in Greek or German). We know our situation. The world looks to Americans because we are prize babies, beautifully brainwashed of Europe, dangerously inoculated with a mere physical anger.

Our poetry is angry not because it has anything to be angry about but because our poetry is foreign. This foreign body in the pure bloodstream of the American baby of art sets up a fever which looks like Protest or Revolt or something but is nothing but diaper rash. Perhaps this might explain why our poetry is so scatological. And as a sub-sub-footnote, it seems that the generosity of America toward the Obscene is that of the organism that cannot distinguish between faecal matter and oil paint. I believe this is or was the Freudian view of art, which might perhaps explain the love of Freud amongst us.

But I am horsing around with sacred cows.

I should be monkeying with W as a *soixante-neuf* of M.

"My hand in yours, Walt Whitman—so," said Hart Crane. Which sounds like the Teamsters Union.

Whitman aspired to greatness and attained it. Greatness is a stance, an annunciation, an immutable gesture. Whitman has this. It doesn't matter whether he is or is not accepted as great; he established the belief in his greatness; he willed it; and we inherit his challenge to dispute him.

Williams, on the other hand, never aspired to greatness, like Whitman or Eliot. He made no such demand. Rather, he asserted the wrongness of the American grain and went against it full force. He was an amateur swimming against professionals. He ended up, it appears, in or near Camden, where Whitman held sway over his Ramakrishna-like school of disciples, all of them slightly cracked. Whitman enthroned himself in vast wicker rocking chairs or Victorian thrones, bearded, matronly, scarcely a ray of darkness in his soul. Williams penned his footnotes furiously and with clearheadedness to the very end, not for any System but for a truth which he held on to for dear life. It was the truth of his *détente*, it meant not that the American is free (he knew better than that) but that the American must be free of poetry.

Y / Yeats

The Ouija Board now switches spastically to Y, the polar star of modern poetry. There is only one Y, the modern and universal contradictory of the American Whitman. (*Contradictory* is now a noun.) Yeats is as far as the modern European sensibility has been able to progress. Yeats is the only poetic solution for modern Europe and is no solution at all for anything, including Yeats.

What is Yeats? This is something like the child's question when she first heard the name of John Keats: What are Keats? What are Yeats? Doctor Williams would point out jeeringly that though they are spelled the same they don't sound that way.

Yeats is like Whitman, up to a point. Yeats was an outlander, a natural enemy of England, a lover of what belonged to his beautiful and bitter island, but one who aspired to escape from the condition of Ireland and transform it into a phoenix nest. He did something like that single-handed. It was a miracle. He took the curse off Ireland. Probably James Joyce would not have had the strength to get off the ground had it not been for (what scholars sometimes call *the example of*) Yeats. Shaw and Wilde abandoned Ireland. Yeats sought out in Ireland what had not been murdered by her history; he blew on that coal and nursed its little fire. And for that small act of heroism he was made a grand knight of the heroes of Europe and of the world. Yeats (unfortunately, from my philosophy) probably gave European poetry another millennium of life.

In Yeats is summed up all the phoniness of the art of poetry and its practitioners and its adherents, its power and its meaninglessness. Not only is Yeats the master of the modern poem; he is the Master in a more esoteric sense (which I think is what Allen Tate meant when he addressed him so). He is the magus not only of his particular Secret Lodge but of the poem as idol. Eliot and Pound failed to do what Yeats did: to bring the idol out of hiding and to dance its ritual. This is very heroic, as I have said, and European Cultural Memory went down on its knees before it. I can almost sympathize with the magnificent gesture. How could you do otherwise than bow while this image passed before you. Even a Jew can bow to a Pope.

This is Yeats: all Pope. Without power he parades before the European imagination images of such glory and defeat that the lowliest lout is metamorphosed into an archetypal prince.

And Yeats is never offstage. Through the smoke of the theater and the smart, severe costuming rises the figure (half man, half Yeats) of the poet. He is, alas, so much like Ezra Pound, another play doctor of poetry. In America, had we the consciousness or unselfconsciousness to say something, people would yell that the play is A-1 but now let's take off the gear and do it straight.

Yeats loved and flirted with politics and knew less

about it than he knew about biochemistry. He had the bourgeois Old World notion that a poet was really royalty in disguise. He became royal at a time when even the idea of kings was more obsolete than—but nothing is obsolete any more.

And here there is a towering irony. This poet, so much a master and artist, so bewildered in his provincial theater of history, so much an anachronism—this man, who courted the American poet most like him, Ezra Pound, invented or repatented the little lyric, metaphysical, symbolist gadget which is the model for the modern American poem.

This brings me back to the starting point of all my criticism or whatever you call what I write. This gadget is the reason why I started on the ruinous road and why I am still on it. I admit that most of my own poems are similar to the gadget. Critics used to accuse me of *thinking* in the poem, which is bad manners in Gadgetville; or they accused me of *feeling* in the poem, which is even worse. I was made aware for a long time that my dissociated sensibility was showing, and I felt appropriately guilty and inferior. Now there is no question that the best poetic gadget of our time is marked "Made in Ireland," but the Americans have done remarkable imitations on a mass scale.

The closed poem encloses, and that is all it can do or wants to do. It will not even mount the stage and exclaim. And when it does the women tear it limb from limb, as they did Orpheus. The closed poem lives in books; and the books, in libraries. It is the perfect poem for the mechanical age, which age this gadget poem pretends to hate.

The antithesis of the closed poem is not necessarily the open poem or the freedom of Whitman or surrealism or just plain spillover of feeling, anger, or illumination. Poetry, if you can stand another epigram, has no antithesis, neither prose nor science nor painting nor anything else. The open poem is obviously preferable in my scale of things to the gadget, but that is only because there

is a greater chance for the poem to sound when the box
is sprung.

All definitions of poetry are right except when a definition sets up antitheses, whether it is Aristotle trying
to contain the poem in order to hold it long enough to
categorize, or Valéry and those who define poetry as
language in a state of crisis. Frost had described the art
as that which is lost in translation. While this too is an
antithesis, it comes close. For poetry to me is that which
abolishes translation. In poetry the understanding process
is forgotten, and you do not so much perceive relationships
as experience them. The artificiality of modern poetry
and its aesthetic were created in good faith as an attempt
to make visible to the mind the processes of unification.
The mind is incapable of creating other than rational,
limited relationships. The rational mind is not far in advance of the thinking machines, which the mind has
invented and assembled and put to work. The poem,
insofar as it has escaped ratiocination and valuation, can
present relationships but only in the context of human
response. Here, too, theory goes off on a tangent and
assumes that poetry is therefore humanistic. Thus in our
colleges we still employ the antique expression Arts *and*
Sciences. There is no aesthetic differential between Art and
Science that I can fathom. Or between Humanism and
its many antitheses. Nor is there any differential between
the value of science and the value of art and the value
of common expressive action. Mathematical formulae are
as much poems as poems are formulations of available
data. Juan Gris, sitting at a café with Apollinaire in Paris,
looked around at the horror of billboards and announced
that those billboards were the poetry of our age. It is
wrong to accept this as a social protest, which on a super-
ficial level it was. Rather he meant that the brutal art
of the advertiser, the brutal sensibility of modern man,
was the only poetry which had the power of our own
speech. Every form of expression aspires to a form which
is both absolutely inclusive and fluid. Science is the poetry
of our time not because nothing succeeds like success

but because it has found more inclusive, more open forms.
Science never says that this is the answer. It says merely
that this answer is for the moment possible. That is
where the gadget poem fails. The gadget poem says that
this is or there is a work of art which is immutably a
classic; there are no classics in science.

I started with Shakespeare, the supreme poet of language
and pageantry. And I end with Yeats, the twentieth-century master of the gadget poem. In between lie Whitman
and Doc Williams, opponents of pageantry and the language of pageantry.

Finally, I will discuss the literature of situation, as I
find it in such writers as Henry Miller, Céline, and the
Marquis de Sade, which is to say, in "anti-literature" or
the literature of non-morality. Non-moral literature is
identical with the non-moral life. It is, I think, the way
out of language and the way into Being.

Henry Miller and Myself

The road from Aristotle to Yeats is a short one, and
it would seem to me that we have gotten nowhere. Poetry
is yet to take the road not taken. There are a few
wild spurs, a few Quixotes who rode off in all directions,
some never to return. (This bit of imagery, I see, can
become an avocation, and I'd better stop it now with
the infernal conclusion that Literature like War is Hell.)

I believe I have covered the ground I wanted, and I
am somewhat impressed by the alphabetical method of
criticism. Confronted with fifty or fifteen hundred or
fifteen thousand books, what do you do but try to find
the configuration that balances them. My remarks have
added up, I hope, to a Poundian "ideogram," a painting
without perspective, a simultaneous presentation of all
the experience of books I could summon up. Not that
this is any great *Biographia Literaria*. My only hope is
that I have been understood; it is too much to expect
more than a few persons to agree with more than some

of my opinions or to change their way of life and adopt
these criteria. I have stopped trying to propagandize as
I used to do in my criticism; right now my only concern
is stating my case.

Having gone through the books I wanted, guided by
ABC's, I come to the last shelves in my *malebolge*, the
bottom and the top. The bottom I will speak of first. The
top is my Rare Book Room or what the Library of Congress calls its Delta Collection. Delta is the symbol of
female fertility and makes a cute design on the index
card. Catholic University in Washington calls its Delta
Collection the Inferno Collection. The largest library of
banned books is, of course, in the Vatican; the next largest,
at the University of Indiana, the Kinsey Collection. I
have no such library because the handful of Delta books
I do have I keep in circulation or give away.

The books on my bottom shelf are almost all useless,
because they are Useful. Literary dictionaries, histories
of this and that literary persuasion, lexicons, anthologies,
and textbooks of modern or more or less modern literature.
The only ones I trust are the foreign dictionaries, probably because I don't know any better. If I look up a word
in German or Italian or Latin or Greek I believe what
I read. I believe it especially if the book has not been
published in the United States. Any book published in
America raises my suspicions as to its honorable intentions.
This is especially true of textbooks. Anyone who has
published more than two books in this country knows
that there are few publishers in America interested in
books. Our publishers are mostly puppets of advisers;
their sole interest seems to be in making money (they
are not even interested in making a reputation). If an
American writer wants to find a publisher who cares
about either literature or good bookmaking, he has to
go to the Orient or to Holland or Germany or England
or Italy. Many of our young American poets are printed
in North Africa or Mexico. Even many of our little magazines are published outside America.

Our university publishers are not much better. Some

of them do produce the works of actual scholars. That is something else. Most of them behave like Madison Avenue publishers, trying to make a fast buck for the university. Good literary publishing in America is still largely in the hands of individuals who pay for the printing themselves and sometimes do the work with their own hands.

This is in a country where whole forests are slaughtered daily to keep the billboards rising.

On my dictionary shelf I have a few works of phrenology and palmistry and astrology. I have already spoken of Wilhelm Reich, who carried Freud from the geography of the mind to the geography of the body. Reich described the physical character of the neurotic and psychotic in terms of muscles. A man or woman develops a typography of musculature which is visible. The apparent physical bearing of a man or woman or child is muscular. The soldier or athlete is protected by certain advanced muscle formations. You can see them in his body and they shine out of his face. The teacher has a dance of the body all his own. This touches on the esoteric and occult. Poe, who is quite a twentieth-century man, frequently ended his book reviews with a description of the author's body and face. He was especially interested in skull formation, as he believed his own skull to have the bumps and shape of genius. This is a form of literary criticism I think we should revive in our time. In medieval face charts there are forehead lines which identify character types: prostitute, criminal, genius, and so forth. Modern medicine is just beginning to come to terms with such things. The lines of the human hand are in some advanced fields of medicine used to help in surgical prognosis.

I have been away from magic books for a long time. Magic properly manipulated has its value in our world of science and in any other kind of controlled phenomena. Magic is an exertion of the will upon matter. Its efficacy is not purely symbolic. It is not merely old science or primitive psychology. All the peripheral sciences, such as psychiatry, use it. Religions would disintegrate without it. The arts employ it more or less at will. There are more varieties of magic than even anthropologists can count, but all have been workable at one time or another.

It took me many years before I discovered why I had become a writer. Literature for me, as it probably is for most literary people, was an escape from the street, from the daily life, from my own psychological twitches, from the past as it had been expressed to me. Literature was a three-hundred-horsepower gadget that fulfilled my fantasy life. Very satisfactorily. Literature also had its effects on others. Literature was a slow way to come at life, to the world past the pile of manuscript or beyond the wall of books.

For writers like me literature was a way out of the labyrinth of self into the world. I am eternally grateful for being forced to become a poet, because without that method of escape from self I could never have known that there was another world. Without literature I would never have been able to escape from it. For I learned to believe not in literature, not in culture, but in the creative act. As my respect for literature decreased, my respect for the act of creativity grew. With me it was a kind of revelation to discover that all standards are fictitious and that standards exist only when we make them. To be rid of those idols of culture seemed to me a state of innocence which I would never be able to attain. It was Henry Miller who taught me—what shall I call it?—the higher innocence.

I first read *Tropic of Cancer* when it came out illegally in 1939. It was not my book, I had never heard of Miller, and it made no impression on me. I was then just beginning to publish my first poetry and had not yet seen daylight. I read the book with a girl friend; it was probably a kind of Paolo and Francesca episode.

It was fifteen years before I read Miller again, with my ears open. I think it must have been *The Air-Conditioned Nightmare* and the fact that I had lived so long in so many parts of America that conditioned me for understanding. Once I had read everything of his I could

lay my hands on, I knew where I was. I was beyond
the wall of books. I was where I should have been fifteen
years before. I had been sleeping in the poem.

It was not Miller alone but the writers in Miller's life.
One of his best works is called *The Books in My Life*, a
work he wrote in gratitude to the writers who had formed
him. It was a kind of bibliographical poem of thanks to
all the Dionysians and rebels of the world who had led
him from a meaningless young manhood to the inferno of
books and thence back to a life of the saint. *Saint* is a
word that only Millerites use in reference to this old goat.
In fact, Miller sanctifies the goat and sports the satyr's
foot. Miller is one of the great satyrics of all time, a
clown, a burlesque comic. This is why he is shunned
by the literati and the professoriat. He is not hated or
demeaned by them, merely unmentioned. He doesn't fit.
That is what Miller is always saying about himself in
a thousand crazy registers: Look! I don't fit; and then
he goes off into one of those belly laughs which might
run for two hundred pages. Pure filth, say the bourgeoisie
(with a certain degree of accuracy at that).

Miller, like Lawrence, substantiated for me all my
suspicions about the great monuments of culture, literary
and otherwise. He doused me with a bucket of cold water
filled with unnameable objects. He gave me the one-two
Zen punch. I am eternally grateful for that.

Four or five years ago I wrote my first essay about him
to top off a series of lectures I was giving in Cincinnati.
When the Grove Press decided to break the ice of American censorship by publishing *Tropic of Cancer*, my essay
was chosen as a frontispiece, along with the brief and
bitterly beautiful preface by Anäis Nin. My essay was
needed not for its literary merit, if it had any, but for
help in butting the book through the courts. It was
quoted in pro and con testimony and did some good.
After all, I am a professor and a writer. Minnesota was
one of the states that had the good sense to give the book
its freedom. Some states did; some didn't.

Some literary critics described my essay as gibberish.

I think I did gibber a bit, but then Miller gives me the gift of tongues.

The only thing I attempted in that essay was a distinction between writers and authors, between language and situation. Miller may be the world's worst writer; he is one of the great authors. The sooner we recognize the difference between the literature of reference or retrospect or whatever and the accidental writings of the amateur, the better. I say accidental: call it natural, primitive, *révolté*, naive, anything. The twentieth century is the greatest period for creativity in so many ways, creativity and destruction; I feel that all the arts, literature included, feel this power to depart from the museum, the anthology, the textbooks, the standard. In this situation the amateur is the best bet.

I have long since given up evangelizing about Miller. I found that it does no good. Miller is a question of wavelength; you get him or you don't. The somnambulists open a weary, wart-studded eyelid when you mention Miller and give you a passing how-dare-you stare before they go back to the late-late show. Women tend to loathe him when they read him closely. He despises women, women say. Woman, they claim, is only a *machine à plaisir* to Miller. Nothing could be further from the facts. If anything, he is as sentimental about women as Sir Walter Scott.

Confronted with multiplex accusations against Miller, I tend to clam up. His use of what is called foul language, the clinical and generally boring reports of coupling, the diatribes against the American landscape and culture and society, the old-fashioned, Frenchified surrealism, the ego and bombast, the artlessness, the effrontery, and so on and so forth—who can answer these charges? As Miller loves to answer in full voice: Guilty!! Guilty on all counts!! And keeps on writing the Brooklyn Canterbury Tales of himself. He is the himself of Walt Whitman, the single, separate person but also the word *en masse*.

Miller, the opposite of a sadist, is a disciple of the Divine Marquis. Unlike Sade, Miller is never pathological,

prurient with the machine of fantasy or the dry lust
of the movies or the automobile. He can distinguish all
too well between love and lust but rejects neither. The
greatness of Sade was that he acted out the drama of
the nonexistence of love. In Sade there is neither love
nor hate, only the various registers of lust and cannibalism.
Miller, on the other hand, is one of the great poets of
love, if not a Rupert Brooke of lust. He sees not only
the mystery but the absurdity, not only the absurdity
but the hilarity. If I may be the literary critic for the
moment, his literary model is the burlesque, both the
strippers and the comedians. The comedians especially.

I know of no other writer of our time who has exposed
the failure of love into sex *without moralizing about it*
and without putting on the trappings and the suits of
Art.

The *magnum opus* of Miller is a single anti-novel, not
yet finished, which will run seven or ten or twelve novels.
The rest of his books, uncountable, are footnotes, orna-
ments, offshoots, cartouches belonging to the main book.
His work will never be able to enter a canon; it will always
defy the traditional; it is sabotage to all that still stands
of the museum of culture. Yet it is the furthest thing from
negation. What really shocks people about Miller is that
he is happy. Happiness is obscene.

I turn now to a question of obligation. As a writer I
have long ago given up the idea of obligation. Any kind
of artist knows that the only obligation of the artist is
between himself and his piece of paper. Morals, ethics,
society, institutions of behavior—all these impinge upon
his work but only by chance. As far as function is concerned, function is subjective, natural at best like anything that grows, forced sometimes when nature takes a
pathological twist. Where the poem goes, where the painting hangs, when the variations are played are as much
a matter of wonder to the creator as to anyone else.
The artist knows only one thing: that he is alone.

But I am a teacher. I manipulate the ideas of young

men and women. Their minds are plastic and impression-
able. I am aware of certain dangers. Should I inflict my
ideas, opinions, and tastes on them?

When I have doubts like these I wish I had never
faced a class or written a line of criticism. Still, I go on
doing these things, sometimes rationalizing to myself
that nobody can really be influenced by ideas except a few
crackpots.

This is a crucial question. Am I to speak out about the
things I do or save them for people who are ready for
them? When are you ready? And the people I choose,
which make most sophisticated and learned people blush:
Wilhelm Reich, Alexander Neill, Henry Miller, Sade,
Lautréamont, Rimbaud, Whitman, Kropotkin, William
Burroughs. Kid stuff.

So in the long run I end up with a credo myself, a
pedagogical creed, even a plan of action. I am a writer
hyphen teacher, consequently a saboteur, a Trojan Horse.

I made a distinction some time back between the
society we live in and the non-society the artist lives in.
The artist today (though it wasn't always so) is a kind
of virus in the body of the social plasma. There he is,
asserting himself. Sometimes virulent, sometimes dormant,
a vector, a fever-producing foreign body. Plato was right:
society can do without that kind of headache.

But Plato was wrong. Because society or the state is
not a *sine qua non* of human life. This is what the artist
says. Community, yes; society, no. Man is a communal
animal; society is a fossil of community.

I am not trying to write a sociology but only groping
my way back to what is natural. Everything I have said
has been an argument in favor of art as a natural, not a
specialized, condition of man. Neill takes the child and
relieves it of its societal hatreds and fears. Reich tries to
relieve the somatic anxieties of the body by removing the
fears and inhibitions of physical contact. Miller celebrates
without moral or aesthetic discrimination the acts of lust
and of love. Céline wipes out the distinction between the

hero and the anti-hero, between patriotism and survival, between death and murder. Genet destroys the notion of crime.

We have been flattering ourselves in America that we have finally broken through the line of Puritan defenses in publishing half a dozen banned books. And it's true that we have liberated James Joyce, a couple of Henry Miller items, and *Lady Chatterley*. But we haven't even scratched the surface. Still, we are trying and are in some ways doing better than even the French. In France you can't buy *Tropic of Cancer* in French, only in English, German, Arabic, and Swahili. But in America you can't buy Sade, even in French.* And so forth.

For almost two centuries the rather pretty English sex novel usually called *Fanny Hill* has been sold as contraband. It is at present for sale in Lincoln, Nebraska. In one of the introductions it lists Benjamin Franklin as an early owner of the book, as ingenious a selling device as you could ask for. I have noticed, by the way, that all the American editions of the banned books are printed in exceptionally large type, making them legible for the elderly and for very young children who can use the books as spellers. All well and good.

I will try to define the obscene, but like everyone else who rejects a religious view I can only say: *There is no such thing!* Henry Miller quotes scripture, Romans 14:14: "I know and am persuaded by the Lord Jesus that there is nothing unclean of itself, but to him that esteemeth anything to be unclean, to him it is unclean." He also quotes a legal expert named Theodore Schroeder on the meaning of banning a book. Schroeder says that "it is not the inherent quality of the book which counts, but its hypothetical influence upon some hypothetical person, who at some problematical time in the future may hypothetically read the book." Miller himself says that if there is an ulterior motive at work in a so-called obscene book, it goes far beyond sex. The purpose of such

---

* The ban has now been lifted.

a book is to awaken, to usher in a sense of reality. He compares the use of the obscene by the writer to the use of the miraculous by the Masters in painting.

Miller, contrary to uninformed opinion, is fully and poetically conscious of the miracle of Sex. He plunges into it lock, stock, and barrel, even like the mystics of old immersing themselves in the One. So, to the charge of obscenity he answers gleefully and at the top of his lungs: *Obscene? Yes! Guilty. Guilty on all counts!*

Nobody knows the meaning of the obscene, neither the Supreme Court, the English Department, nor the American Academy of Arts and Letters. The only people who claim to know the meaning are clerics, male and female, politicians, and journalists—anyone who has an ax to grind. Psychologically, there is one constant fact about those who use the term, namely, that to them sexuality is inseparable from filth. Sex is filthy and filth is sexual —this is as close to the meaning of obscenity as the censors can get. Which only puts the finger on the clergy, police, politicians, and journalists and gets us nowhere.

The writer uses the word *obscene* to turn the tables on his enemies. What is obscene to him is not what the righteous call obscene. To the writer or artist the modern obscenities are the very things which are supposedly the foundations of society: industrialism, advertising, journalism, militarism, mass entertainments, film, and television; things which keep mankind in a froth of excitation and hysteria; the world of the aphrodisiac without fulfillment. This is the atmosphere which creates our homicidal restlessness or contributes heavily to it. Society, of course, and religion as one of its central institutions, supports the psychology of repression and denial. Society fights the freedom of sexual expression on every front, just as it fights individual freedom of action in favor of what it thinks of as Order.

All artists who have sometimes felt it necessary to work in the medium of the obscene have done so after exploring every other avenue of expression. True, there are artists who create the obscene out of resentment and revenge, and behind them a legion of opportunists. We cannot legislate against any of these either. We can only look to the authentic obscenicist—I think I have just invented a word—the writer who uses the obscene in good faith to disclose and to celebrate reality.

Compare Charles Baudelaire and Walt Whitman on this score.

Baudelaire's famous poems *The Flowers of Evil* were published at almost exactly the same time as Whitman's *Leaves of Grass*. Baudelaire's book wallows in unfulfilled sex and religion and is, in style, of the most extreme and exquisite formality. Whitman's book extols physical love and the physical beauty of all things, denies religion, and is in the first free style in American poetry. *The Flowers of Evil* demonstrates obscenity in bad faith; Whitman, the opposite. It is typical of modern elite culture that Baudelaire is exalted and Whitman sneered at. Baudelaire retreated hypocritically from the charges of blasphemy and lubricity. Whitman did not, although outside his poetry he tried to cover up his homosexuality, which was not very heroic.

The door to the obscene has been opened, at any rate, not very far but enough to disclose a panorama of horror to the righteous. Yet respectable professors and renowned writers nowadays come to court to defend the art of the obscene. And as we know, they have achieved a certain small success.

But nobody has yet gone to court to defend the pornographic—pornography, as I understand it, being the realistic graphic or written portrayal of sexual activity, supposedly with the aim of arousing sexual feeling in the spectator.

I would like to give a talk sometime in defense of homosexuality, although I am no authority on the subject. I have no doubt that American society is highly homosexual—we do a perfunctory job of hiding it—and that a great many of our most productive and responsible people, male and female, are members of the third sex.

That is definitely their right, though they are considered criminal.

American avant-garde publishers have been making a first breakthrough here. We presently have an English version of the French novel *Notre Dame des Fleurs,* which the philosopher Jean-Paul Sartre has taken the trouble to write a massive tome about. *Our Lady of the Flowers* is an exquisite and terrifying document, a work of art if you like, written by a thief, a jailbird, a queer, possibly even a murderer. There are many fine and derivative works by Americans now being printed: *Naked Lunch, City of Night,* books of poems by the hundreds—all needed—fierce works which will perhaps help our Puritan countrymen finally to admit the Third Sex to equal citizenship.

Those who fear the obscene do so out of fear of the pornographic, which is the ultimate expression of eroticism. The pornographic strikes fear even into the hearts of many famous obscene writers. They too will close the door on this aspect of the inferno. But here, I believe, their logic and their sincerity falter. The Obscene writer or artist has no choice but to embrace, however loathingly, the uttermost depths of the actual, though the heat of the furnace destroy him. But if he has a pure heart, an open mind, and a willing corpus, he can stroll through the fire as coolly as Shadrack, Meshach, or Abednego.

There is one writer in literary history who dared face the consequences of the pornographic. He is the Marquis de Sade, who is known in some quarters as a dangerous maniac, in others as the Anti-Christ, but who among poets and artists is commonly called the Divine Marquis, patron saint of surrealism, precursor of sexual psychology, and so forth. To those of you who haven't read him I suggest the quiet and brilliant essay by Simone de Beauvoir called "Must We Burn Sade?" This essay appears in an English translation in a good introductory anthology of Sade's work.

Sade's nature (de Beauvoir points out) was thoroughly irreligious. There was no trace of metaphysical anxiety in

him; he was too concerned with justifying his existence
to speculate on its meaning. The fear of the beyond never
appears in his work. But Sade's atheism, unlike that of
contemporary eighteenth-century philosophers, did not
substitute the worship of Nature for the worship of God.
Unlike Diderot or Rousseau, sexual pleasure for Sade is
selfish, tyrannical, and criminal. That is, Sade agrees with
the Deists and nature worshipers that sexuality is natural,
but to him Nature is *evil* and not good. He quoted Hobbes's
declarations that man is a wolf to man and that the
state of Nature is one of war. The Rousseauistic creed
that *Nature is Good; let us follow Her* he turned into
the opposite, *Nature is Evil; let us follow Her*. From this
he derived his peculiar brand of hedonism which the
world today knows by his name as Sadism.

Sade's pessimism rose from the most extreme form of
individuality we have an example of. Knowing his own
perverseness and admitting that he was a creature of
Nature, he fought savagely to remain "natural." Submis-
sion to society was unthinkable, as his long years in jail
and the asylum proved. Sade fought to retain his authenticity and his freedom, and given his character and his
situation he could not but condone incest, sodomy, and
sexual vagary, including murder. Such is the price of
freedom. At the same time he apparently regarded himself as an extreme case and did not feel that in an ideal
anarchic community he and his ilk would present too
great a danger. Indeed, in such a community, in a world
without hatred his violent acts would lose their significance. If the prohibitions which make crime attractive
were abolished, lust itself would be eliminated. De Beauvoir points out that Sade must be given a place in the
great family of those who want to cut through the
banality of everyday life to a truth which is immanent
in this world. His ethic can be summed up in his bitter
cry that in a criminal society you must be a criminal.

Simone de Beauvoir defends Sade because he "drained
to the dregs the moment of selfishness, injustice, and
misery, and insisted upon its truth." Sade forces us to

reexamine the basic problem of our age: the true relation between man and man. But Sade knew only two alternatives: abstract morality and crime. He was unaware of action. Sade hated the collectivity because he knew by experience that the person who insists upon his singularity is banned from society. If society recognizes only the *transcendent* qualities of each man and not his singularities, man will be led only to new idols, new prisons, and new guillotines. The French Revolution ended in the Terror and Napoleon. Bolshevism with its abstract morality became a tyranny overnight. It is better to assume the burden of "evil" than to subscribe to this abstract good. The question that Sade leaves in our mind is: What are my natural rights as a separate man? This is the question facing us who inherit an awesome burden of freedom at a time when freedom is all but nonexistent everywhere. Everything is being institutionalized from top to bottom. There is no singularity, individuality, or even eccentricity in America; we are all machine-tooled, shined, and burnished by religion, education, medicine, and business. Even sex is machined in America.

Just a century ago, Thoreau printed a talk in *The Atlantic Monthly*, called "Life Without Principle." Nowadays all college students read Thoreau, but they might as well be reading Tacitus for all it means to them. This in spite of the fact that Thoreau has probably had a greater influence on history than George Washington. Certain writings of Thoreau wakened Gandhi to his struggle to free India from Europe. The present awakening of the Negro population can also be traced largely to the example of Thoreau. The essay on civil disobedience can be set beside the Constitution as one of the greatest American documents.

Thoreau is the best American scripture and I never tire of the text. For instance, when he says: "I take it for granted, when I am invited to lecture anywhere . . . that there is a desire to hear what I *think* on some subject, though I may be the greatest fool in the country. . . ."

Thoreau on Business, that is, busy-ness and American

Business, for which we are most famous: "This world is a
place of business, what an infinite hustle! I am awakened
almost every night by the panting of the locomotive. It
interrupts my dreams. There is no sabbath. . . . It is nothing but work, work, work. . . ." A beautiful paragraph
that ends: "I think that there is nothing, not even crime,
more opposed to poetry, to philosophy, ay, to life itself,
than this incessant business." Imagine Thoreau at a meet-
ing of the NAM or the Chamber of Commerce or practically any place in America today, the America which
President Coolidge summed up in his basic English: The
business of America is Business!

About working purely for money, which is the American
way of life, he says: "You are paid for being something
less than a man." Thoreau advises not to hire a man
who does your work for money, but him who does it for
love of it. Now you can look high and low for a man who
puts the love of his work above money, whether a carpenter or a doctor—especially a doctor—and you won't
find him. Craftsmanship, even of the lowliest kind, has
disappeared so completely in America that we have to
import artisans whenever we need a job done by someone
who puts the result above the cash.

About journalism Thoreau is merciless. You have to read
the essay to get the full flavor of it. But he sums up the
newspaper—*and politics*—in the words: "Of what consequence, though our planet explode, if there is no character involved in the explosion. . . . *I would not run round
the corner to see the world blow up.*"

Running around the corner to see the world blow up
seems to be the favorite pastime of our countrymen,
newspapers, Congress, and the populace alike.

And on moral tyranny in the United States, which is
my subject, he says: Even if we have freed ourselves from
a political tyrant (meaning George III) we are still the
slaves of economic and moral tyranny. He says that we
have achieved the *res publica* but have done nothing for
the *res privata*, the private state.

Of institutions he says, country-style: "As a snow-drift is

formed where there is a lull in the wind, so . . . where there is a lull of truth, an institution springs up. But the truth blows right on over it, . . . and at length blows it down." By *institution* he means anything from a church to a cartel to a government.

Thoreau ends with a double-barreled blast at newspapers and politics, both of which he spews out of his mind: "Those things which now most engage the attention of men, as politics and the daily routine, are, it is true, vital functions of human society, but should be unconsciously performed, like the corresponding function of the physical body. [I take this to mean the outhouse.] They are *infra-human*, a kind of vegetation. . . ." Proudly he asserts: "I have not got to answer for having read a single President's Message."

Henry Miller published an edition of this essay, "Life Without Principle," in 1946. In it he said that we should try not to imitate Thoreau but to *surpass* him. "We should not strive to become like Thoreau or even like Jesus Christ, but to become what we are in truth and in essence." Which is precisely the message of the infamous Marquis de Sade.

Almost to a man, American artists and writers are in full-fledged opposition to the American Way of Life, that is, life according to Business, Politics, Journalism, Advertising, Religion, Patriotism, and Morality. It is for this reason that our creative people are recognized *outside* the United States—and always have been—before they are recognized here. And almost to a man they revere the primitive America, which claimed freedom of action for all men, at some distant time in the future which has not yet arrived, freedom of expression, which we do not have; freedom of the *res privata*, which we have less than any European peasant or South American peon. Nor do we even have the freedom of the ballot except for palefaces—but I don't want to start up that road.

The drama being played out in America, ever since George Washington refused the crown and crossed the Rubicon, is the drama of the Private State versus the Re-

public, Artist versus Bourgeois. The Republic is Abstract
Morality incarnate and as such is the natural enemy of
the artist (private man). This comic-tragic play is richly
documented in all our literature, good, bad, and indifferent. The underlying query in all American art amounts
to this: Do we mean to take the consequences of freedom? Or was it all one of the errors of history, like the
French and Russian revolutions? And if we mean to take
the consequences of liberty, how far are we willing to go?
How far with the vote, with a churchless society, with obscenity and pornography; in short, what commitment are
we willing to make to a free, non-moral world?

I prefer the term *non-moral* to *amoral*. *Amoral* has picked
up some of the unhealthy iridescence of *moral* or *immoral*,
quasi-religious words of the dark ages of the mind. I would
have *non-moral* mean neither moral nor immoral nor
amoral but rather free from all such judgments. Non-
morality is, for instance, the detachment from politics
which Thoreau and Sade advocate. Non-morality is non-
political, as non-political as sexual intercourse, and for this
reason can exert greater political force than politics itself.
American politicians to their dismay are finding this out;
in the face of non-moral action, defying the law without
violence, politics puts its tail between its legs and slinks
off, like Lord Mountbatten surrendering to Gandhi.

Guilty on all counts! yells Henry Miller, rolling in the
courthouse aisle and holding his sides. *He* didn't make the
laws. Let the laws try themselves. And they do. And end
up in the archives.

Released from morality, man bursts into unimaginable
creativity. The great Renaissance of Europe was the re-
birth of joy at the death of the universal morality. Those
vast, twisted, schizophrenic nightmares called Gothic
Cathedrals are the monuments of humankind entrapped
in the moral order and dreaming feverishly of escape.
Higher and higher went the naves and pinnacles. Thinner
and thinner grew the prison walls; brighter and brighter
grew the light from outside, until man knew: why not the
light itself? And they all left off those sickly masterpieces.

Now when will we leave off the even more sickly pinnacles of Manhattan and Chicago?

In literature, if we are committed to the non-moral as we are supposed to be as Americans, we can draw no line of demarcation between the Comédie Française, the French novel, and the "French postcard." Between the *Encyclopedia of Social Sciences*, the Bible, and *The Hundred and Twenty Days of Sodom*. As for the pornographic, the moralist argues that you don't hand an infant a loaded pistol. To which the least obscene reply must be: infants can't read. As for excessiveness or debauchery, nature has a way with that. As Picasso says, you can't eat twelve dinners a day. And as for sex crimes, it is always in the best regulated towns, with the most numerous churches, that the worst sex crimes occur.

A free society is nothing less than a non-moral society, one in which private, individual liberty is absolute. But this is not liberty, cry the moralists and politicians; it is *license*. It is what the Romans called *libido*, meaning *violent* desire, which is true. Violence is in a direct proportion to suppression. Freudian libido describes the *crippled* sexuality of modern Western man, crippled by a suppressive society from the cradle to the grave with social security benefits and a limestone cross thrown in.

The therapeutics of the obscene is not my concern. What is the point of accommodating reality to a nightmare? Of course, people can be made to adjust to this nightmare society. From the analyst's office, scientifically constructed to resemble a motel room recommended by the AAA, to the home living room, made to resemble the analyst's office, there is a clear channel of communication. Between these islands you fall asleep, and *fast*, in a sealed car, always at analytic temperature, and with the radio leaking Muzak and plenty of news of French Indo-China or whatever they call it nowadays. And no *dirty books* unless they happen to be Literature!—which is to say, approved for discussion by the PTA, which is at present being analyzed by the FBI for College Board Examinations.

In the matter of books, printed or oral, we know that

the ultimate restraint has always been religious. Writing and drawing are rare and sacred skills (or in the era of religion used to be). These skills were quickly appropriated by the elites, even as they are today. The elites by definition are dynastic and self-perpetuating, and it is to their interest to keep literature sacred and fundamentally secret. The quasi-sacred nature of even secular poetry is a vestige of the awe for writing which we have inherited from the deep primitive past.

Sacred literature, of course, encompasses the obscene and tries to assimilate it, just as sacred art is an attempt to restrict the natural creativity of mankind. The Song of Songs, one of the most beautiful of erotic poems, was finally included by its original editors in what we call the Bible. It is fairly agreed that this poem was a series of pagan marriage songs, appropriated by certain priests, attributed to Solomon, and later made into a Christian symbolistic fetish, and so on.

The rich "obscene" contents of all religions are perversions of the natural, and each religion revels in accusations against all others, accusations which are symbolically if not actually true. The sexuality of the Inquisitions or of Protestant witch burning; Moslem polygamy and a sex heaven; medieval accusations of the Jew as sexual monster, a theme revived by Hitler; to touch on a few religious niceties. In one of the recent novels I mentioned in passing, capital punishment is shown to be the sexual pleasure of the police and the law, with Righteousness springing the trapdoor.

There is a strong tendency for literature to turn back into religion. It is one of the things artists are constantly battling. And religion is constantly attempting to encircle and to biblicize creativity to hold it in check. Only in a Renaissance, which is a revolution of the free, does religion totter and lose its grip on the arts of man. It is then that the arts leap up like giants; then we have Shakespeare and Michelangelo and the rest. Although the churches thereupon change their tactics, building chapels that resemble boudoirs, making the angels more voluptuous and the music indistinguishable from that of the opera.

The writer knows that religion is always ready to seize him and his work. He knows too that the moralistic elites are lying in wait. In our time the escape from these authorities has taken the course of rediscovering the primitive. Modern art is in this sense deeply vandalistic, for all the great arts of our time are visibly destructive of authority. Surrealism, Dada, the various forms of anti-art, and the resurgence of the obscene—all these mean that Art is natural; it is not sacred.

Religion has lost the power to enforce by murder, but it still retains the power to punish. Sex in every form and fashion is illegal in our moralistic society except by benefit of law or clergy. Which is to say that religion is still at it. Doctors and lawyers everywhere recognize the survival of the most brutal practices of the dark ages of the mind. Our law books are weighty with anachronisms left over from a history all of us would like to forget. Yet the legal and medical professions do nothing to abolish these laws or even to modify them, with the exception of an occasional lawyer or doctor who takes his hand away from the cash register for a moment. When will they, whose responsibility it is, do something about the laws against contraception, laws against abortion, laws against adolescent love and marriage, laws against homosexuality, and laws against so-called obscene books? Our society is probably more backward in this respect than in any other.

But morality too may be on the wane, and here the third line of defense makes its appearance. Aestheticians, anthologists, literature professors (some of us are so misguided) make their appeal not to God or Morality but to Good Taste. One device used by these protectors of the aesthetic realm is that of Style. A Dirty Book must be hard to read. The aesthetic rule is that if a Dirty Book is slow going and has stylistic ornamentation then it is *Literature* and may be admitted to the curriculum. But if the Dirty Book is in plain English or American (which "even cats and dogs can read") then the book is taboo. You can admit Joyce's *Ulysses* because it is literature. It has 'style. Not only that; it's a parallel to the *Gilgamesh Epic* or *Beowulf* or something. It's *serious*.

I am opposed to book-banning of any kind, by any institution or by any person. So are all writers and all artists I know of. This makes the writer the sworn enemy of the censor, whether a religious censor of the United States Post Office or the Pure Food and Drug Administration or the local police. In our time the word *obscene* almost invariably refers to sex, and people who make an issue of the obscene are mostly those who live the lives of others, possibly because they have none of their own.

The writer opposed to Mrs. Grundy and Uncle George takes a dim view of American society. He sees it as suicidal, anesthetic, materialistic, and simultaneously prurient and anti-sexual. It is a society in which the chief occupation is the frustration of life and beauty. All modern writers without exception have elaborated this theme.

I have quoted at length from Sade or rather his present interpreter, Simone de Beauvoir. Sade is the perfect example of the extreme argument for personal liberty. I have quoted Thoreau, partly to temper Sade. Both Sade and Thoreau are tremendously influential in the world today, the one psychologically, the other politically. I thank Henry Miller for leading me to them.

Finally, I have advanced an argument for the Non-moral way. Non-morality implies a gradual and total relaxation of authority. It implies, optimistically, a belief in self-regulation by the individual and by society. And it implies the release of consciousness and of joy, without the shackles of tradition, without benefit of historical Memory or what has always been miscalled Principle. As Thoreau said: If I have anything to regret, it is my good behavior.